In Defence of Sociology

In Defence of Sociology

Essays, Interpretations and Rejoinders

ANTHONY GIDDENS

Polity Press

First published in 1996 by Polity Press in association with Blackwell Publishers Ltd.

2 4 6 8 10 9 7 5 3 1

Editorial office:
Polity Press
65 Bridge Street
Cambridge CB2 1UR, UK

Marketing and production:
Blackwell Publishers Ltd
108 Cowley Road
Oxford OX4 1JF, UK

Published in the USA by
Blackwell Publishers Inc.
238 Main Street
Cambridge, MA 02142, USA

ISBN 0–7456–1761–1
ISBN 0–7456–1762–X (pbk)

A CIP catalogue record for this book is available from the British Library and the Library of Congress

Typeset in 11 on 12½pt Times
by Photoprint, Torquay, Devon
Printed in Great Britain by T. J. Press (Padstow) Ltd., Padstow, Cornwall
This book is printed on acid-free paper.

Contents

Sources and Acknowledgements

The chapters which compose this work come from the following sources: 'In Defence of Sociology', *New Statesman and Society*, 7 April 1995; 'Living in a Post-Traditional Society', Ulrich Beck, Anthony Giddens and Scott Lash: *Reflexive Modernization*, Cambridge: Polity Press, 1994; 'What is Social Science?' was previously unpublished; 'Functionalism: *Après la Lutte*', *Studies in Social and Political Theory*, London: Hutchinson, 1979; ' "Britishness" and the Social Sciences' is the text of a talk broadcast on Radio 4 in April 1995; 'The Future of Anthropology', Akbar Ahmed and Chris Shore: *The Future of Anthropology*, London: Athlone Press, 1995; 'Four Myths in the History of Social Thought', *Studies in Social and Political Theory*; 'Auguste Comte and Positivism', *Profiles and Critiques in Social Theory*, London: Macmillan, 1982; 'The Suicide Problem in French Sociology', *Studies in Social and Political Theory*; 'Reason without Revolution?: Habermas's "Theory of Communicative Action" ', Richard Bernstein: *Habermas and Modernity*, Cambridge: Polity Press, 1985; 'Literature and Society: Raymond Williams', *Profiles and Critiques in Social Theory*; 'T.H. Marshall, the State and Democracy' was the Marshall Lecture, delivered at the University of Southampton in 1994; 'Brave New World: The New Context of Politics', David Miliband: *Rethinking the Left*, Cambridge: Polity Press, 1994; 'The Labour Party and British Politics', combined from three articles in *New Statesman and Society*, originally published on 30 September, 7 October and 14 October 1994.

Preface

The articles included here first appeared in a diversity of different contexts and at diverse dates. In selecting the pieces I have been guided by two main criteria. I have chosen articles which in some way or another reflect the title of the book – they contribute to elucidating what I take to be the central position of sociology in the social sciences as a whole. But I have also tried to respond to the many enquiries I had about essays that had gone out of print and have included those most in demand among people who have written to me. I have incorporated several long and substantial essays as well as a selection of shorter writings.

ONE

In Defence of Sociology

There's something about sociology that raises hackles other academic subjects fail to reach. Economics may be the dismal science, full of obscure terms few can understand and seemingly irrelevant to the practical tasks of day-to-day life. Yet sociology is often indicted on all counts – diffuse and lacking a coherent subject-matter, as well as being jargon-ridden. What do you get when you cross a sociologist with a member of the Mafia? An offer you can't understand.

What is it with sociology? Why is it so irritating to so many? Some sociologists might answer: ignorance; others: fear. Why fear? Well, because they like to think of their subject as a dangerous and discomfiting one. Sociology, they are prone to say, tends to subvert: it challenges our assumptions about ourselves as individuals and about the wider social contexts in which we live. It has a direct connection with political radicalism. In the 1960s, the discipline seemed to many to live up to this firebrand reputation.

In truth, however, even in the 1960s and early 1970s sociology wasn't intrinsically associated with the left, let alone with revolutionaries. It came in for a great deal of criticism from Marxists of various persuasions who, far from regarding the subject as subversive, saw it as the very epitome of the bourgeois order they found so distasteful.

In some aspects and situations of its development sociology has in fact a long history of being bound up with the political right. Max Weber, commonly regarded as one of its classical founders, inclined more to the right than to the left and was savagely critical of the self-proclaimed revolutionaries of his time. Vilfredo Pareto and Robert Michels both flirted with Italian fascism towards the end of their lives. Most sociologists have probably been liberals by temperament and political inclination: this was true of Emile Durkheim and in later generations of R.K. Merton, Talcott Parsons, Erving Goffman and Ralf Dahrendorf among many other prominent sociological thinkers.

Sociology has currently been going through a hard time in the very country where it has long been most well developed, the US. A prominent American sociologist, Irving Louis Horowitz, recently published a book entitled *The Decomposition of Sociology*, a work which he reports was 'more a matter of pain rather than pride to have felt the need to write'. The discipline, he argues, has gone sour. Three sociology departments, including a distinguished one, at Washington University, St Louis – where Horowitz himself once worked – have recently been closed down. Yale University houses the oldest sociology department in the United States: its resources have just been cut by almost half.

Undergraduate student numbers in sociology in the US have fallen substantially over the two decades since the 1970s – from a record high of 36,000 students in 1973 to below 15,000 in 1994. According to Horowitz, however, the travails of sociology aren't just expressed in declining student appeal. They are to do with the parlous intellectual state of the discipline. Sociology, he says, might not in the past have been linked to an overall political standpoint, but since the 1960s it has increasingly become so. The subject has become the home of the discontented, a gathering of groups with special agendas, from the proponents of gay rights to liberation theology. Sociology is decomposing because it has come to be just what its critics always saw it as, a pseudo-science; and because there has been an outflow of respectable, empirically-oriented social scientists into other, more narrowly defined areas – such as urban planning, demography, criminology or jurisprudence. The deterioration of sociology doesn't imply the disintegration of social research, which is still flourishing in many domains; but much of such research has degenerated into pure empiricism, no longer guided by worthwhile theoretical perspectives. What has disappeared is the capacity of sociology to provide a unifying centre for the diverse branches of social research.

Shutting down of the sociology departments at Washington University and elsewhere has provoked a heated debate in the US – to which Horowitz's is one among a variety of contributions. William Julius Wilson, well-known for his writings on the urban poor, has argued that sociology has become too detached from issues on the public agenda and should focus its concerns on matters of practical policy. After all, as he says, there's hardly a dearth of social problems for sociologists to study, with the cities falling into ruin, divisions between white and black as rigid as they ever were and violent crime a commonplace.

Is sociology in the doldrums? And if so, is this in some sense a peculiarly American phenomenon or something that applies worldwide? Or was sociology perhaps always the rag-tail affair its critics have long proclaimed it to be?

Let's deal first of all with the old chestnut that sociology doesn't have a proper field of investigation. The truth of the matter is that the field of study of sociology, as understood by the bulk of its practitioners, is no more, but no less, clearly defined than that of any other academic area. Consider, for example, history. That discipline has an obvious subject-matter, it would seem – the past. But the past embraces everything! No clear or bounded field of study here, and history is every bit as riven by methodological disputes about its true nature as sociology has ever been.

Sociology is a generalizing discipline that concerns itself above all with modernity – with the character and dynamics of modern or industrialized societies. It shares many of its methodological strategies – and problems – not only with history but with the whole gamut of the social sciences. The more empirical issues it deals with are very real. Of all the social sciences, sociology bears most directly on the issues that concern us in our everyday lives – the development of modern urbanism, crime and punishment, gender, the family, religion, social and economic power.

Given that sociological research and thinking are more or less indispensable in contemporary society, it is difficult to make sense of the criticism that it is unenlightening – that it is common sense wrapped up in somewhat unattractive jargon. Although specific pieces of research could always be questioned, no one could argue that there is no point in carrying out, say, comparative studies of the incidence of divorce in different countries. Sociologists engage in all sorts of research which, once one has some awareness of them, would prove interesting, and be thought important, by most reasonably neutral observers.

There is, however, another, more subtle reason why sociology may appear quite often to proclaim what is obvious to common sense. This is that social research doesn't, and can't, remain separate from the social world it describes. Social research forms so much a part of our consciousness today that we take it for granted. All of us depend upon such research for what we regard *as* common sense – as 'what everyone knows'. Everyone knows, for example, that divorce rates are high in today's society; yet such 'obvious knowledge', of course, depends upon regular social research, whether it happens to be carried out by government researchers or academic sociologists.

It is therefore to some degree the fate of sociology to be taken as less original and less central to our social existence than actually it is. Not only empirical research but sociological theorizing and sociological concepts can become so much part of our everyday repertoire as to appear as 'just common sense'. Many people, for instance, now ask whether a leader has charisma, discuss moral panics or talk of someone's social status – all notions that originated in sociological discourse.

These considerations, obviously, don't help with the issue of whether sociology as an academic discipline is in a state of sorry decline or even dissolution since its heyday in the 1960s, if that period was indeed its apogee. Things *have* changed in sociology over the past thirty years, but not all for the worse. For one thing, the centre of power has shifted. American sociology used to dominate world sociology, but it does so no longer. Especially so far as sociological theorizing is concerned, the centre of gravity has shifted elsewhere, particularly to Europe. The major sociological thinkers now are over here rather than over there, authors like Pierre Bourdieu, Niklas Luhmann or Ulrich Beck.

Sociology in the US appears to have become over-professionalized, with research groups concentrating on their own patch, having little knowledge of, or interest in, anyone else's. Everyone in American sociology has a 'field' and whatever the sociologist's speciality happens to be effectively defines that identity. Quantophrenia is rife in American sociology departments. For many if you can't count it, it doesn't count; the result, to say the least, can be a certain lack of creativity.

There's a good deal of justification for William Julius Wilson's advice to sociologists to engage in research immediately relevant to public policy issues and to participate forcefully in the wide debates their work may arouse. After all, many questions raised in the political arena are sociological – questions to do, for instance, with welfare, crime or the family. Sociological work is relevant, not just to their formulation as particular types of policy question, but to grasping the likely consequences of whatever policies might be initiated in relation to them.

Reconnecting sociology to a public policy-making agenda wouldn't address the other issues raised about the so-called decline of sociology. What of the disaggregation of sociology, of which Horowitz makes so much? Is it a discipline without a common conceptual core, in danger of breaking up into unconnected specialities? And have the most innovative authors moved elsewhere? Most important of all, perhaps, has it lost its cutting edge?

If one compares sociology to economics, it has to be conceded that sociology is much more internally diverse. In economics there exists a variety of different schools of thought and theoretical approaches, but the neo-classical view tends to dominate almost everywhere and forms the basic stuff of virtually all introductory texts. Sociology isn't to the same degree in the thrall of a single conceptual system. However, this surely should be seen more as a strength than a weakness. I don't believe such diversity has produced complete disarray, but instead gives voice to the pluralism that must exist when one studies something as complex and controversial as human social behaviour and institutions.

Is there any evidence that talented scholars who might once have been attracted to working in sociology have now migrated elsewhere? There's no doubt that in the 1960s some were drawn into sociology because they saw it, if not offering a route to revolution, as trendy and new; and it doesn't have that reputation any longer. But most such individuals probably weren't interested in a career within the confines of the academy. More relevant are factors that have affected the academic world as a whole, not sociology in particular. Many talented people who might once have gone into academic life probably won't do so today, because academic salaries have fallen sharply in relative terms over the last two decades and working conditions have deteriorated.

Yet a good case could actually be made for saying that British sociology is doing better than in previous generations. Compare, for instance, the fortunes of sociology in Britain over recent years with those of anthropology. In the early postwar period, this country boasted anthropologists of worldwide reputation; no crop of comparably distinguished sociological authors was to be found at that time.

Now things are more or less reversed. There are few, if any, anthropologists of the current generation who can match the achievements of the preceding one. British sociology, however, can offer a clutch of individuals with a worldwide reputation, such as John Goldthorpe, Steven Lukes, Stuart Hall, Michèle Barrett, Ray Pahl, Janet Wolff and Michael Mann.

Moreover, in sheer statistical terms, sociology is not in decline in this country in the way it has been in the US. A-level sociology is extremely popular and flourishing rather than shrinking. University admissions in sociology are, at worst, stable in relation to other subjects.

Everything in the sociological garden isn't rosy – although was it ever? Funding for social research has dropped off sharply since the early 1970s; there isn't the scale of empirical work there once was. But it would be difficult to argue that sociology is off the pace intellectually, especially if one broadens the angle again and moves back to a more international perspective. Most of the debates that grab the intellectual headlines today, across the social sciences, and even the humanities, carry a strong socio-logical input. Sociological authors have pioneered discussions of postmodernism, the post-industrial or information society, globalization, the transformation of everyday life, gender and sexuality, the changing nature of work and the family, the 'underclass' and ethnicity.

You might still ask: what do all these changes add up to? Here there is a lot of sociological work to be done. Some of that work has to be investigatory or empirical, but some must be theoret-ical. More than any other intellectual endeavour, sociological reflection is central to grasping the social forces remaking our lives today. Social life has become episodic, fragmentary and dogged with new uncertainties, which it must be the business of creative sociological thought to help us understand. William Julius Wilson's argument is certainly important: sociologists should focus their attention on the practical and policy-making implications of the changes currently transforming social life. Yet sociology would indeed become dreary, and quite possibly dis-aggregated, if it didn't also concern itself with the big issues.

Sociology should rehone its cutting edge, as neo-liberalism disappears into the distance along with orthodox socialism. Some questions to which we need new answers have a perennial quality, while others are dramatically new. Tackling both of these, as in previous times, calls for a healthy dose of what C. Wright Mills famously called the sociological imagination. Sociologists, don't despair! You still have a world to win, or at least interpret.

TWO

Living in a Post-Traditional Society

In the social sciences today, as in the social world itself, we face a new agenda. The end not just of a century but of a millennium: something which has no content, and which is wholly arbitrary – a date on a calendar – has such a power of reification that it holds us in thrall. *Fin de siècle* has become widely identified with feelings of disorientation and malaise, to such a degree that one might wonder whether all the talk of endings, such as the end of modernity, or the end of history, simply reflects them. No doubt to some degree such is the case. Yet it is certainly not the whole story. We are in a period of evident transition – and the 'we' here refers not only to the West but to the world as a whole.

In this discussion I speak of the emergence of a post-traditional society. This phrase might at first glance seem odd. Modernity, almost by definition, always stood in opposition to tradition; hasn't modern society long been 'post-traditional'? It has not, at least in the way in which I propose to speak of the 'post-traditional society' here. For most of its history, modernity has rebuilt tradition as it has dissolved it. Within Western societies, the persistence and recreation of tradition was central to the legitimation of power, to the sense in which the state was able to impose itself upon relatively passive 'subjects'. For tradition placed in stasis some core aspects of social life – not least the family and sexual identity – which were left largely untouched so far as 'radicalizing Enlightenment' was concerned.[1]

Most important, the continuing influence of tradition within modernity remained obscure so long as 'modern' meant

'Western'. Modernity has been forced to 'come to its senses' today, as a result of its generalization across the world. No longer the unexamined basis of Western hegemony over other cultures, the precepts and social forms of modernity stand open to scrutiny.

The orders of transformation

The new agenda for social science concerns two directly connected domains of transformation. Each corresponds to processes of change which, while they have their origins with the first development of modernity, have become particularly acute in the current era. On the one hand there is the extensional spread of modern institutions, universalized via globalizing processes. On the other, but immediately bound up with the first, are processes of intentional change, which can be referred to as the radicalizing of modernity.[2] These are processes of *evacuation*, the disinterring and problematizing of tradition.

Few people anywhere in the world can any longer be unaware of the fact that their local activities are influenced, and sometimes even determined, by remote events or agencies. The phenomenon is easily indexed, at least on a crude level. Thus, for example, capitalism has for centuries had strong tendencies to expand, for reasons documented by Marx and many others. Over the period since World War I, however, and particularly over the past forty years or so, the pattern of expansionism has begun to alter. It has become much more decentred as well as more all-enveloping. The overall movement is towards much greater interdependence. On the sheerly economic level world production has increased dramatically, albeit with various fluctuations and downturns; and world trade, a better indicator of interconnectedness, has grown even more. 'Invisible trade', in services and finance, has increased most of all.[3]

Less evident is the reverse side of the coin. The day-to-day actions of an individual today are globally consequential. My decision to purchase a particular item of clothing, for example, or a specific type of foodstuff, has manifold global implications. It not only affects the livelihood of someone living on the other side of the world but may contribute to a process of ecological decay which itself has potential consequences for the whole of humanity. This extraordinary, and still accelerating, connectedness between everyday decisions and global outcomes, together with its reverse, the influence of global orders over individual life, form the key subject-matter of the new agenda. The connections involved are often very close. Intermediate collectivities and groupings of all sorts, including the state, do not disappear as a result; but they do tend to become reorganized or reshaped.

To the Enlightenment thinkers, and many of their successors, it appeared that increasing information about the social and natural worlds would bring increasing control over them. For many, such control was the key to human happiness; the more, as collective humanity, we are in a position actively to make history, the more we can guide history towards our ideals. Even more pessimistic observers connected knowledge and control. Max Weber's 'steel-hard cage' – in which he thought humanity was condemned to live for the foreseeable future – is a prison-house of technical knowledge; we are all, to alter the metaphor, to be small cogs in the gigantic machine of technical and bureaucratic reason. Yet neither image comes close to capturing the world of high modernity, which is much more open and contingent than any such image suggests – and is so precisely *because of*, not in spite of, the knowledge that we have accumulated about ourselves and about the material environment. It is a world where opportunity and danger are balanced in equal measure.

The more we try to colonize the future, the more it is likely to spring surprises upon us. This is why the notion of risk, so central to the endeavours of modernity, moves through two stages.[4] First of all it seems no more than part of an essential calculus, a means of sealing off boundaries as the future is invaded. In this form risk is a statistical part of the operations of insurance companies; the very precision of such risk calculations seems to signal success in bringing the future under control.

This is risk in a world where much remains as 'given', including external nature and those forms of social life coordinated by tradition. As nature becomes permeated, and even 'ended', by human socialization, and tradition is dissolved, new types of incalculability emerge. Consider, for example, global warming. Many experts consider that global warming is occurring, and they may be right. The hypothesis is disputed by some, however, and it has even been suggested that the real trend, if there is one at all, is in the opposite direction, towards the cooling of the global climate. Probably the most that can be said with some surety is that we cannot be certain that global warming is *not* occurring. Yet such a conditional conclusion will yield not a precise calculation of risks but rather an array of 'scenarios' – whose plausibility will be influenced, among other things, by how many people become convinced of the thesis of global warming and take action on that basis. In the social world, where institutional reflexivity has become a central constituent, the complexity of 'scenarios' is even more marked.

On the global level, therefore, modernity has become experimental. We are all, willy-nilly, caught up in a grand experiment, which is at the one time our doing – as human agents – yet to an imponderable degree outside of our control. It is not an experiment in the laboratory sense, because we do not govern the outcomes within fixed parameters – it is more like a dangerous adventure, in which each of us has to participate whether we like it or not.

The grand experiment of modernity, fraught with global hazards, is not at all what the progenitors of Enlightenment had in mind when they spoke of the importance of contesting tradition. The social world has become largely organized in a conscious way, and nature fashioned in a human image, but these circumstances, at least in some domains, have created greater uncertainties, of a very consequential kind, than ever existed before.

The global experiment of modernity intersects with, and influences, as it is influenced by, the penetration of modern institutions into the tissue of day-to-day life. Not just the local community, but intimate features of personal life and the self, become intertwined with relations of indefinite time-space extension.[5] We are all also caught up in *everyday experiments* whose outcomes, in a generic sense, are as open as those affecting humanity as a whole. Everyday experiments reflect the changing role of tradition and, as is also true of the global level, should be seen in the context of the *displacement and reappropriation of expertise*, under the impact of the intrusiveness of abstract systems. Technology, in the general meaning of 'technique', plays the leading role here, in the shape both of material technology and of specialized social expertise.

Everyday experiments concern some very fundamental issues to do with self and identity, but they also involve a multiplicity of changes and adaptations in daily life. Some such changes are lovingly documented in Nicholson Baker's novel *The Mezzanine*. The book deals with no more than a few moments in the day of a person who actively reflects, in detail, upon the minutiae of his life's surroundings and his reactions to them. A paraphernalia of intrusion, adjustment and readjustment is revealed, linked to a dimly perceived backdrop of larger global agencies.

Take the example of the ice-cube tray:

> The ice-cube tray deserves a historic note. At first these were aluminium barges inset with a grid of slats linked to a handle like a parking brake – a bad solution; you had to run the grid under warm water before the ice would let go of the metal. I remember seeing these used, but never used them myself. And then suddenly there were plastic and rubber 'trays', really moulds, of several designs – some producing very small cubes, others producing large squared-off cubes and bathtub-buttoned cubes. There were subtleties that one came to understand over time: for instance, the little notches designed into the inner walls that separated one cell from another allowed the water level to equalise itself: this meant that you could fill the tray by running the cells quickly under the tap, feeling as if you were playing the harmonica, or you could turn the faucet on very slightly, so that a thin silent stream of water fell in a line from the tap, and hold the tray at an angle, allowing the water to enter a single cell and well from there into adjoining cells one by one, gradually filling the entire tray. The intercellular notches were helpful after the tray was frozen, too; when you had twisted it to force the cubes, you could selectively pull out one cube at a time by hooking a fingernail under the frozen projection that had formed in a notch. If you couldn't catch the edge of a notch-stump because the cell had not been filled to above the notch level, you might have to mask all the cubes except one with your hands and turn the tray over, so that the single cube you needed fell out. Or you could twist all the cubes free and then, as if the tray were a frying pan and you were flipping a pancake, toss them. The cubes would hop as one above their individual homes about a quarter of an inch, and most

would fall back into place; but some, the loosest, would loft higher and often land irregularly, leaving one graspable end sticking up – these you used for your drink.[6]

What is at issue here is not just, or even primarily, technology, but more profound processes of the reformation of daily life. Tradition here would appear to play no part whatever any more; but this view would be mistaken, as we shall see.

Insulting the meat

Among the !Kung San of the Kalahari desert, when a hunter returns from a successful hunt his kill is disparaged by the rest of the community, no matter how bountiful it may be. Meat brought in by hunters is always shared throughout the group, but rather than being greeted with glee, a successful hunt is treated with indifference or scorn. The hunter himself is also supposed to show modesty as regards his skills and to understate his achievements. One of the !Kung comments:

> Say that a man has been hunting, he must not come home and announce like a braggart, 'I have killed a big one in the bush!' He must first sit down in silence until I or someone else comes up to his fire and asks, 'What did you see today?' He replies quietly, 'Ah, I'm no good for hunting. I saw nothing at all . . . maybe just a tiny one'. Then I smile to myself because I know he has killed something big.

The twin themes of deprecation and modesty are continued when the party goes out to fetch and divide up the kill the next day. Getting back to the village, the members of the carrying group loudly comment upon the ineptness of the hunter and their disappointment with him:

> You mean you have dragged us all the way out here to make us cart home your pile of bones? Oh, if I had known it was this thin I wouldn't have come. People, to think I gave up a nice day in the shade for this. At home we may be hungry, but at least we have nice cool water to drink.[7]

The exchange is a ritual one, and follows established prescriptions; it is closely connected to other forms of ritual interchange in !Kung society. Insulting the meat seems at first sight the perfect candidate for explanation in terms of latent functions. It is a slice of tradition which fuels those interpretations of 'traditional cultures' which understand 'tradition' in terms of functional conceptions of solidarity. If such notions were valid, tradition could be seen essentially as unthinking ritual, necessary to the cohesion of simpler societies. Yet this idea will not work. There is certainly a 'functional' angle to insulting the meat: although it also leads to conflicts, it can be seen as a means of sustaining egalitarianism in !Kung (male) community. The ritualized disparagement is a counter to arrogance and therefore to the sort of stratification that might develop if the best hunters were honoured or rewarded.

Yet this 'functional' element does not in fact operate in a mechanical way (nor could it); the !Kung are well aware of what is going on. Thus, as a !Kung healer pointed out to the visiting anthropologist, when a man makes many kills, he is liable to think of himself as a chief, and see the rest of the group as his inferiors. This is unacceptable; 'so we always speak of his meat as worthless. In this way we cool his heart and make him gentle.'[8] Tradition is about ritual and has connections with social solidarity, but it is not the mechanical following of precepts accepted in an unquestioning way.

To grasp what it means to live in a post-traditional order we have to consider two questions: what tradition actually is and what are the generic characteristics of a 'traditional society'. Both notions have for the most part been used as unexamined concepts – in sociology because of the fact that they have been foils for the prime concern with modernity; and in anthropology because one of the main implications of the idea of tradition, repetition, has so often been merged with cohesiveness. Tradition, as it were, is the glue that holds premodern social orders together; but once one rejects functionalism it is no longer clear what makes the glue stick. There is no necessary connection between repetition and social cohesion at all, and the repetitive character of tradition is something which has to be explained, not just assumed.[9]

Repetition means time – some would say that it *is* time – and tradition is somehow involved with the control of time. Tradition, it might be said, is an orientation to the past, such that the past has a heavy influence, or, more accurately put, is made to have a heavy influence, over the present. Yet clearly, in a certain sense at any rate, tradition is also about the future, since established practices are used as a way of organizing future time. The future is shaped without the need to carve it out as a separate territory. Repetition, in a way that needs to be examined, reaches out to return the future to the past, while drawing on the past also to reconstruct the future.

Traditions, Edward Shils says, are always changing;[10] but there is *something* about the notion of tradition which presumes endurance; if it is traditional, a belief or practice has an integrity and continuity which resists the buffeting of change. Traditions have an organic character: they develop and mature, or weaken and 'die'. The integrity or *authenticity* of a tradition, therefore, is more important in defining it as tradition than how long it lasts. It is notable that only in societies with writing – which have actually become thereby less 'traditional' – do we usually have any *evidence* that elements of tradition have endured over very long periods. Anthropologists have virtually always seen oral cultures as highly traditional, but in the nature of the case have no way of confirming that the 'traditional practices' they observe have existed over even several generations; no one knows, for instance, for how long the !Kung practice of insulting the meat might have been in place.

I shall understand 'tradition' in the following way. Tradition, I shall say, is bound up with memory, specifically what Maurice Halbwachs terms 'collective memory'; involves ritual; is connected with what I shall call a *formulaic notion of truth*; has 'guardians'; and, unlike custom, has binding force which has a combined moral and emotional content.

Memory, like tradition – in some sense or another – is about organizing the past in relation to the present. We might think, Halbwachs says, that such conservation simply results from the existence of unconscious psychic states. There are traces registered in the brain which make it possible for these states to be called to consciousness. From this point of view, 'the past falls into ruin', but 'only vanishes in appearance', because it continues to exist in the unconscious.[11]

Halbwachs rejects such an idea; the past is not preserved but continuously reconstructed on the basis of the present. Such reconstruction is partially individual, but more fundamentally it is *social* or collective. In fleshing out this argument, Halbwachs offers an interesting analysis of dreams. Dreams are in effect what meaning would be like without its organizing social frameworks – composed of disconnected fragments and bizarre sequences. Images remain as 'raw materials' that enter into eccentric combinations with one another.

Memory is thus an active, social process, which cannot merely be identified with recall.[12] We continually reproduce memories of past happenings or states, and these repetitions confer continuity upon experience. If in oral cultures older people are the repository (and also often the guardians) of traditions, it is not only because they absorbed them at an earlier point than others but because they have the leisure to identify the details of these traditions in interaction with others of their age and teach them to the young. Tradition, therefore, we may say, is an *organizing medium of collective memory*. There can no more be a private tradition than there could be a private language. The 'integrity' of tradition derives not from the simple fact of persistence over time but from the continuous 'work' of interpretation that is carried out to identify the strands which bind present to past.

Tradition usually involves ritual. Why? The ritual aspects of tradition might be thought to be simply part of its 'mindless', automaton-like character. But if the ideas I have suggested so far are correct, tradition is necessarily active and interpretative. Ritual, one can propose, is integral to the social frameworks which confer integrity upon traditions; ritual is a practical means of ensuring preservation. Collective memory, as Halbwachs insists, is geared to social practices. We can see how this is so if we consider not just the contrast between memory and dreaming but the 'in-between' activity of day-dreaming or reverie. Day-dreaming means that an individual relaxes from the demands of day-to-day life, allowing the mind to wander. By contrast continuity of practice – itself actively organized – is what connects the thread of today's activities with those of yesterday, and of yesteryear. Ritual firmly connects the continual reconstruction of the past with practical enactment, and can be seen to do so.

Ritual enmeshes tradition in practice, but it is important to see that it also tends to be separated more or less clearly from the pragmatic tasks of everyday activity. Insulting the meat is a ritualized procedure, and understood to be so by the participants. A ritual insult is different from a real insult because it lacks denotative meaning; it is a 'non-expressive' use of language. This 'isolating' consequence of ritual is crucial because it helps give ritual beliefs, practices and objects a temporal autonomy which more mundane endeavours may lack.

Like all other aspects of tradition, ritual has to be interpreted; but such interpretation is not normally in the hands of the lay individual. Here we have to establish a connection between tradition's *guardians* and the truths such traditions contain or disclose. Tradition involves 'formulaic truth', to which only certain persons have full access. Formulaic truth depends not upon referential properties of language but rather upon their opposite; ritual language is performative, and may sometimes contain words or practices that the speakers or listeners can barely understand. Ritual idiom is a mechanism of truth because, not in spite, of its formulaic nature. Ritual speech is speech which it makes no sense to disagree with or contradict – and hence contains a powerful means of reducing the possibility of dissent. This is surely central to its compelling quality.

Formulaic truth is an attribution of causal efficacy to ritual; truth criteria are applied to events caused, not to the propositional content of statements.[13] Guardians, be they elders, healers, magicians or religious functionaries, have the importance they do in tradition because they are believed to be the agents, or the essential mediators, of its causal powers. They are dealers in mystery, but their arcane skills come more from their involvement with the causal power of tradition than from their mastery of any body of secret or esoteric knowledge. Among the !Kung the elders are the main guardians of the traditions of the group. Insulting the meat may be 'rationally understood' in terms of its consequences for the collectivity, but it derives its persuasive power from its connections to other rituals and beliefs which either the elders or the religious specialists control.

The guardians of tradition might seem equivalent to experts in modern societies – the purveyors of the abstract systems whose impact upon daily life Nicholson Baker chronicles. The difference between the two, however, is clear-cut. Guardians are not experts, and the arcane qualities to which they have access for the most part are not communicable to the outsider. As Pascal Boyer puts it, 'a traditional specialist isn't someone who has an adequate picture of some reality in his or her mind, but someone whose utterances can be, in some contexts, directly determined by the reality in question.'[14]

Status in the traditional order, rather than 'competence', is the prime characteristic of the guardian. The knowledge and skills possessed by the expert might appear mysterious to the layperson; but anyone could in principle acquire that knowledge and those skills were she or he to set out to do so.

Finally, all traditions have a normative or moral content, which gives them a binding character.[15] Their moral nature is closely bound up with the interpretative processes by means of which past and present are aligned. Tradition represents not only what 'is' done in a society but what 'should be' done. It does not follow from this, of course, that the normative components of tradition are necessarily spelled out. Mostly they are not: they are interpreted within the activities or directives of the guardians. Tradition has the hold it does, it can be inferred, because its moral character offers a measure of ontological security to those who adhere to it. Its psychic underpinnings are affective. There are ordinarily deep emotional investments in tradition, although these are indirect rather than direct; they come from the mechanisms of anxiety-control that traditional modes of action and belief provide.

So much for an initial conceptualizing of tradition. The question of what a 'traditional society' is remains unresolved. I do not intend to deal with it at any length here, although I shall come back to it later. A traditional society, inevitably, is one where tradition as specified above has a dominant role; but this will hardly do in and of itself. Tradition, one can say, has most salience when it is not understood as such. Most smaller cultures, it seems, do not have a specific word for 'tradition' and it is not hard to see why: tradition is too pervasive to be distinguished from other forms of attitude or conduct. Such a situation tends to be particularly characteristic of oral cultures. A distinctive feature of oral culture, obviously, is that communications cannot be made without an identifiable speaker; this circumstance plainly lends itself to formulaic versions of truth. The advent of writing creates hermeneutics: 'interpretation', which is first of all largely scriptural, takes on a new meaning. Tradition comes to be known as something distinctive and as potentially plural. All premodern civilizations, however, remained thoroughly shot through with tradition of one kind or another.

If we ask the question, 'in what ways have modern societies become de-traditionalized?', the most obvious way of providing an answer would be to look at specific forms of symbol and ritual and consider how far they still form 'traditions'. However, I shall defer answering such a question until later, and for the moment shall reorient the discussion in quite a different way. Tradition is repetition, and presumes a kind of truth antithetical to ordinary 'rational enquiry' – in these respects it shares something with the psychology of compulsion.

Repetition as neurosis: the issue of addiction

The question of compulsiveness lies at the origin of modern psychotherapy. Here is how one self-help book of practical therapy begins. 'This is a recording', it says, speaking of an individual's life-experiences – in our present activities we are constantly (in a largely unconscious way) recapitulating the past. The influence of past over present is above all an emotional one, a matter of 'feelings'.

> Reasons can exist in two 'places' at the same time. You can be physically present with someone in the here and now, but your mind can be miles and years removed. One of our problems in relationships is that 'something' removes us from the present and we are not with whom we were with.
>
> These recorded experiences and the feelings associated with them are available for replay today in as vivid a form as when they happened, and they provide much of the data that determine the nature of today's transactions. Events in the present can replicate an old experience and we not only remember how we felt, but we feel the same way. We not only remember the past, we relive it. We are there! Much of what we relive we don't remember.[16]

Compulsiveness in its broadest sense is an inability to escape from the past. The individual, who believes himself or herself to be autonomous, acts out a surreptitious fate. Concepts of fate have always been closely allied with tradition and it is not surprising to find that Freud was preoccupied with fate. 'The *Oedipus Rex*', he observes,

> is a tragedy of fate. Its tragic effect depends upon the conflict between the all-powerful will of the gods and the vain efforts of human beings threatened with disaster. Resignation to the divine will, and the perception of one's unimportance, are the lessons which the deeply moved spectator is supposed to learn from the play.

'The oracle has placed the same curse on us',[17] he continues, but in our case it is possible to escape. From Freud onwards, the dilemma of the modern condition has been widely seen as overcoming the 'programming' built into our early lives.

Freud of course was much concerned with dreams, 'the royal road to the unconscious'. Freud's theory of dreams may or may not be valid in its own terms, but it is worthwhile considering its relation to the ideas of Halbwachs. For both Halbwachs and Freud dreams are memories with the social context of action removed. Let me now historicize this view. The period at which Freud wrote was one at which traditions in everyday life were beginning to creak and strain under the impact of modernity. Tradition provided the stabilizing frameworks which integrated memory traces into a coherent memory. As tradition dissolves, one can speculate, 'trace memory' is left more nakedly exposed, as well as more problematic in respect of the construction of identity and the meaning of social norms. From then onwards, the reconstruction which tradition provided of the past becomes a more distinctively individual responsibility – and even exigency.

As a good medical specialist, Freud set out to cure neuroses; what he actually discovered, however, was the emotional under-tow of disintegrating traditional culture. The emotional life of modern civilization was essentially written out of Enlightenment philosophy, and was alien to those scientific and technological endeavours that were so central to the coruscating effects of modernity. Science, and more generally 'reason', were to replace the supposedly unthinking precepts of tradition and custom. And so, in a sense, it proved to be: cognitive outlooks were indeed very substantially and dramatically recast. The emotional cast of tradition, however, was left more or less untouched.[18]

Freud's thought, of course, is open to being understood in Enlightenment terms. From this point of view, Freud's importance was that he discovered a psychological 'track of development' comparable to that of the social institutions of modernity. The 'dogmatics' of the unconscious could be dissolved and replaced by veridical self-awareness; in Freud's celebrated, perhaps notorious, phrase, 'where id was ego shall be'. Some, more suspicious of the claims of Enlightenment, see Freud in a quite contrasting way. Freud shows us, they say, that modern civilization can never overcome those dark forces which lurk in the unconscious. Freud's own line of intellectual development in fact seems to veer from the first view towards the second over the progression of his career.

Yet perhaps neither of these perspectives is the most effective way of looking at things. Freud was dealing with a social, not only a psychological, order; he was concerned with a social universe of belief and action at the point at which, in matters directly affecting self-identity, *tradition was beginning to turn into compulsion*. Compulsion, rather than the unconscious as such, turned out to be the other side of the 'cognitive revolution' of modernity.

Freud's concrete investigations and therapeutic involvements – unlike most of his writings – concentrated upon the emotional problems of women, as mediated through the body. Yet the hidden compulsiveness of modernity was also manifest – although in a different way – in the public domain. What is Weber's discussion of the Protestant ethic if not an analysis of the obsessional nature of modernity? The emotional travails of women, of course, have no place in Weber's study – nor do the private or sexual lives of the purveyors of the entrepreneurial spirit. It is as if these things have no bearing upon the demeanour or motivation of the industrialist: a conceptual schism which reflected a real division in the lives of men and women.

Weber's work deals quite explicitly with the transition from tradition to modernity, although he does not put it in quite those terms. Religious beliefs and practices, like other traditional activities, tend to fuse morality and emotion. They have, as

Weber makes clear, an adequate and visible motivational base. Just as we can quite easily understand the desire to accumulate wealth in the traditional world, where it is used to cultivate distinctive prerogatives, so we can also make sense of religious asceticism and its driven quality. The Hindu ascetic, for example, strives to overcome the toils of the world and enter a state of religious devotion.

The driven asceticism of the entrepreneur has no such obvious origins even though, just as obviously, it is inspired by passion and conviction. The outlook of the capitalist, Weber says, seems to the non-modern observer 'so incomprehensible and myster- ious, so unworthy and contemptible. That anyone should be able to make it the sole purpose of his life-work, to sink down into the grave weighed down with a great material load of money and goods, seems to him explicable only as the product of a perverse instinct, the *auri sacra fames*.'[19] Weber himself shared this attitude of something akin to contempt in spite of his clarification of the intellectual puzzle posed by the capitalist spirit. Once the fulfilment of the calling of the entrepreneur 'cannot directly be related to the highest spiritual and cultural values', and is not the result of sheerly economic constraint, 'the individual generally abandons the attempt to justify it at all'. And so follows the famous quotation from Goethe: 'Specialists without spirit, sen- sualists without heart; this nullity imagines that it has attained a level of civilisation never before achieved.'[20]

What Weber calls 'economic traditionalism' is in his view characteristic of the vast bulk of economic activity in premodern civilizations. Economic traditionalism quite often recognizes material gain as a legitimate motive, but always grounds it in a wider morality, and includes, usually, a notion of excess. This was true both of Lutheranism and of all varieties of Puritanism. Luther, for example, understood work as a calling in a tradition- alistic way, as part of an objective historical order of things governed by God.[21] The obsessional pursuit of divine grace has been part of many religions, but Lutheranism preserved some of that relatively relaxed attitude towards day-to-day life character- istic of non-monastic Catholicism. Puritanism is more driven. It was antagonistic towards most forms of traditionalism and more or less eliminated ritual within the religious sphere; it was also hostile to all types of sensuous culture.

It is tempting to link Weber's discussion of Puritan asceticism to psychological repression, and many have in fact done so. Puritanism – and, following this, capitalism as an economic system – might seem to maximize self-denial. The pursuit of material gain on the part of the entrepreneur, after all, goes along with a frugal lifestyle and a horror of hedonism. In fact, some commentators have suggested that there have been two phases in the development of modern institutions over the past three centuries or so. The first was marked by the dominance of discipline and repression, the second by an upsurge of hedonism, perhaps associated with the rise of the consumer society.[22] Yet we might interpret the implications of Weber's work in quite a different fashion. The core of capitalist spirit was not so much its ethic of denial as its *motivational urgency*, shorn of the traditional frameworks which had connected striving with morality.

The capitalist, so to speak, was primed to repetition without – once the traditional religious ethic had been discarded – having much sense of why he, or others, had to run this endless treadmill. This was a positive motivation, however; success brought pleasure rather than pain. Hedonism differs from pleasure enjoyed in much the same way as the striving of the entrepreneur differs from economic traditionalism. In other words, almost by definition it too is obsessional: this is why it is much more closely related to the traits upon which Weber concentrated than may seem the case at first blush.

Modernity as compulsive: what does this mean and what are its implications? Although the connections need to be spelled out in greater detail, as with Freud we are speaking here of an *emotional drive to repetition*, which is either largely unconscious or poorly understood by the individual concerned. The past lives on, but rather than being actively reconstructed in the mode of tradition it tends to dominate action almost in a quasi-causal fashion. Compulsiveness, when socially generalized, is in effect *tradition without traditionalism*: repetition which stands in the way of autonomy rather than fostering it.

Freud spoke of obsession or compulsion; today we more commonly speak of addictions. The terminological difference is important, and helps bring out what is at issue. Compare the anorectic individual with Weber's entrepreneur. Each is driven by a this-worldly asceticism. Anorexia, however, is seen as a pathology, and (at present at least) is concentrated mainly in young women. It seems odd at first to regard anorexia as an addiction, because it appears more as a form of self-denial than as being 'hooked' on pleasure-giving substances. In this respect, however, it is no different from the capitalist spirit, and the point made about hedonism applies. In a world where one can be addicted to anything (drugs, alcohol, coffee, but also work, exercise, sport, cinema-going, sex or love) anorexia is one among other food-related addictions.

Addiction, it has been said, 'is anything we feel we have to lie about'.[23] It is, one could say, repetition which has lost its connection to the 'truth' of tradition; its origins are obscure to the individual concerned, although he or she may lie to others too. Thus alcoholics often hide their addiction even from those to whom they are closest, as part of denying it to themselves. Addiction, the author quoted above (a therapist) says, 'keeps us out of touch with ourselves (our feelings, morality, awareness – our living process)'; the individual's relations with others also tend to be obsessional rather than freely entered into. 'Ingestive addictions' (to food or chemicals) can be psychologically based, but addiction is primarily a social and psychological phenomenon rather than a physiological one. Thus in the field of alcoholism, a well-known syndrome is that of the 'dry drunk', a person who exhibits most of the traits of the alcoholic, but without consuming alcohol. Many people, at least for some while, become more compulsive about their behaviour-patterns after giving up alcohol than they were before.[24]

Why juxtapose addiction and tradition? There are two reasons. One is to focus on the compulsive traits of modernity as such, a matter to which I shall return later. The other, more important at this juncture, is because the topic of addiction provides an initial illumination of characteristics of a post-traditional order. In premodern societies, tradition and the routinization of day-to-day conduct are closely tied to one another. In the post-traditional society, by contrast, routinization becomes empty unless it is geared to processes of institutional reflexivity. There is no logic, or moral authenticity, to doing today what one did yesterday; yet these things are the very essence of tradition. The fact that today we can become addicted to anything – any aspect of lifestyle –

indicates the very comprehensiveness of the dissolution of tradition (we should add, and this is not as paradoxical as it seems, 'in its traditional form'). The progress of addiction is a substantively significant feature of the postmodern social universe, but it is also a 'negative index' of the very process of the de-traditionalizing of society.

Family and marriage counsellors sometimes use 'genograms' in helping individuals get along with – or split up from – one another. A genogram is very much like an anthropologist's map of a lineage in a traditional culture, save that it concentrates on the emotions. It traces out the emotional attachments of, say, the partners in a marriage backwards in time, reaching into the parents' and grandparents' generations. A genogram supposedly allows us to see how the emotional life of the present-day individuals recapitulates that of past generations – and provides the possibility of fruitfully escaping from this 'inheritance'.

One therapist, writing of experience with genograms, says 'I became aware, over and over again, of how tenaciously the past searches for its expression in the present.'[25] Most of the connections involved, again, are emotional and unconscious. Consider the case of Tom and Laura, described by Maggie Scarf.[26] Scarf began to construct a genogram for the couple by first of all asking what attracted the two to one another. Tom was a person who kept his emotions to himself, and he believed that this self-sufficiency was one of the things that Laura initially found attractive about him. Yet Laura's ideas about the relationship stressed 'sincerity', 'openness' and 'making oneself vulnerable'. 'It was as if each of them', Scarf says, 'had found, in the other, a missing aspect of something lacking in his or her own inner being.' Each had unconsciously recognized a complementary need in the other – the one for emotional communication, the other for independence of mind.

Repetition as disclosed by family analysis is often strikingly literal. Thus, for example, a woman whose upbringing has been affected by the fact that her father was an alcoholic marries a man who also turns out to be an alcoholic; perhaps she then divorces him, only to repeat a similar pattern. More commonly, the 'mode of being with the other' replicates what has been transmitted from the family context of childhood. As in the case of tradition, this is not a passive process but an active, albeit mainly unconscious, activity of recreation. Scarf observes:

> To some large or small degree, when we attain adult status, most of us have not put our childhood things behind us. In the very process of choosing our mates, and of being chosen – and then, in elaborating on our separate, past lives in the life we create together – we are deeply influenced by the patterns for being that we observed and learned about very early in life and that live on inside our heads. The fact that there may be *other options*, other systems for being in an intimate relationship, often doesn't occur to us, because we don't realise that we *are* operating within a system, one which was internalised in our original families. What has been, and what we've known, seems to be the 'way of the world'; it is reality itself.

Repetition is a way of staying in 'the only world we know', a means of avoiding exposure to 'alien' values or ways of life. Laura's parents had each been married before, but she didn't find this out until she was in her early twenties. The discovery was a shocking one; she felt that they had deceived her previously. Although she was an outgoing person on the surface, she maintained an attitude of inner reserve. In her relationship with her husband, she seemed to want complete closeness and integrity, but actually they had an unconscious 'arrangement'. When she made a move towards closeness, he would react by asserting his autonomy. She depended upon him to preserve a necessary distance between them, while she expressed emotions in a public way which he could not do. He saw his own desire for emotional closeness to her as *her* need, for he seemed emotionally self-sufficient.

Going back through the relations between their parents and grandparents, parallel forms of symbiosis came to light – as well as many other similarities. Both had quite 'old' fathers, who were in their early forties when their children were born. Each had a parent who had regularly suffered from depression. These traits also went back a further generation. The relations between their parents 'reversed' their own, but otherwise paralleled it. Tom's mother was the depressed one in his family, while in Laura's case it was her father. Tom became an 'outsider', an 'observer', in his family, where neither conflict nor attachment between his parents was openly acknowledged; Laura was called upon to express emotions that were displaced on to her during family scenes.

I am not concerned here with how illuminating the therapist's analysis of the couple's relationship might be, or even whether genograms have any validity as representations of the past. So far as the post-traditional society is concerned, what is interesting is what I shall call the process of *excavation* involved. 'Excavation', as in an archaeological dig, is an investigation, and it is also an evacuation. Old bones are disinterred, and their connections with one another established, but they are also exhumed and the site is cleaned out. Excavation means digging deep, in an attempt to clean out the debris of the past.

The factors involved are several-fold: first, as mentioned, the past becomes emotional inertia when tradition becomes weakened. Second, however, as in premodern societies, the past cannot simply be blanked out (although some psychological mechanisms have this effect) but must be reconstructed in the present. Third, the reflexive project of self, a basic characteristic of everyday life in a post-traditional world, depends upon a significant measure of emotional autonomy. Fourth, the prototypical post-traditional personal relation – the pure relationship – depends upon intimacy in a manner not generally characteristic of premodern contexts of social interaction.[27] The succession of the generations is stripped of the crucial significance it had in premodern orders, as one of the most central means for the transmission of traditional symbols and practices.

Choices and decisions

Let me follow the theme of therapy just a little further. Works of therapy almost always emphasize the issue of choice. Choice is obviously something to do with colonizing the future in relation to the past and is the positive side of coming to terms with inertial emotions left from past experiences. 'Who are you and what do you want?': the query sounds the ultimate in specious individualism. Yet there is something more interesting than this going on, which is essentially a way of looking at the social world.

The following is just a small sample of a very long list of 'choices' given by one author:

> Who you spend most of your time with
> What your favourite foods are
> Your posture
> How much or how little you smile
> How late you stay up at night
> Whether you smoke
> Whether you gossip
> Who you admire most
> How calm you are
> How you spend your holidays
> How often you feel sorry for yourself
> How much you worry
> How much patience you have
> How happy you are
> Who to talk to when you have a problem
> Whether you eat breakfast
> What you think about just before you go to sleep at night[28]

In post-traditional contexts, we have no choice but to choose how to be and how to act. From this perspective, even addictions are choices: they are modes of coping with the multiplicity of possibilities which almost every aspect of daily life, when looked at in the appropriate way, offers. The therapist advises:

> Look at what you can do, starting at any time you choose, by making conscious, *active* choices every time the opportunity comes up. It is what we do with these choices (and many other choices just like them) that will always determine not only how well each day works for us, but how successful we will be at anything we do.[29]

The logic is impeccable; for active choice surely produces, or is, autonomy. So why does the advice grate somewhat? One reason might be an objection from classical psychoanalysis. Choices are blocked, or programmed, by unconscious emotions, which cannot first be thought away by listing indefinite numbers of 'options'. Depending upon how fixed unconscious traits are presumed to be, one's genogram could be seen as setting clear limits to feasible options. To see day-to-day life as an amalgam of free choices thus flies in the face of psychological reality. Another reason might be the inevitability of routinization. Daily life would be impossible if we didn't establish routines, and even routines which are nothing more than habits cannot be wholly optional: they wouldn't be routines if we didn't, at least for longish periods of time, place them effectively 'beyond question'.

There is a third reason, however, which is to do with constraint and power. The choices that are constitutive of lifestyle options are very often bounded by factors out of the hands of the individual or individuals they affect. Everyday experiments, as I described them earlier, are ways of handling options, and in this sense are certainly 'active'. Yet the nature of the options in question is clearly variable. Take the matter of the ice-cubes. The technological changes which impinge upon people's lives are the result of the intrusion of abstract systems, whose character they may influence but do not determine. The shifting design of ice-cube trays presumably responds in some way to consumer demand; but the design of the trays, and their construction, are controlled by large industrial corporations far removed from the control of the lay individual.

In coming to grips with the post-traditional order, then, we have to make a distinction between *choices* and *decisions*. Many of our day-to-day activities have in fact become open to choice or, rather, as I have expressed it previously, choice has become obligatory. This is a substantive thesis about everyday life today. Analytically, it is more accurate to say that all areas of social activity come to be governed by decisions – often, although not universally, enacted on the basis of claims to expert knowledge of one kind or another. *Who* takes those decisions, and *how*, are fundamentally a matter of power. A decision, of course, is always somebody's choice and in general all choices, even by the most impoverished or apparently powerless, refract back upon pre-existing power relations. The opening-out of social life to decision-making therefore should not be identified *ipso facto* with pluralism; it is also a medium of power and of stratification. Examples are legion, and span the whole gamut of social activity from minute features of day-to-day life through to global systems.

Nature and tradition as complementary

In respect of the progression of decision-making, we see a direct parallel between tradition and nature – one that is very important. In premodern societies, tradition provided a relatively fixed horizon of action. Tradition, as has been emphasized, involves active processes of reconstruction, particularly as filtered by its guardians. It is common to see tradition as intrinsically conservative, but we should say instead that it renders many things external to human activity. Formulaic truth, coupled to the stabilizing influence of ritual, takes an indefinite range of possibilities 'out of play'. Tradition as nature, nature as tradition: this equivalence is not as extreme as it may sound. What is 'natural' is what remains outside the scope of human intervention.

'Nature' in the modern era has become contrasted with the city; it is equivalent to 'countryside' and quite often has the connotation of a rural idyll:

> Oh there is blessing in this gentle breeze,
> A visitant that while it fans my cheek
> Doth seem half-conscious of the joy it brings
> From the green fields, and from yon azure sky.
> Whate'er its mission, the soft breeze can come
> To none more grateful than to me; escaped
> From the vast city, where I long had pined
> A discontented sojourner.[30]

There is some sense in such a usage. 'Nature' means that which lies undisturbed, that which is created independently of human activity. In one way the image is quite false, for the countryside is nature subordinated to human plans. Yet 'nature' in this meaning does preserve traits long associated with its separation from human contrivance. In many traditions, of course, nature was personalized; it was the domain of gods, spirits or demons. It would be misleading to see animism or other comparable outlooks as a merging of the human and natural worlds, however. Rather, the personalizing of nature expressed its very independence from human beings, a source of change and renewal set off from humanity, yet having a pervasive influence upon human lives. If nature was determined by decisions, these were not human ones.

One way to read human history, from the time of the rise of agriculture, and particularly the great civilizations, onwards is as the progressive destruction of the physical environment. Environmental ecology in the current period has arisen mainly as a response to perceived human destructiveness. Yet the very notion of 'the environment', as compared to 'nature', signals a more deep-lying transition. The environment, which seems to be no more than an independent parameter of human existence, actually is its opposite: nature as thoroughly transfigured by human intervention. We begin to speak about 'the environment' only once nature, like tradition, has become dissolved.[31]

The socialization of nature means much more than just the fact that the natural world is increasingly scarred by humanity. Human action, as mentioned, has long left an imprint upon the physical environment. The very invention of agriculture means clearing the natural ecosystem so as to create a habitat where humans can grow plants or raise animals as they want. Many now familiar landscapes of 'natural beauty', such as some of those in southern Greece, have actually been created by soil erosion following the placing of the land under cultivation in ancient times. Earlier on, the Sumerians, the originators of agrarian civilization, had destroyed the very land they had laboured to make fruitful.[32]

Until modern times, however, nature remained mainly an external system that dominated human activity rather than the reverse. Even in the most sophisticated of hydraulic civilizations floods or droughts were common; a bad harvest could produce devastation. Risk here is of the old type. Natural disasters obviously still happen, but the socialization of nature in the present day means that a diversity of erstwhile natural systems are now products of human decision-making. Concern over global warming comes from the fact that the climate of the earth is no longer a naturally given order. If global warming is indeed occurring, it is the result of the extra quantities of 'greenhouse gases' that have been added to the atmosphere over a period of no more than some two hundred years. Energy consumption has increased by a factor of some three hundred in the twentieth century alone; the fuel burned to provide the energy releases carbon dioxide into the atmosphere. A concomitant reduction in the world's natural 'sinks', which can absorb carbon dioxide, has exacerbated this effect. The overall consequence, even should the thesis of global warming prove mistaken, is the creation of new types of feedback effect and system influence.

The International Panel on Climate Change set up four possible emissions 'scenarios' and tried to assess the implications of each.[33] In the 'business as usual' scenario, where there is not much change from what seem to be the trends at the moment, the amount of carbon dioxide in the atmosphere will double in about twenty years into the new century. The introduction of very tight restrictions, one scenario, would stabilize the level; in each of the others, the level of increase would be geometric. All are just that – scenarios – which could reflexively influence what it is they are about. None of them, however, predicts a reversion. That is to say, henceforth and for the foreseeable future, with all its imponderabilities, we are dealing with a human rather than a natural order.

Some have said that the very idea of inanimate nature, so significant to the outlook and technology of the modern West, should be rejected today. Thus Rupert Sheldrake has suggested that 'once again it makes sense to think of nature as alive'; we might think of 'the entire cosmos' as 'more like a developing organism than an external machine'.[34] This process he specifically connects with the rebirth of tradition and ritual, as well as with an exploration of religion. 'A number of Westerners, myself included, have rejected the Christian religion and explored instead the religious traditions of the East, particularly Hinduism and Buddhism; others have attempted to revive aspects of pre-Christian paganism and the religion of the goddess.'[35] Whether or not such ideas and proclivities become widespread, such a process of selection is not a reawakening of tradition but something new. It is the adoption of tradition as itself a lifestyle decision; and no attempt to reanimate nature will reintroduce nature as it used to be.

The 'externality' of nature in premodern times did not only include the physical environment. It concerned also the body and, in close conjunction with tradition, whatever was counted as part of 'human nature'. All cultures have had systems of medicine and regimes of bodily training. But in the modern era the body and its physiological processes have been much more deeply invaded than before. Nowhere is this more evident than in the sphere of reproduction. The effects of detraditionalization and technology merge quite closely here, as in many other areas. The decision to have only a few children, for example, a demographic change of the first significance in modern societies in the nineteenth and early twentieth centuries, was part of the dissolution of traditional family systems, not a result of changes in technologies of contraception.

Technical changes, however, together with other innovations in reproductive technologies, have radically cut into 'external nature'. *In vitro* fertilization and embryo transplantation provide good examples. Not only can an individual or couple decide to have a child without having sexual intercourse, thus making a reality of virgin birth, but a variety of new possibilities, and dilemmas, open up as regards established kin categories and identities.

Tradition as contextual

Tradition is contextual in the sense that it is guaranteed by a combination of ritual and formulaic truth. Separated from these, tradition lapses into custom or habit. Tradition is unthinkable without guardians, because the guardians have privileged access to truth; truth cannot be demonstrated save in so far as it is manifest in the interpretations and practices of guardians. Priests or shamans may claim to be no more than the mouthpiece of the gods, but their actions *de facto* define what the traditions actually are. Secular traditions have their guardians just as much as those concerned with the sacred; political leaders speak the language of tradition when they claim the same sort of access to formulaic truth.

The connection between ritual and formulaic truth is also what gives traditions their qualities of exclusion. Tradition always discriminates between 'insider' and 'other', because participation in ritual and acceptance of formulaic truth are the conditions for its existence. The 'other' is anyone and everyone who is outside.

Traditions, one could say, almost demand to be set off from others, since being an insider is crucial to their character.

Tradition hence is a medium of identity. Whether personal or collective, identity presumes meaning; but it also presumes the constant process of recapitulation and reinterpretation noted earlier. Identity is the creation of constancy over time, that very bringing of the past into conjunction with an anticipated future. In all societies the maintenance of personal identity, and its connection to wider social identities, is a prime requisite of ontological security. This psychological concern is one of the main forces allowing traditions to create such strong emotional attachments on the part of the 'believer'. Threats to the integrity of traditions are very often, if by no means universally, experienced as threats to the integrity of the self.

Obviously in even the most traditional of societies not all things are traditional. Many skills and tasks, particularly those more removed from ritual or ceremonial occasions, are forms of 'secular expertise'. Such skills and tasks may often be informed by claims to generalizing knowledge, regarded as revisable in the light of new experience or changing conditions of operation. Malinowski showed as much many years ago. Yet the majority of skills are crafts; they are taught by apprenticeship and example, and the knowledge-claims they incorporate are protected as arcane and esoteric. The mystique demands initiation on the part of the fledgling participant. Hence the possessors of craft skills are often in effect guardians, even if those skills are kept relatively separate from the more overtly traditional apparitions of the society. Among the !Kung, for example, hunting is a skill developed by practice over many years, protected but not structured by initiation rites. A !Kung male can identify any local species by means of its footprints in the sand; he can deduce its sex, age, how rapidly it is travelling, whether or not it is healthy, and how long ago it passed through the area.[36]

Tradition claims a privileged view of time; but it tends to do so also of space. Privileged space is what sustains the differences of traditional beliefs and practices. Tradition is always in some sense rooted in contexts of origin or central places. Hunting and gathering societies may not have a fixed place of abode, but the area within which the group circulates is ordinarily accorded sacral qualities. At the other extreme, the 'great traditions' have created cultural diasporas spanning very large areas; premodern Christianity or Islam, for instance, stretched across massive geographical regions. Yet such diasporas remained centred, either upon a single point of origin – Rome, Mecca – or upon a cluster of holy places.

The 'salvation religions' connected privileged place to quite impermeable cultural boundaries between insiders and outsiders. One is either a believer or a heathen. Other 'great traditions', most notably the 'exemplary religions' of the East, such as Buddhism or Hinduism, had more fuzzy zones of inclusion and exclusion. Yet the relation between tradition and identity always made the categories of friend and stranger (if not necessarily enemy) sharp and distinct. The stranger, it has been said (by Robert Michels), is the representative of the unknown. Although it might seem that the category of the stranger depends upon the territorial segmentation of premodern social systems, in fact it results more from the privileged and separatist character of traditionally conferred identities. The unknown is that culturally defined space which separates off the outside from the world of the 'familiar', structured by the traditions with which the collectivity identifies.

Tradition thus provided an anchorage for that 'basic trust' so central to continuity of identity; and it was also the guiding mechanism of other trust relations. Georg Simmel's definition of the stranger is somewhat different from that of Michels: the stranger is someone 'who comes today and stays tomorrow'.[37] The stranger, in other words, isn't just someone who belongs to 'the unknown world out there' but a person who, by staying on, forces the locals to take a stand. One has to establish whether or not the stranger is a 'friend' if he or she does not go away again – which is not the same as accepting the stranger as one of the community, a process that may take many years, or even never happen. The stranger, as has been observed, is someone who:

did not belong in the life-world 'initially', 'originally', 'from the start', 'since time immemorial', and so he questions the extemporality of the life-world, brings into relief the 'mere historicality' of existence. The memory of the event of his coming makes of his very presence an event in history, rather than a fact of nature . . . However protected the stay of the stranger is temporary – an infringement of the division which ought to be kept intact and preserved in the name of secure, orderly existence.[38]

The problem is: under what circumstances can the stranger be trusted? For tradition and the structural elements with which it is involved (such as kinship ties) sustain the networks of social relations along which trust flows. 'Familiarity' is the keynote of trust, which is often sustained by its own rituals. Ritual is important to trust because it supplies evidence of shared cultural community, and also because participation represents something of a public commitment which it is difficult later to go back on. In premodern societies, the extension of trust to newly encountered strangers normally takes the form of an extension of the 'familiar', either through ritual encounters or through the uncovering of kin connections.[39] A person may be trusted, at least provisionally, if some kind of kin relation, even very remote, is identified. Institutions like the Kula ring sustain trust between the different communities involved through ritual means, but the ritual is bolstered also by a more or less deliberate forging of kin bonds.

As Hans-Georg Gadamer has quite rightly stressed, tradition is closely bound up with authority. 'Authority' has a double sense: it is the authority which an individual or group has over others, the capacity to issue binding commands; however, it means also a reference-point of knowledge. Sometimes the two become merged, as a matter of ideology or as a means of impersonalizing power; a directive will say 'issued by authority'. On the other hand, where an individual, for whatever reason, loses the aura which authority conveys, he or she is seen as a charlatan. The two are therefore inevitably interdependent. A person who wields effective authority holds the aura of 'authority' in its more impersonal sense; correspondingly, of course, 'authority' must take the empirical forms of the giving of directives or judgements on the part of specific individuals.

Guardians and experts

In general we can make a distinction between rulers or officials (who give commands) and guardians (who supply interpretations), although the two categories are quite often merged in the same person. Max Weber was much concerned with the role of expertise in modern societies, but the contrasts he drew between tradition and expertise were primarily to do with the legitimacy of command systems. Those he discusses under the category of 'traditional authority' are mainly rulers rather than guardians, save in the context of his sociology of religion. Traditional authority is where 'masters are designated according to traditional rules and obeyed because of the traditional status'. Trust is generated not just by these traditional rules but by personal loyalty. The individual who has authority over others is, in Weber's words, a 'personal master' rather than a superior, one reason why traditional authority cannot be understood in terms of 'formal procedures'. Traditional rules are rarely clearly specified and always allow the master a wide area of freedom to do what he likes; he is free to do good turns for his subordinates, in return for gifts or dues. Household officials and favourites are often tied to the ruler in a patrimonial way, as slaves or dependants.

Authority in its more generic sense, in traditional cultures, is, however, the province of the guardians, and about this Weber says little. Those who hold authority – or effectively 'are' authority – in this way do or are so in virtue of their special access to the causal powers of formulaic truth. 'Wisdom' is the characteristic term which applies here. The wise person or sage is the repository of tradition, whose special qualities come from that long apprenticeship which creates skills and states of grace. Authority in its non-specific meaning is clearly a generative phenomenon. Whatever degree of trust may come from personal loyalty, the stability of traditional leadership depends in a much more integral way upon access to symbols which perpetuate the necessary 'aura'. Rulers may turn on their sages, Weber says, kings on their churchmen, because at any given point the masters possess greater secular power; but were the influence of traditions' guardians dispelled altogether, the power of a chief or prince would quickly come to naught.

Since he gives so much emphasis to domination, when he contrasts traditional with more modern forms of authority Weber focuses particularly upon 'rational-legal' authority. The dominance of the expert, in other words, is largely equated with the replacement of patrimonialism by bureaucracy. The prototypical expert is the bureaucratic official, performing the specialized

duties of his office; the Puritan version of the calling played its
due part in this transition. From this interpretation comes
Weber's nightmare vision of a world imprisoned in the 'steel-hard
cage' of bureaucratic domination.

Rational-legal authority rests upon 'a belief in the legality of
enacted rules and the right of those elevated to authority under
such rules to issue commands'.[40] Personal loyalty is downplayed
as compared to due process of law or formal procedure. The
keynote institution of rational-legal authority is the bureaucratic
organization; discipline and control are characteristic of the
conduct of the official and the organization as a whole.

The contrast Weber draws between traditional and rational-
legal authority has been justly influential, as of course has his
theory of bureaucracy. Yet his bureaucratic nightmare has not
come to pass and it is not obvious that the 'official' is either the
dominant figure of the age or the faceless autocrat whose diffuse
power Weber feared. The compulsiveness that Weber unearthed
in the Puritan ethic is coupled not to a 'disciplinary society' –
whether in the manner of Weber or of Foucault – but to
something else.

We need here to separate the expert from the official. Officials
are experts, in a wide sense of that term, but expertise, in the
context of the modern social order, is a more pervasive phenomenon than is officialdom. We should not equate experts and
professionals. An expert is any individual who can successfully
lay claim to either specific skills or types of knowledge which the
layperson does not possess. 'Expert' and 'layperson' have to be
understood as contextually relative terms. There are many layers
of expertise, and what counts in any given situation where expert
and layperson confront one another is an imbalance in skills or
information which – for a given field of action – makes one an
'authority' in relation to the other.

When we compare tradition with expertise we find major
differences, just as in the case of comparing guardians with
experts. We can sum these up, for the purposes of the present
discussion, in the following way: first, expertise is disembedding;
in contrast to tradition it is in a fundamental sense non-local and
decentred. Second, expertise is tied not to formulaic truth but to
a belief in the corrigibility of knowledge, a belief that depends
upon a methodical scepticism. Third, the accumulation of expert

knowledge involves intrinsic processes of specialization. Fourth, trust in abstract systems, or in experts, cannot readily be generated by means of esoteric wisdom. Fifth, expertise interacts with growing institutional reflexivity, such that there are regular processes of loss and reappropriation of everyday skills and knowledge.

In its modern guise at least, expertise is in principle devoid of local attachments. In an ideal-typical way, it could be said that all forms of 'local knowledge' under the rule of expertise become local recombinations of knowledge derived from elsewhere. Obviously in practice things are more complicated than this, owing to the continuing importance of local habits, customs or traditions. The decentred nature of expertise derives from the traits to which Weber gives prominence, save that those do not concern only rational-legal procedures. That is to say, expertise is disembedding because it is based upon impersonal principles, which can be set out and developed without regard to context. To say this is not to downgrade the importance of art or flair; but these are qualities of the specific expert rather than the expert system as such.

The decentred character of expertise does not preclude the existence of 'authoritative centres', such as professional associations or licensing bodies; but their relation to the knowledge-claims they seek to influence or regulate is quite different from that of centres of tradition in regard of formulaic truth. Although such might not always happen in practice, in principle their role is to protect the very impartiality of coded knowledge. In many ways expertise thus cuts across the formation of the bureaucratic hierarchies upon which Weber placed emphasis. It has become a commonplace to say as much about the role of professionals, whose global affiliations cannot be contained within the hierarchy of command within the organization. However, the phenomenon goes well beyond this example. In virtue of its mobile form, expertise is as disruptive of hierarchies of authority as it is a stabilizing influence. Formal bureaucratic rules, in fact, tend to deny that very openness to innovation which is the hallmark of expertise; they translate *skills* into *duties*.

Disembedding mechanisms depend on two conditions: the evacuation of the traditional or customary content of local contexts of action, and the reorganizing of social relations across broad time-space bands. The causal processes whereby disembedding occurs are many, but it is not difficult to see why the formation and evolution of expert systems are so central to them. Expert systems decontextualize as an intrinsic consequence of the impersonal and contingent character of their rules of knowledge-acquisition; as decentred systems, 'open' to whosoever has the time, resources and talent to grasp them, they can be located anywhere. Place is not in any sense a quality relevant to their validity; and places themselves, as we shall see, take on a different significance from traditional locales.[41]

Wisdom and expertise

There were various sorts of communication, but also dispute, between the diverse guardians of tradition in premodern contexts. Wrangles of interpretation were extremely common, and most traditional symbols and practices, even in small cultures, had strongly defined fissiparous tendencies. Difference in the interpretation of dogma, however, is not the same as disputes relating to expert knowledge (or, as should always be stressed here, claims to knowledge). The 'natural state' of tradition, as it were, is *deference*. Traditions exist in so far as they are separated from other traditions, the ways of life of separate or alien communities. The expert purveys universalizing knowledge. Experts are bound often to disagree, not only because they may have been trained in varying schools of thought but because disagreement or critique is the *motor* of their enterprise.

We sometimes speak, not without reason, of 'traditions of thought' in academic study, science and other areas relevant to the distribution of expertise. Gadamer has even made tradition, in his sense, the origin of all forms of linguistic understanding. The debate about 'presuppositions' and the importance of working within relatively fixed perspectives has spilled over into the philosophy of science. Yet the use of 'tradition' to describe such perspectives, while justifiable enough as shorthand, is clearly elliptical. The combination of scepticism and universalism that characterizes modern modes of enquiry ensures that traditions of thought are understood by sympathizer and critic alike to be relatively arbitrary. Experts trained in one particular approach may often be critical or dismissive of the views of those schooled in others; yet critique of even the most basic assumptions of a perspective is not only acceptable, but called for, expected and responded to.

The point is not just that, as Popper says, everything is open to doubt, fundamental though that is, not just to intellectual enquiry but to everyday life in conditions of modernity. It is the *mixture of scepticism and universalism* which gives the disputes of experts their particular flavour. Experts disagree not just because they are defending different pre-established positions but in the very service of overcoming those differences. Pluralism here has a different form from the cultural diversity of premodern systems, and is clearly related to broad principles of democratization. Experts frequently disagree, but in the interests of a universalism that lends itself to public discourse. Such discourse is both the means of and produced by the conjunction of critique and universalism.

Discomforts for expert and layperson come from the very same source. Expert knowledge, and the general accumulation of expertise, are supposed to provide increasing certainty about how the world is, but the very condition of such certainty, not to put too fine a point on it, is doubt. For a long while, the tensions inherent in such a situation were masked by the distinctive status which science, understood in a specific way, enjoyed in modern societies – plus a more or less unquestioned dominance that the West held over the rest of the world. Furthermore, the very persistence of tradition, especially in contexts of everyday life, held back processes of evacuation that have today become far advanced. So long as traditions and customs were widely sustained, experts were people who could be turned to at certain necessary junctures; and, in the public eye, at least, science was in effect not very different from tradition – a monolithic source of 'authority' in the generic sense. The differences between guardians and experts were much less obvious than they have since become.

A non-traditional culture dispenses with final authorities, but the significance of this for day-to-day life was first of all muted by the factors described above. Even for those working in intellectual disciplines, 'science' was invested with the authority of a final court of appeal. What seems to be a purely intellectual matter – the fact that, shorn of formulaic truth, all claims to knowledge are corrigible (including any metastatements made about them) – has become an existential condition in modern societies. The consequences for the lay individual, as for the culture as a whole, are both liberating and disturbing. Liberating, since obeisance to a single source of authority is oppressive; anxiety-provoking, since the ground is pulled from beneath the individual's feet. Science, Popper says, is built upon shifting sand; it has no stable grounding at all. Yet today it is not only scientific enquiry but more or less the whole of everyday life to which this metaphor applies.

Living in a world of multiple authorities, a circumstance sometimes mistakenly referred to as postmodernity, is very consequential for all attempts to confine risk to the narrow conception referred to previously, whether in respect of an individual's life-course or of collective attempts to colonize the future. For since there are no super-experts to turn to, risk calculation has to include the risk of which experts are consulted, or whose authority is to be taken as binding. The debate over global warming is one among an indefinite range of examples that could be quoted. The very scepticism that is the driving force of expert knowledge might lead, in some contexts, or among some groups, to a disenchantment with all experts; this is one of the lines of tension between expertise and tradition (also habit and compulsion).

Science has lost a good deal of the aura of authority it once had. In some part, probably, this is a result of disillusionment with the benefits which, in association with technology, it has been claimed to bring to humanity. Two world wars, the invention of horrifically destructive weaponry, the global ecological crisis, and other developments in the present century might cool the ardour of even the most optimistic advocates of progress through untrammelled scientific enquiry. Yet science can and indeed must be regarded as problematic in terms of its own premises. The principle 'nothing is sacred' is itself a universalizing one, from which the claimed authority of science cannot be exempt.

A balance between scepticism and commitment is difficult enough to forge within the philosophy of science, where it is endlessly debated; it is surely unsurprising, therefore, to find that such a balance is elusive when sought after in practical contexts of day-to-day life. Again, this is as much true of the collective efforts of humanity to confront global problems as it is of the individual seeking to construct a personal future. How can a layperson keep up with, or reconcile the diverse theories about, for example, the influence of diet upon long-term health? Some findings are at any time quite well-established and it is sensible to act on them; for instance, giving up smoking almost certainly lessens the chance of contracting a specific range of serious illnesses. Yet it is only forty years ago that many doctors were recommending smoking as a means of enhancing mental and bodily relaxation. Many forms of scientific knowledge, particularly when they are bracketed to observable technologies, are relatively secure; the shifting sand is leavened with a measure of concrete. However, all must be in principle regarded as open to question and at every juncture a puzzling diversity of rival theoretical and practical claims is to be found in the 'moving' areas of knowledge.

In modern social conditions all experts are specialists. Specialization is intrinsic to a world of high reflexivity, where local knowledge is re-embedded information derived from abstract systems of one type or another. There is not a one-way movement towards specialization; all sorts of generalisms ride on the back of the division of labour in expertise. An example would be the general physician in the field of medicine; he or she is a non-specialist in medical terms, whose role is to know whether a patient needs a specialist and, if so, of what kind. Yet a general physician is clearly a specialist when compared to lay members of the public.

It is of the first importance to recognize that all specialists revert to being members of the ordinary lay public when confronted with the vast array of abstract systems, and diverse arenas of expertise, that affect our lives today. This is far more than just an expansion of the division of labour in general. The guardians of tradition had their specialisms; the skills and position of the craft worker, for example, were usually quite separate from those of the priest. Specialist guardians, however, never became mere 'lay people'. Their possession of 'wisdom' gave them a distinct and general status in the community at large. In contrast to wisdom, 'competence' is specifically linked to specialization. A person's competence as an expert is coterminous with her or his specialism. Consequently, although some forms of expertise might command wide public esteem, a person's status within one abstract system is likely to be completely beside the point within another.

This situation decisively influences the nature of trust relations between experts and lay individuals, as well as trust in the abstract systems which the experts 'front'. Trust no longer depends upon a respect for the 'causal relation' believed to hold between a guardian and formulaic truth. The skills or knowledge possessed by experts are esoteric only in so far as they express their commitment to the mastery of a specialism; the individual who consults an expert could have sat in that person's place, had he or she concentrated upon the same learning process. Trust based purely on the assumption of technical competence is *revisable* for much the same reasons as knowledge purchased through methodical scepticism is revisable; it can in principle be withdrawn at a moment's notice. Hence it is not surprising that the purveyors of expertise often feel led to place a special premium on the services they have to offer, or to make particular efforts to reassure patrons at the point of contact with them. The degrees and diplomas hung on the wall of a psychotherapist's office are more than merely informational; they carry an echo of the symbols with which figures of traditional authority surrounded themselves.

The problematic nature of trust in modern social conditions is especially significant when we consider abstract systems themselves, rather than only their 'representatives'. Trust in a multiplicity of abstract systems is a necessary part of everyday life today, whether or not this is consciously acknowledged by the individuals concerned. Traditional systems of trust were nearly always based on 'facework'; because of having special access to the esoteric qualities of tradition, the guardian was tradition made flesh. The disembedded characteristics of abstract systems mean constant interaction with 'absent others' – people one never sees or meets but whose actions directly affect features of one's own life. Given the divided and contested character of expertise, the creation of stable abstract systems is a fraught endeavour. Some types of abstract system have become so much a part of people's lives that, at any one time, they appear to have a rock-like solidity akin to established tradition; yet they are vulnerable to the collapse of generalized trust.

On the level of day-to-day life, forfeit of trust may take various forms, some of which are entirely marginal to the persistence of abstract systems themselves. It does not make much odds, for example, if a few people opt out more or less completely from surrounding abstract systems – by, say, establishing a small, self-sufficient commune in a rural area. The fact that Jehovah's Witnesses reject much of the electronic technology of modernity has no particular impact on the wider society. Some dislocations or relapses in trust, however, are much broader in their implications. A progressive acceleration of mistrust in a bank, or a government, can lead to its collapse; the world economy as a whole is subject to vagaries of generalized trust, as of course are the relations between nation-states in the global political order.

Most important of all, trust in abstract systems is bound up with collective lifestyle patterns, themselves subject to change. Because of their local and centred character, traditional practices are embedded: they correspond to normative qualities that sustain daily routines. The notion of 'lifestyle' has no meaning when applied to traditional contexts of action. In modern societies, lifestyle choices are both constitutive of daily life and geared to abstract systems. There is a fundamental sense in which the whole institutional apparatus of modernity, once it has become broken away from tradition, depends upon potentially volatile mechanisms of trust. The compulsive character of modernity remains largely hidden from view so long as the Promethean impulse holds sway, especially when it is backed by the pre-eminent authority of science. When these factors are placed in question, however, as is happening today, the coincidence of lifestyle patterns and global processes of social reproduction come under strain. Alterations in lifestyle practices can then become deeply subversive of core abstract systems. For instance, a general move away from consumerism in modern economies would have massive implications for contemporary economic institutions.

Compulsiveness, I want to argue, is *frozen trust*, commitment which has no object but is self-perpetuating. Addiction, to recapitulate, is anything we have to lie about: it is the obverse of that integrity which tradition once supplied and which all forms of trust also presume. A world of abstract systems, and potentially open lifestyle choices, for reasons already explained, demands active engagement. Trust, that is to say, is invested in the light of the selection of alternatives. When such alternatives become filtered out by unexplicated commitments – compulsions – trust devolves into simple, repetitive urgency. Frozen trust blocks re-engagement with the abstract systems that have come to dominate the content of day-to-day life.

Outside areas of compulsive repetition, the dialectic of loss and reappropriation offers clear contrasts with more traditional social orders. The esoteric quality of traditions is not something which is communicable from guardians to others; it is their very access to formulaic truth that sets them off from the rest of the population. Lay individuals come to share in this quality only infrequently – as in religious ceremonials, where they may temporarily have direct access to the realm of the sacred.

This situation is altered in a basic way when expertise comes widely to replace tradition. Expert knowledge is open to reappropriation by anyone with the necessary time and resources to become trained; and the prevalence of institutional reflexivity means that there is a continuous filter-back of expert theories, concepts and findings to the lay population. The reappropriation of expert knowledge, where compulsive behaviour-patterns do not apply, is the very condition of the 'authenticity' of everyday life. Habits and expectations tend to be reshaped in terms of the pervasive filter-back of information in a more or less automatic way. However, more deliberate and focused forms of re-engagement are common. As emphasized before, these can be individual or collective; they may cover idiosyncratic elements of a person's everyday life or be global in character.

Tradition in modernity

Modernity destroys tradition. However (and this is very important), a collaboration between modernity and tradition was crucial to the earlier phases of modern social development – the period during which risk was calculable in relation to external influences. This phase is ended with the emergence of high modernity or what Beck calls reflexive modernization. Henceforth, tradition assumes a different character. Even the most advanced of premodern civilizations remained resolutely traditional. Some brief comments upon the character of such civilizations will be worthwhile before taking up directly the issue of 'tradition in modernity'.

In premodern civilizations, the activities of the political centre never fully penetrated the day-to-day life of the local community.[42] Traditional civilizations were segmental and dualistic. The vast majority of the population lived in local, agrarian communities making up, as Marx said, 'a sack of potatoes'. Traditions participated in, and expressed, this dualism. The 'great traditions' were above all associated with the rationalization of religion, a process which depended upon the existence of scriptural texts. Rationalization here was not inimical to tradition; on the contrary, although the evidence cannot be forthcoming, we may suspect that it made possible the long-term existence of specific traditional forms well beyond anything found in purely oral cultures. For the first time a tradition could know itself to exist 'from time immemorial'. The great traditions were 'monumental' – in a material sense in so far as they produced great edifices, but also in a more non-physical way in the sense in which their classical texts were a testament to their power.

Because of the structural character of these civilizations, however, the great traditions were communicated only imperfectly to the local community, over which their hold was insecure. Local communities, in any case, remained oral societies. They bred a variety of traditions which either remained distant from or actively contested the filter-down of the more rationalized systems. Thus Weber showed in his studies of the 'world religions' that the rationalization of 'scriptoral tradition' became recontextualized within the community; magic, sorcery and other local practices broke up the unifying influence of the centralized symbolic order.

A very large part of the content of tradition, therefore, continued to be at the level of the local community. Such 'little traditions' were often influenced by the guardians of rationalized religions (priests, officials) but also responded to a variety of local conditions. Often there were linguistic differences as well as other cultural schisms between local communities and central elites.

As a result of the association that developed between capitalism and the nation-state, modern societies differ from all forms of pre-existing civilization. The nation-state and the capitalist enterprise were both power-containers, in which the development of new surveillance mechanisms ensured much greater social integration across time-space than had previously been possible.[43] In the early modern state, surveillance processes continued to draw upon traditional sources of legitimation, such as the divine right of the sovereign, and his or her household, to rule. Perhaps even more importantly, certainly to my analysis here, the power system of the early modern state continued to presume the segmentation of the local community. Only with the consolidation of the nation-state, and the generalization of democracy in the nineteenth and twentieth centuries, did the local community effectively begin to break up. Before this period, surveillance mechanisms were primarily 'from the top down'; they were means of increasing centralized control over a non-mobilized spectrum of 'subjects'. The time of the accelerating development of the nation-state was thus also one in which the general population became more closely drawn into systems of integration that cross-cut the local community level. Institutional reflexivity became the main enemy of tradition; the evacuation of local contexts of action went hand in hand with growing time-space distanciation (disembedding).

However, this was a complex process. Early modern institutions did not only depend upon pre-existing traditions but also created new ones. Formulaic truth, and associated rituals, were pressed into service in new arenas – the most important being the symbolic domain of the 'nation'. Eric Hobsbawm, among others, has drawn attention to the phenomenon. He notes that nineteenth- and twentieth-century ' "traditions" which appear or claim to be old are quite often recent in origin and sometimes invented'.[44] 'Invented traditions' are not necessarily constructed in a deliberate way, although this is sometimes the case. Thus for example many nineteenth-century buildings in Britain were put up or rebuilt in Gothic style. The contact claimed with the past in invented tradition, Hobsbawm says, is 'largely factitious' – in contrast to 'genuine traditions'. Invented traditions, Hobsbawm argues, proliferate in the context of early modern institutions.

'Ancient materials' are used for modern ends – most especially, to create legitimacy for emerging systems of power.

Hobsbawm's substantive thesis may be correct, but his concepts are more open to question. 'Invented tradition', which at first sight seems almost a contradiction in terms, and is intended to be provocative, turns out on scrutiny to be something of a tautology. For *all* traditions, one could say, are invented traditions. What gives tradition its 'genuineness', its authenticity, as I have remarked earlier, is not that it has been established for aeons; nor is it anything to do with how far it accurately encapsulates past events. In those most 'traditional' of all societies, oral cultures, after all, the 'real past', if those words have any meaning, is effectively unknown. Tradition is the very *medium* of the 'reality' of the past. In societies which have a recorded history, of course, 'continuity with a suitable past' can be established – and can be dissected by the historian with a critical eye. Yet how far such continuity is ever 'genuine' in Hobsbawm's sense is problematic and, to repeat, has nothing to do with a tradition's authenticity, which depends upon the connection of ritual practice and formulaic truth.

The interconnections between early modernity and tradition can be briefly described in the following way:

First, the fact that traditions, old and new, remained central in the early development of modernity indicates again the limitations of the 'disciplinary model' of modern society. Surveillance mechanisms did not by and large depend for their effectiveness upon the internalization of emotional control or conscience. The emerging emotional axis was rather one which linked compulsiveness and *shame* anxiety.

Second, the legitimating role of science, generally understood in a positivistic fashion, perpetuated ideas of truth which, in popular culture at any rate, retained strong ties with formulaic truth. The struggles between 'science and religion' concealed the contradictory character of science's claims to unquestioned 'authority'. Hence many experts were effectively guardians and elicited appropriate forms of deference.

Third, the compulsive nature of modernity was not something that remained completely hidden or unresisted. One way of indexing this, as Christie Davies has shown, is by reference to common forms of humour and joking. Those places where

Calvinism, the 'purest form' of the capitalist spirit, was strongest (e.g., Scotland, Switzerland, Holland) also became the butt of a certain style of joking. Jokes about the Scots, for example, in some part belong to a wider category of ethnic joking; but such jokes often focus full square on the Protestant ethic. A Scot sat at the bedside of an ailing friend. 'You seem more cheerful, John.' 'Aye, man, I thought I was going to die, but the doctor can save my life. It's going to cost £100.' 'Eh, that's a terrible extravagance. Do ye think it's worth it?'

What are such jokes about if not compulsiveness, a rejection of the dogged stupidity characteristic of all compulsive behaviour? As Davies points out, the central characters in such jokes act out a caricature of the Protestant ethic – but clearly indicate that alternative attitudes are alive and well.[45]

Fourth, the compulsiveness of modernity was from its first origins gender-divided. The compulsiveness documented by Weber in *The Protestant Ethic* is that of a male public domain. In those institutional contexts where the capitalist spirit was dominant, women were effectively left with the emotional burdens which a 'striving instrumentalism' produced. Women began modes of emotional experimentation that were subsequently to have a great impact.[46] Yet traditional modes of gender difference, and gender domination, were at the same time actively reinforced by the development of newer traditions – including the emergence of an ethos of female 'domesticity'.

Fifth, tradition was called upon particularly in respect of the generation, or regeneration, of personal and collective identity. The sustaining of identity is thrown up as a fundamental problem by the maturation of the institutions of modernity, but – in tensionful and contradictory ways – this problem was 'resolved' by invoking the authority of tradition. The 'sense of community' of working-class neighbourhoods, for example, took the form, in some part, of a reconstruction of tradition; as did nationalism on the level of the state.

Globalization and the evacuation of tradition

The phase of 'reflexive modernization', marked as it is by the twin processes of globalization and the excavation of most traditional contexts of action, alters the balance between tradition and modernity. Globalization seems at first sight an 'out-there' phenomenon, the development of social relations of a worldwide kind far removed from the concerns of everyday life. To the sociologist, therefore, it might appear as simply another 'field' of study, a specialism among other specialisms. The study of global-ization would be the analysis of world systems, modes of interconnection which operate in the global stratosphere. So long as traditional modes of life, and especially the 'situated local community' persisted, such a view was not too far from the truth. Today, however, when the evacuation of local contexts has become so far advanced, it is quite inaccurate. Globalization is an 'in-here' matter, which affects, or rather is dialectically related to, even the most intimate aspects of our lives. Indeed, what we now call intimacy, and its importance in personal relations, have been largely created by globalizing influences.

What ties globalization to processes of the excavations of traditional contexts of action? The connection is the disembed-ding consequences of abstract systems. The causal influences here are complex, and bound up with the multidimensional character of modernity.[47] I shall not analyse this directly here, but rather spell out the structural relations concerned. Tradition is about the organization of time and therefore also space: so too is globaliza-tion, save that the one runs counter to the other. Whereas tradition controls space through its control of time, with global-ization it is the other way around. Globalization is essentially 'action at distance'; absence predominates over presence, not in the sedimentation of time, but because of the restructuring of space.

Processes of globalization today still to an extent follow certain early patterns established during the initial phase of modern social development. Capitalist enterprise, for example, is a disembedding mechanism *par excellence*, and is powering its way through previously resistant parts of the world just as thoroughly as it ever did. Paradoxically, state socialism, which saw itself as the prime revolutionary force in history, proved much more accommodating towards tradition than capitalism has been.

The first phase of globalization was plainly governed primarily by the expansion of the West, and institutions which originated in the West. No other civilization made anything like as pervasive an impact upon the world, or shaped it so much in its own image. Yet, unlike other forms of cultural or military conquest, disembedding via abstract systems is intrinsically decentred, since it cuts through the organic connection with place upon which tradition depended. Although still dominated by Western power, globalization today can no longer be spoken of only as a matter of one-way imperialism. Action at a distance was always a two-way process; now, increasingly, however, there is no obvious 'direction' to globalization at all, as its ramifications are more or less ever-present. The current phase of globalization, then, should not be confused with the preceding one, whose structures it acts increasingly to subvert.

Hence post-traditional society is the first *global society*. Until relatively recently, much of the world remained in a quasi-segmental state, in which many large enclaves of traditionalism persisted. In these areas, and also in some regions and contexts of the more industrially developed countries, the local community continued to be strong. Over the past few decades, influenced by the development of instantaneous global electronic communication, these circumstances have altered in a radical way. A world where no one is 'outside' is one where pre-existing traditions cannot avoid contact not only with others but also with many alternative ways of life. By the same token, it is one where the 'other' cannot any longer be treated as inert. The point is not only that the other 'answers back', but that mutual interrogation is possible.

The 'interrogations' of other cultures which the West carried out were for a long time one-sided – a series of investigations of a cryptic other which resembled nothing so much as the queries that men pursued into women. (Indeed there may very well have been quite close connections between these two sorts of endeavour.)[48] So far as non-Western cultures are concerned, the development of anthropology – a process which leads towards its effective dissolution today – gives a rough index of the phenomenon.

Anthropology has passed through three general phases. The first was one of taxonomy of the alien; early ethnography was a sort of collective voyage of the *Beagle*, circumnavigating the world in pursuit of the classification of exotic species. Taxonomic anthropology was often evolutionary. Evolutionism succeeded beautifully as a means of categorizing the other as, if not inert, no more than a 'subject' of enquiry. Not that the enquiry was ever a casual or particularly comfortable one. The alien character of other traditions was a persistent source of compelling interest, puzzlement and generalized anxiety; any threat to Western dominance was, however, quashed by the neutralizing and distant effect of 'naturalized alienness'. One could say that the alienness of non-Western traditions was a real counterpart to the 'given' form of nature, an external environment of Western expansionism to be 'understood' and probably trampled over in much the same way.

A new phase was initiated when anthropology discovered what might be called the essential *intelligence* of other cultures or traditions. The other is discovered as just as knowledgeable as 'us', although living of course in different circumstances. Realization of such capability, and therefore of the implicit claims to equality of the other, were convergent with the invention of functionalism in anthropology. Functionalism recognizes the authenticity of other traditions, but relates that authenticity only to their inner cohesion, as situated cultural wholes. The integrity of traditions thus becomes acknowledged, but the 'dialogic' relation established is one that presumes the separateness of the alien. 'Intelligence' is entirely contextual; each culture is adapted to the milieu in which it is 'discovered'. The anthropological monograph can be deposited in the Western library where it stands alongside an indefinite array of other studies. In social or material terms the juxtaposition of recording and real consequences remains cruel: the anthropologist, as Lévi-Strauss sadly remarked, is the chronicler, and even in some part the causal agent, of a disappearing world. The anthropological monograph preserves, in much the same way as a protected relic does, a testament to a way of life to which we can no longer directly bear witness.

Compare the journeys of an itinerant anthropologist today. Nigel Barley carried out anthropological research in Indonesia.[49] Barley's work is different both in style and content from orthodox anthropology. It is chatty, witty and informal; it records his own feelings, puzzles and mistakes in his encounters with the individuals whose lives he went to study. He talks of the incidents, funny and dangerous, which happened during his time 'in the field' and of his 'subjects' as flesh-and-blood people rather than merely ciphers of a larger collectivity. Interestingly, his books read more like novels than academic texts – the presence of the author creates a biographical style as well as a strong narrative form. *He* is the *ingénu*, rather than those whom he goes to 'investigate'; he is like a Lucky Jim of the anthropological world. As an aside, but a very important one, it might be noted that the recovery of a narrative style here turns structuralism on its head. The 'absence of the author' in most pre-existing anthropological studies is not a reflection of the fact that texts speak for themselves; rather, the author is absent because such studies are not full dialogic engagements with 'other cultures'.

A feature of Barley's writing is that the everyday world from which he comes is pictured as just as baffling and problematic as the one he enters in Indonesia. His attempts to buy cheap air tickets in London meet with disaster; the only detailed map he can find of the area he is going to visit dates from the 1940s and the place-names are in Dutch; the advice he gets from anthropologists who have worked in the area previously is contradictory. His ingenuousness, and puzzled curiosity about the details of everyday life, actually parallel very closely the outlook of the hero of *The Mezzanine*. The alien culture is no more or less in need of interpretation than is his culture of origin; at the same time, even the most exotic forms of behaviour, when approached in a determined way, prove to have elements of easy familiarity. Embarrassment and a certain diffuse anxiety, occasionally laced with an awareness of danger, emerge as the prime negative aspects of the anthropological encounter; on the positive side, along with self-illumination, there are humour and the pleasures of discovering a common humanity.

Wherever he goes, including the most apparently isolated of areas, he is never completely out of the tracks of tourists, and sometimes even stumbles across anthropologists. Local customs continue alongside images and information coming from both the national society and the wider world. Barley himself is introduced into the group he came to study as a 'famous Dutch tourist', come to 'honour the community and its old ways'.[50] One man whom the anthropologist met offered him hospitality in a charming traditional house in the village; he seemingly had resisted the intrusions of the modern world. Of course, it turned out that he had a degree in satellite communications from the Massachusetts Institute of Technology and actually lived most of the time in the city, where he had a modern house:

> His attachment to the traditional world was just as much an outsider's as mine was . . . He rubbed salt into my wounds by his relentless self-awareness: 'You see. I only learned to value the old way by going abroad. If I had sat in my village I would have thought of America as the Kingdom of Heaven. So I come back for the festivals'.[51]

Barley's anthropological trip was not just a one-way one; a group of his 'subjects' returned with him to London. Barley organized the visit by arranging with the Museum of Mankind that they would build a traditional rice-barn as an exhibit. Unlike the sophisticated individual just referred to, his companions had never previously been far away from their home village. They, presumably, wrote no books on their return, but we get at least some sense of their reactions to Barley's own mode of life and its wider cultural setting. They had their own puzzles, their own share of incidents and reactions; and, naturally, these only sometimes followed lines the 'anthropologist' expected. Yet their activities in London furthered Barley's grasp of their indigenous culture; for the process of building the rice-barn allowed him to document their methods of production in their entirety and to gather information that would have been very hard to come by in 'the field'.

'Return visits' are by no means unknown in anthropology. Franz Boas, for example, once shepherded some of the Kwakiutl around New York (they were apparently singularly indifferent to the grandeur of the city). Anthropologists have sometimes told candid inside stories of their field-work, although quite often these originated as private diaries, kept separate from their ethnographic reports. Thus Malinowski's field-work diaries of his experiences in the Trobriands (and in England) remained unpublished until some while after his death. Today, however, anthropology is directly embroiled in the institutional reflexivity of modernity, and anthropology thus becomes indistinguishable from sociology. Australian aboriginals and other groups across the world are contesting land-rights on the basis of anthropological studies.

In a post-traditional order, in Richard Rorty's memorable phrase, we see the formation – as a possibility rather than a fully fledged actuality – of a cosmopolitan conversation of humankind. It is a social order where the continuing role of tradition, for reasons I shall go on to mention, is, however, edged with a potential for violence.

De-traditionalization

In the post-traditional order, even in the most modernized of societies today, traditions do not wholly disappear; indeed, in some respects, and in some contexts, they flourish. In what sense, however, or in what guises, do traditions persist in the late modern world? On a schematic level, the answer can be given as follows. Whether old or new, traditions in the modern world exist in one of two frameworks.

(1) Traditions may be discursively articulated and defended – in other words, justified as having value in a universe of plural competing values. Traditions may be defended in their own terms, or against a more dialogical background; here reflexivity may be multilayered, as in those defences of religion which point to the difficulties of living in a world of radical doubt. A discursive defence of tradition does not necessarily compromise formulaic truth, for what is most consequential is a preparedness to enter into dialogue while suspending the threat of violence.

(2) Otherwise, tradition becomes *fundamentalism*. There is nothing mysterious about the appearance of fundamentalism in the late modern world. 'Fundamentalism' only assumes the sense it does against a background of the prevalence of radical doubt; it is nothing more or less than 'tradition in its traditional sense', although today embattled rather than in the ascendant. Fundamentalism may be understood as an assertion of formulaic truth without regard to consequences.

In the concluding section I shall return to a discussion of the implications of these observations. For the moment, again in a rather schematic way, let me indicate some of the relations between tradition and the quasi-traditional traits of post-traditional society. I hope the reader will accept that such a relatively cursory account passes over a great deal which in another context would need to be unpacked – especially if a direct confrontation were to be made with some of the claims of postmodernism.

In the present-day, the destruction of the local community, in the developed societies, has reached its apogee. Little traditions which either survived, or were actively created, during earlier phases of modern social development have increasingly suc-cumbed to forces of cultural evacuation. The division between great and little traditions, which in some premodern civilizations survived for thousands of years, has today almost completely disappeared. Distinctions between 'high and low culture' of course still exist, and are associated with the persistence of a certain classicism in the former as compared to the latter; but this has only marginal connections with tradition as I have defined it.

The dissolution of the local community, such as it used to be, isn't the same as the disappearance of local life or local practices. Place, however, becomes increasingly reshaped in terms of distant influences drawn upon in the local arena. Thus local customs that continue to exist tend to develop altered meanings. They become either *relics* or *habits*.

Habits may be purely personal forms of routinization. Many of the items listed on page 28 for example, are today likely to be matters of habit. They are individual routines of one kind or another, which have a certain degree of binding force simply by virtue of regular repetition. The psychological significance of such routines should not be underestimated. They are of basic import-ance for ontological security because they provide a structuring medium for the continuity of life across different contexts of action. In a post-traditional order habits are regularly infused with information drawn from abstract systems, with which also they often clash. A person might resolutely stick to a certain type of diet, for instance, even though a good deal of medical opinion condemns it. However, she or he may effectively be forced to shift if, as in the case of the ice-cube tray, manufacturing or design processes change.

Many personal habits effectively become collective as they are shaped by commodification, or as a result of generalizable influences of institutional reflexivity. Local customs are more

genuinely collective habits when they are created by influences
within an area or community; but those that are remnants of
more traditional practices are likely to devolve into items in what
some have called the *living museum*. Whether they are personal
traits or more closely connected with social customs, habits have
lost most ties with the formulaic truth of tradition. Their brittle
character is indicated by the fuzzy boundary which separates
them from compulsive behaviour; their compelling force can
devolve into compulsive ritual, or in specific instances into the
obsessional neuroses which Freud was one of the first to describe
and try to account for.

Artefacts once associated with both great and little traditions in
the post-traditional order tend to become relics, although 'relic'
should be extended to cover more than only physical objects. A
relic, as I use the word here, covers any item in a living museum.
Relics are not just objects or practices which happen to live on as
a residue of traditions that have become weakened or lost; they
are invested with meaning as exemplars of a transcended past.
Consider the story of Wigan pier. George Orwell's *The Road to
Wigan Pier*, first published in 1937, described Wigan as a
dilapidated area which bore witness to the evils of industrialism.
The road to Wigan pier was a personal journey but also described
a downward trajectory of modern civilization. Orwell's account
of the town was so scathing that it in fact aroused a great deal of
local resentment.

Orwell was disappointed to find that Wigan pier no longer existed
when he got to the town. The pier was not actually a walkway, still
less was it anywhere near the sea; the term referred to an iron frame
employed to empty coal into barges along a canal. It had been
scrapped several years before Orwell arrived there. In the 1980s,
however, the pier was rebuilt. The surrounding dock and ware-
houses were cleaned up and refitted, trees planted, and the area
designated as a 'heritage centre'. The centre harks back not to the
1930s but to 1900; an exhibition, which recreates a mine and
miners' cottages, occupies part of it. It invites the visitor to
experience 'the way we were'. Ironically, Orwell has been
drummed into service as part of the very 'heritage' he found so
distasteful: visitors can take a drink in the Orwell pub.[52]

Relics are signifiers of a past which has no development, or at
least whose causal connections to the present are not part of what

gives them their identity. They are display items in a showcase, and Wigan pier is in this respect no different from 'true monuments', such as ruins preserved or refurbished palaces, castles and country homes. A material relic might seem to be something which literally 'stays in place' – which remains untouched by the vagaries of change around it. It would be more correct to say the opposite. A relic has no effective connection with the area in which it exists, but is produced as a visible icon for observation by whosoever happens to wish to visit. Like other museum pieces, it may be on the site where it originated, but whether it is or not has little relevance to its nature, which is as a signifier of difference. A relic is like a memory trace shorn of its collective frameworks.

A living museum is any collage of such 'memory traces' presented for public display. In so far as they do not become habits, customs may fall into this category. The point about relics today is that only their association with a lapsed past gives them any significance. Relics were (and are) common in religious traditions, but there they had quite a different significance; they derived their importance not from simple connection with the past but from the fact that they participated in the domain of the sacred. As Durkheim pointed out, the sacred is indivisible; a small piece of Christ's cloak is as holy as any other seemingly more impressive religious object or practice.

The advent of modernity plainly does not spell the disappearance of collective ritual. Sometimes such ritual is proclaimed to go back for centuries, or even millennia; more commonly it is a relatively recent invention in the Hobsbawm mode. Max Gluckman makes a useful distinction between 'ritualism' and the 'ritualization of social relations' which has some purchase here.[53] 'Ritualism' exists where ritual activities are bound up with 'mystical notions', or what I would call formulaic truth. The 'ritualization of social relations' is where social interaction has a standardized form adopted as a way of defining the roles that people have on ceremonial occasions. Ritualism persists, or becomes revised, in some contexts, but in most instances has been displaced by ritualization (the two can come into conflict where, say, a person who never attends church wishes to have a church wedding). Ritualism and therefore tradition continue to exist and even flourish wherever formulaic truth forms a means of constructing interpretations of past time.

At about the same date as *The Road to Wigan Pier* was published, a crowd of some one hundred thousand people gathered just outside Pretoria, in South Africa, to celebrate the laying of the foundation stone for the Voortrekker Monument. Men and women turned out in the Voortrekker dress, fires were lit and '*Die Stem*', the Afrikaner anthem, was sung. The monument was built to celebrate the anniversary of the Great Trek undertaken by the Boers a hundred years before and the victory of the covered wagons over the massed forces of the Zulu army. The ritual, and the construction of the memorial building, were not just continuations of pre-existing traditions; they actually helped create a new version of Afrikaner nationalism.

Such examples demonstrate that tradition is not just about celebrating an unchangeable past or defending the status quo. South Africa at that point was still under the colonial control of the British; the Afrikaners looked forward to the time at which they would govern an independent country. In the words of one Afrikaner political leader: 'The Great Trek gave our people its soul. It was the cradle of our nationhood. It will always show us the beacons on our path and serve as our lighthouse in our night.'[54]

Tradition, plainly, is bound up with power; it also protects against contingency. Some have argued that the sacred is the core of tradition, because it invests the past with a divine presence; from this point of view political rituals have a religious quality. However, one should rather see formulaic truth as the property which links the sacred with tradition. Formulaic truth is what renders central aspects of tradition 'untouchable' and confers integrity upon the present in relation to the past. Monuments turn into relics once formulaic truths are disputed or discarded, and the traditional relapses into the merely customary or habitual.

Tradition, discourse, violence

Tradition is effectively a way of settling clashes between different values and ways of life. Ruth Benedict expressed this in celebrated fashion when she proposed that cultures make a selection from the 'arc of possible values' and outlooks on the world.[55] Once made, however, and notwithstanding the changes that might occur, the resultant traditions form a prism; other ways of life are distinct, have an alien quality and their own centres. Tradition incorporates power relations and tends to naturalize them. The world of 'traditional society' is one of traditional *societies*, in which cultural pluralism takes the form of an extraordinary diversity of mores and customs – each of which, however, exists in privileged space.

The post-traditional society is quite different. It is inherently globalizing, but also reflects the intensifying of globalization. In the post-traditional order cultural pluralism, whether this involves persisting or created traditions, can no longer take the form of separated centres of embedded power.

Looked at analytically, there are only four ways, in any social context or society, in which clashes of values between individuals or collectivities can be resolved. These are through the *embedding of tradition*; *disengagement* from the hostile other; *discourse* or dialogue; and *coercion* or *violence*. All four are found in most environments of action, in all cultures, at least as immanent possibilities. However, quite different weightings of these factors are possible. In those societies in which tradition is a dominant influence, traditional beliefs and practices, as filtered through the activities of the guardians, take a great deal 'out of the play'. Embedded power is largely *concealed* and cultural accommodation takes the form above all of geographical segmentation. Disengagement here is not so much an active process as an outcome of the time-space organization of premodern systems, coupled to barriers which stand in the way of non-local communication.

With the emergence of modernity, however, and particularly with the intensifying of globalizing processes, these circumstances become more or less completely undermined. Traditions are called upon to 'explain' and justify themselves in a manner already alluded to. In general, traditions only persist in so far as they are made available to discursive justification and are prepared to enter into open dialogue not only with other traditions but with alternative modes of doing things. Disengagement is possible in some ways and in some contexts, but these tend to become more and more limited.

The Voortrekker Monument subsequently became a symbol of the dominant ideology in South Africa in the postwar period. One could see the apartheid doctrine fostered by that ideology as a deliberate 'refusal of dialogue' on the basis of enforced geographical and cultural segregation.

Take as another instance the case of gender as tradition. Up to and well beyond the threshold of modernity, gender differences were deeply enshrined in tradition and resonant with congealed power. The very absence of women from the public domain suppressed any possibility that masculinity and femininity could be opened out to discursive scrutiny. Today, however, as a result of profound structural changes, combined with the struggles of feminist movements over many decades, divisions between men and women, up to and including the most intimate connections between gender, sexuality and self-identity, are publicly placed in question.

To place them in question means asking for their discursive justification. No longer can someone say in effect, 'I am a man, and this is how men are', 'I refuse to discuss things further' – statements that are normally carried in actions rather than stated in words. Behaviour and attitudes have to be justified when one is called upon to do so, which means that reasons have to be given; and where reasons have to be provided, differential power starts to dissolve, or alternatively power begins to become translated into authority. Post-traditional personal relations, the pure relationship, cannot survive if such discursive space is not created and sustained.

Yet, in very many cases it is not sustained. What happens? One possibility, obviously, is disengagement: today we live in the separating and divorcing society. A person can move on and look elsewhere. Even whole groups of people might do so. Where disengagement does not occur, and traditional relations are asserted, we enter the domain of potential or actual violence. Where talk stops, violence tends to begin. Male violence towards women today, both in the context of relationships and in the wider public arena, could be interpreted in this way.[56]

What applies in the area of personal relations and everyday life applies also to the global order and all levels in between. What I have just described could be seen as a male Clausewitzean theory of personal life: force or violence are resorted to once a 'diplomatic' exchange of views stops. Clausewitz's theorem still has its defenders, as well as its contexts of practical application, in the relations between states today. Cultural clashes in the global arena can breed violence; or they can generate dialogue. In general, 'dialogic democracy' – recognition of the authenticity of the other, whose views and ideas one is prepared to listen to and debate, as a mutual process – is the only alternative to violence in the many areas of the social order where disengagement is no longer a feasible option. There is a real and clear symmetry between the possibility of a 'democracy of the emotions' on the level of personal life and the potential for democracy on the level of the global order.

The post-traditional society is an ending; but it is also a beginning, a genuinely new social universe of action and experience. What type of social order is it, or might it become? It is, as I have said, a global society, not in the sense of a world society but as one of 'indefinite space'. It is one where social bonds have effectively to be *made*, rather than inherited from the past – on the personal and more collective levels this is a fraught and difficult enterprise, but one also that holds out the promise of great rewards. It is decentred in terms of *authorities*, but recentred in terms of opportunities and dilemmas, because focused upon new forms of interdependence. To regard *narcissism*, or even *individualism*, as at the core of the post-traditional order is a mistake – certainly in terms of the potentials for the future that it contains. In the domain of interpersonal life, opening out to the other is the condition of social solidarity; on the larger scale a proffering of the 'hand of friendship' within a global cosmopolitan order is ethically implicit in the new agenda sketched in right at the opening of this discussion.

Potentiality and actuality, needless to say, are two very different things. Radical doubt fuels anxiety, socially created uncertainties loom large; yawning gaps separate rich and poor on both local and more global levels. Yet we can discern clear prospects for a renewal of political engagement, albeit along different lines from those hitherto dominant. Breaking away from the aporias of postmodernism, we can see possibilities of 'dialogic democracy' stretching from a 'democracy of the emotions' in personal life to the outer limits of the global order. As collective humanity, we are not doomed to irreparable fragmentation, yet neither on the other hand are we confined to the iron cage of Max Weber's imagination. Beyond compulsiveness lies the chance of developing authentic forms of human life that owe little to the formulaic truths of tradition, but where the defence of tradition also has an important role.

THREE

What is Social Science?

We can distinguish three main characteristics of mainstream social science, or what I have sometimes called the 'orthodox consensus'. These views have been pre-eminent in sociology for much of the postwar period, but I think it would be true to say that they have stretched across a wide range of other social sciences as well.

The first is *naturalism*, the notion that the social sciences should be modelled after the natural sciences and that the logical framework of social science addresses problems similar to those of natural science. I prefer the term 'naturalism' to 'positivism', although they mean much the same thing.

The second feature of the orthodox model is the idea that when we explain human activity, we should do so in terms of some sort of conception of *social causation*. That is to say, although as human agents we might seem to know a good deal about what we are doing and about why we act as we do, the social scientist is able to show that really we are moved by causes of which we are unaware. The role of social sciences is to uncover forms of social causation of which actors are ignorant.

A third element (about which I shall not say much in this discussion) associated with the model is *functionalism*. Although it has been generally held that the social sciences should be like natural sciences, most have accepted that they cannot be too much like classical physics because social scientists deal with systems; and systems resemble biological wholes more than the

phenomena which concern physicists. Notions of systems supposedly derived from biology, often modelled as well upon
cybernetics, were assumed by many sociologists to be central to
social analysis.

The orthodox consensus is today a consensus no more. It used
to be a majority position in social science, but now has become a
minority one (certainly in the area of social theory, perhaps not
so much in empirical social research). Those who would now
defend such a standpoint represent only one among a diverse
range of perspectives. In its place stands a plurality of different
theoretical perspectives – such as ethnomethodology, various
forms of symbolic interactionism and neo-Weberianism, phenomenology, structuralism, hermeneutics and critical theory – the list
seems almost endless.

This situation is disquieting. We no longer know exactly where
to situate ourselves in relation to such diversity of perspectives. I
speak of 'perspectives' or 'traditions', rather than 'paradigms',
because when Kuhn introduced the notion of paradigm into the
philosophy of science, he used the term in reference to the
natural sciences. Kuhn's philosophy and definition of the term
'paradigm' actually grew out of such a focus. He saw the very
disagreements between social scientists as different from those in
natural science, where there are coordinating perspectives which
dominate the professional core of scientific fields.

There are two reactions to this situation. One is to welcome it.
If there is a plurality of theoretical perspectives, well and good. A
plurality of theories is more desirable than the dogmatism which
stems from the dominance of one particular theoretical tradition.
That kind of reaction can be found even among some of the most
fervent defenders of the orthodox consensus.

Robert K. Merton was one of the main figures who tried to
produce a codification of the orthodox consensus – which he
called (before Kuhn) a paradigm for sociology. He was the first
author, in fact, to use the term 'paradigm' in its current sense.
Merton's later views are substantially different. Albeit somewhat
reluctantly, he came to recognize a variety of competing perspectives in sociology, regarding this as positively desirable. Others
have embraced pluralism much more whole-heartedly, drawing
justification from the work of Feyerabend in philosophy of

science. According to Feyerabend, in science too there should be a plurality rather than a single ordering of perspectives.

The other reaction – the negative one – comes more frequently from those working in more empirical areas of social sciences. This is the reaction of disdain, disinterest, or 'I told you so'. The 'I told you so' view is one which follows this sort of logic: 'I am an empirical researcher. I see social theorists cannot agree with one another; they can't even agree over the basic definitions of what the field of social science is. This confirms the irrelevance of social theory to empirical analysis. I can get on with my empirical work and leave the theorists to squabble over their divergent perspectives.' The second reaction, therefore, confirms for those engaged in empirical work that theoretical debates are really irrelevant to them.

Yet neither of these positions really can be justified. The first is defective because it dismisses the possibility that there are rational criteria for assessing theories. I for one don't believe such to be the case. Some theories are better than others, and some perspectives are more fruitful than others.

The second view is questionable because it can easily be demonstrated that theoretical debates do make a difference to empirical research. What C. Wright Mills called 'mindless empiricism' leads to unenterprising, non-cumulative work. The best kind of empirical research is theoretically informed empirical research. There is a relative autonomy of theory and research; the two cannot be merged. Yet all empirical researchers should be sensitive to theoretical debates, just as theoreticians should be sensitive to the problems of empirical research.

In social theory at the current time we do find signs of a renewed synthesis concerning what the social sciences are about, what their theoretical components are, and what implications there are for empirical analysis. The babble of voices that confronts us today is in some ways more apparent than real. We do know some of the merits and defects of these rival perspectives and have a sense of the main lines of development emerging from the debates.

I don't think that this is liable to produce a new orthodoxy. If I have any sympathies with either of the rival views I described, it is with the first rather than the second. I think there *is* something essentially contestable in what it is to be a human being. There is something elementally difficult in explicating human agency, which is bound to involve us in controversies over the nature of human action. Nevertheless, that does not, and should not, lead us to a blanket approval of theoretical pluralism. The way to document the movement towards synthesis is to identify what was wrong with the orthodox consensus, and then to specify the main elements of emergent agreement.

Mainstream social science, the orthodox consensus, first of all involved a mistaken model of what natural science was like. Social scientists believed themselves to be trying to reproduce the sorts of findings that the natural sciences claim to achieve, but their model of natural science was a philosophically defective one. The model of natural science deployed by the orthodox consensus was essentially an empiricist one, which sees as the highest aspiration of science the creation of deductive systems of laws.

I do not think you could find a single reputable philosopher of science who believes any longer in the conception of natural science to which many social scientists aspired. Natural science, as it clearly demonstrated in the post-Kuhnian philosophy of science, is a hermeneutic or interpretative endeavour. There are, of course, laws in areas of natural science, but laws must be interpreted, and they must be so in the context of theoretical systems. Natural science, therefore, involves interpretative systems of meaning, and the nature of science is involved in the creation of theory frames. The framing of meaning is actually more fundamental than the discovery of laws. The uncovering of laws as constituting 'science' was given an undue primacy in traditional models of natural science, and social scientists naively accepted this emphasis.

The last home of the orthodox consensus is methodology textbooks in the social sciences. Open such a textbook and you might still find in the first few pages the idea that 'explanation' is deduction of an event from a law or a system of complexly related laws. This is simply a false view of most forms of explanation in natural science, and for more than one reason it is a hopeless model to adopt in social science.

The second shortcoming of the orthodox consensus was that mainstream social science involved a false interpretation of human action. For the orthodox consensus, as mentioned, human activity is to be explained in terms of social causation. As lay actors, we may think we know what we are doing in our actions, but the social scientist can show us that in reality we are driven by influences of which we are unaware. What orthodox social science did was to treat us as though our behaviour was the outcome of structural causation or structural constraint, as though it derived directly from social forces.

What we have to do in social theory is to recover a notion of the knowledgeable human agent. By this I mean that the social sciences must emphasize phenomena which in our everyday lives we acknowledge to be primary features of human action, but which, as social scientists, we tend to forget all about. Social scientists forget that most of what we do as human beings we do intentionally, and that we are aware of our reasons for doing so. All human agents know a great deal about the conditions of their activity, that knowledge being not contingent upon what they do, but constitutive of it.

Our knowledgeability is always bounded. It is bounded institutionally, and those boundaries (structural constraints) it is still necessary to study. But recovering the notion of the knowledgeable human agent is quite fundamental to reformulating what the social sciences are about. This recovery has to be based on the idea of practical consciousness. By 'practical consciousness' I mean a notion that has been 'discovered' in a number of traditions of thought. It was identified by Wittgenstein in philosophy, emerges as an empirical concern in ethnomethodology, and is documented in the writings of Goffman. The idea refers to all the things that we know as social actors, and must know, to make social life happen, but to which we cannot necessarily give discursive form.

For example, to speak and understand a language such as English in a grammatically correct way involves knowing an enormously complex set of syntactical rules, tactics of language use, contextual cues and so on. We must know all of these things in order to speak English; but if anyone asked us to give a discursive account of what it is that we know, we would find it very difficult to do so. We could only give the most marginal of accounts of what we actually know – and must know – as language speakers for language to exist at all. It is no contradiction to say that the linguist studies 'what we already know'.

The reason why the questions which orthodox social scientists asked, and the solutions they gave, were often misconceived is that discursive consciousness – the discursive giving of reasons and accounts – was assumed to exhaust the knowledgeability of human agents. The investigator would then move to structural causes. Yet everyone knows much more about why he or she follows any particular course of action than is expressed discursively. Practical consciousness is fundamental to the way in which we make the social world predictable. The predictability of the social world does not just 'happen', as the predictability of the natural world does. It is brought about by the knowledgeably organized practices of human agents.

A third flaw in the traditional conception of social science was the idea that is possible to discover laws of social life more or less directly analogous to those existing in the natural sciences. Two types of generalization exist in social science. They can be called 'laws' if one likes; but each differs from laws in natural science. Consider the example which the philosopher Peter Winch gives, of cars stopping at traffic lights. One might suppose that there is a 'law' involved here. When the lights are red, cars stop; when they go green, the traffic moves ahead again. If you came from an alien culture, and had never seen cars before, you might imagine that there was some kind of ray between the traffic lights that stopped the cars. If that were true it would indeed be naturalistic-style law. However, we are all aware that what makes the cars stop is that traffic drivers know the rules of traffic behaviour, and that these rules and conventions of behaviour supply reasons for what they do.

It is going to be pretty uninteresting to most lay actors in modern societies if social scientists study their behaviour as motorists and come up with the discovery that they mostly stop at traffic lights. Drivers already know, of course, that they stop at traffic lights and they know why – because it is something they do in and through the use of conventions which they apply. Generalizations of such a sort are entirely trite, save where they are part of a process of anthropological retrieval. There is a role for sociologists and anthropologists in documenting how cultures differ, how conventions differ, and therefore how far predictability in different cultural settings depends upon different awareness of convention.

The second sense of 'law' is much closer to the view of generalizations established in the orthodox consensus. This concerns the unintended consequences of human action. It is true that all of us act knowledgeably all the time – that all of us know in some way what we are doing, and why. Yet, as Max Weber rightly stressed, although we are all intentional actors, the scope of our action continually escapes the intentions and purposes which prompt it.

The proponents of the orthodox consensus were preoccupied with social factors brought about by intended consequences – which also, of course, form conditions of action for agents in society. The type of generalization with which naturalistic social science was concerned depends upon the presumption of generalized unintended consequences. 'Laws' here can be understood in a form approximating to law-like generalizations in natural science. I shall call generalizations of this type those of type two. Generalizations of type one are those depending upon the knowledgeable observance of rules or conventions on the part of social actors.

Generalizations of type two clearly do exist in the social sciences. Indeed, their uncovering has to be a basic ambition of social-scientific work. Take as an example the existence of a 'poverty cycle'. Schools in poor areas have poor facilities, students are not motivated towards academic values, teachers have control problems in the classroom. When they leave school, children from such schools are ill-qualified, move into relatively low-paid jobs and live in poor areas. Their children then attend schools in these neighbourhoods – and so the cycle repeats itself.

Type two generalizations can never be exactly parallel to laws in the natural sciences, however, precisely because the causal connections they presume depend upon unintended consequences of purposive action. Virtually all generalizations of this type are mutable in terms of the altered knowledgeability of human agents. There is an intrinsic relation between generalizations of type one (rules and conventions of behaviour) and those of type two (depending upon unintended consequences). In a specific context of action, what people do knowledgeably in the light of convention alters across time, thereby influencing type two generalizations.

Social science cannot be purely 'interpretative'. To suppose otherwise was the basic mistake of those who supposed that generalizations of type one exhaust the contributions which social sciences can make to understanding human behaviour. On the other hand, the naturalistic standpoint was mistaken in presuming that we can explain human behaviour in a comprehensive fashion by means of establishing laws of type two. All social science depends upon grasping, in specific historical circumstances, the relation between knowledgeable activity in the light of convention and social reproduction brought about in an unintended fashion.

As a consequence of its logical shortcomings, the orthodox consensus held a primitive view of the nature of the Enlightenment which social science can deliver to lay individuals. The model upon which the traditional outlook was based derived again from a fairly direct comparison with natural science. The natural sciences, it was presumed, produce Enlightenment by showing us that many of our pre-established beliefs about the world were false. Enlightenment in social science can be equated with the critique of false beliefs.

This view is plainly mistaken when we consider the differences between generalizations of types one and two. Where behaviour happens regularly as a result of the knowledgeable use of convention, there is a logical sense in which it *cannot* be based upon false beliefs. People must know not only what they are doing but why they are doing it for regularities of this kind to occur in the first place. Hence it is not surprising that the redescription of their actions by the social scientist will prove uninteresting. Such information will only be news to those who do not belong to the cultural milieu within which the action observed takes place and is plainly distinct from the critique of false belief.

The ethnographic tasks of social science, of course, are important. All of us live within specific cultures which differ from other cultures distributed across the world, and from others recoverable by historical analysis. Social science in addition can display – that is, give discursive form to – aspects of mutual knowledge which lay actors employ non-discursively in their conduct. The term 'mutual knowledge' covers a diversity of practical techniques of making sense of social activities. Perhaps more than any other single writer, Erving Goffman made clear how complicated, how subtle, but how routinely managed are the components of mutual knowledge. The parallel here with linguistics is quite close. Linguistics is about what the language-user knows, and must know, to be able to speak whatever language is in question. However, most of what we know in order to speak a language, we know non-discursively. Linguistics tells us what we already know, but in a discursive form quite distinct from the usual modes in which such knowledge is expressed.

To these potential forms of enlightenment we have to add the influence of unintended consequences. Actors always know what they are doing (under some description or potential description), but the consequences of what they do characteristically escape what they intend. A nest of interesting problems and puzzles is to be found here.

Naturalistic versions of social science depend for their cogency precisely upon the observation that many of the events and processes in social life are not intended by any of the participants involved. It is in the escape of social institutions from the purposes of individual actors that the tasks of social science, according to naturalism, are to be identified.

The pervasiveness of unintended consequences means that we must continue to defend the version of social science advanced by the 'mainstream' against more 'interpretative' conceptions. But the issue can't be properly handled in the terms of naturalistic social science. For naturalistic sociologists, the unintended character of social processes sustains the view that social life is governed by influences of which social actors are ignorant. But it is one thing to argue that some aspects of social life or institutions are unintended by those who participate in them; it is quite another to presume that consequently individual agents are acted upon by 'social causes' which somehow determine the course of what they do. Far from reinforcing such a conclusion, an appreciation of the unintended consequences of action should lead us to emphasize the importance of a sophisticated treatment of the purposive nature of human conduct. What is unintentional can't even be characterized unless we are clear about the nature of what is intentional; and this, I would argue, also presumes an account of agents' reasons.

There are several different types of enquiry that relate to the role of unintended consequences in human action. For example, we might be interested in asking why a singular event occurred in spite of the fact that no one intended it to occur. Thus an historian might pose the question: why did World War I break out, when none of the main parties involved intended its actions to produce such an outcome?

However, the type of question with which naturalistic social scientists have traditionally been preoccupied concerns the conditions of social reproduction. That is to say, they have sought to demonstrate that social institutions have properties which extend beyond the specific contexts of interaction in which individuals are involved. The connection between functionalism and naturalism has specific application here. For the point of functional explanation has normally been to show that there are 'reasons' for the existence and continuance of social institutions that are quite distinct from the reasons actors might have for whatever they do. (For further discussion, see chapter 4.)

Partly as result of a renewed critical examination of functionalism, it has become apparent that an account of institutional reproduction cannot make reference to social needs, except as counter-factually posited 'as-if' properties. It is perfectly appropriate, and often necessary, to enquire what conditions are needed for the persistence of a given set of social institutions over a specific period of time. But such an enquiry presumes the analysis of the mechanics of social reproduction; it does not in and of itself supply an explanation for them. All large-scale social reproduction occurs under conditions of 'mixed intentionality'. In other words, the perpetuation of social institutions involves some kind of mix of intended and unintended outcomes of action. This mix, however, has to be carefully dissected and is historically variable.

There is a range of circumstances which separate 'highly monitored' conditions of system reproduction from those involving a feedback of unintended consequences. The monitoring of conditions of system reproduction is undoubtedly a phenomenon associated with the emergence of modern society and with the formation of modern organizations generally.

A two-fold objection can be made to explaining a social reproduction in terms of statements of the form 'the function of x

is . . .'. The first is, as already stated, that such a statement has no explanatory value, and can only be rendered causally intelligible when applied to social activity in the form of a counterfactual proposition. The second is that the statement is ambiguous in respect of intentionality. In conditions in which reproduction is highly monitored, the tie between purposes (of some agents) and the continuity of social institutions will be direct and pervasive. Where an unintended feedback operates, the mechanics of the reproduction process will be quite different. It is normally essential to distinguish the difference.

These considerations have significant, although complex, implications for analysing the practical impact of the social sciences. Mainstream social science tended to operate with a defective view of the corrigibility of common sense. I mean by common sense propositional beliefs that actors hold about social life and the conditions of social reproduction. Given their naturalistic presumptions, the proponents of the orthodox consensus assumed that the practical connotations of social science have a technological form. The social sciences correct false beliefs that agents have about social activity or institutions. As we get to know the social world better, just as in the case of the natural world, we are in a position to change it. Such a view has a deeply founded ancestry in the social sciences, dating back at least to Montesquieu, and reiterated by Comte, Durkheim and all naturalistic versions of Marxism.

If the arguments set out earlier are valid, however, such a viewpoint cannot be sustained, at least in anything like the form in which it is developed by these authors. Social science does involve the critique of false beliefs about the social world held by lay actors. But the context in which these critical ideas and theories are formulated, and their practical implications, are quite different from what is involved in natural science. Social science is concerned with concept-bearing and concept-inventing agents, who theorize about what they do as well as the conditions of doing it. Now natural science, as has been made clear in the newer philosophy of science, involves a hermeneutic. Science is an interpretative endeavour, in which the theories comprise meaning-frames. Unlike natural science, however, the social sciences involve a double hermeneutic, since the concepts and theories developed therein apply to a world constituted of the activities of conceptualizing and theorizing individuals. The social scientist does not have to interpret the meanings of the social world to actors within it. On the contrary, the technical concepts of social sciences are, and must be, parasitical upon lay concepts. This is exactly the sense in which, as Winch says, technical social science concepts are logically tied to those of the common-sense world. Generating veridical descriptions of human action presumes that the sociological observer has access to the mutual knowledge whereby actors orient what they do. The condition of being able to describe what actors are doing, in any given context of action, is being able to 'go on' within the form of life in question.

What Winch does not consider at all is the reciprocal absorption of social-scientific concepts into the social world they are coined to analyse. The concepts and theories of natural science are entirely insulated from 'their' world, the object-world of nature. This absorption process helps explain the apparent banality of social-scientific findings, as contrasted with what appear to be the far more innovative achievements of natural science.

The banality of social science was a major source of worry to practitioners of mainstream sociology. Why have not the social sciences generated discoveries about the social world which parallel those of natural science? If such discoveries do not exist, we seem unable to produce the social technologies upon which the practical connotations of social science (in the orthodox model) depend. But this view is a mistake. From its first inception in modern times social science has had, and continues to have, a very far-reaching practical impact upon the social world. It could be argued, in fact, that the transformative consequences of social science for the social world have been considerably greater than those of the natural sciences for 'their' world. But the practical impact of social science has not primarily been a technical one. It has proceeded by the absorption of social-scientific concepts into the social world, of which they have become constitutive. As they become taken over by lay actors and incorporated into social activity, they of course also become familiar elements of social routines. Their originality becomes lost, even though when first constructed they might have been as brilliantly innovative as anything that has existed in natural science.

The early history of social science was bound up with the emergence of political theory in the fifteenth and sixteenth centuries. In the writings of Machiavelli and others, a new discourse of politics emerged, involving notions like sovereignty and the very notion of politics itself. An orthodox social scientist might suppose that these theorists were just describing changes occurring in social life. Of course they were describing such changes, but they were not only doing that. The invention of the discourse of political science helped constitute what the modern state is. Thinkers were not just describing an independently-given world. The modern state is inconceivable, for example, without a notion of sovereignty. The notion of sovereignty, moreover, is one which in some sense all of us now have mastered. Whenever we use a passport to travel from one country to another, we demonstrate some kind of practical mastery of the notion of sovereignty, of the notion of citizenship, and of a range of associated notions. These are not just descriptions of an independently given world of state institutions; they have come to constitute those institutions.

The discourse of economics provides a second example. One might suppose that the early economists were describing a series of changes going on in nineteenth-century society. They were of course doing so, but they were also doing far more. The discourse of economics entered constitutively into what industrial society is. Industrial society could not exist if everyday actors hadn't mastered concepts of investment, risk, cost, even the meaning of economics.

The concepts of social science thus inevitably become familiar in the theories and practices of lay actors and are not restricted to a professional discourse. Social science does not stand in a neutral relation to the social world, as an instrument of technological change; critique cannot be limited to the criticism of false lay beliefs. The implications of the double hermeneutic is that social scientists can't but be alert to the transformative effects that their concepts and theories might have upon what it is they set out to analyse.

FOUR

Functionalism: *Après la lutte*

The debate over the merits and shortcomings of functionalism, which overshadowed most theoretical discussions in sociology for many years, today appears spent. The battlefield is largely empty, even if from time to time isolated bolts continue to be launched. The dust having settled, perhaps we can take stock of the residue of the controversy. Although one might argue that the diversity of critical attacks to which functionalism, in its various guises, was subjected increasingly forced its advocates on to the defensive, it would be difficult to claim that the controversy has lost its vigour because one side has retired defeated. Rather, new types of theoretical approach have emerged into prominence, and have caused the focus of debate to move elsewhere. That this should have happened is surely for the most part a blessing: the functionalism controversy was never an enthralling one at best, and – if I may abandon the martial metaphor in favour of another – occasionally plumbed the depths of dull formalism. But it would be a mistake to suppose that all the issues raised can be quietly forgotten. For whatever the limitations of functionalism (and I shall conclude in this discussion that they are irremediable), it always placed in the forefront problems of institutional organization, and was firmly opposed to subjectivism in social theory. I believe these emphases still to be necessary. My aim is not to rescue functionalism from its critics, nor to re-examine the course of the debate as a whole; it is, by identifying certain of the inherent flaws in functionalist thought, to develop a theoretical scheme that can replace it.

The origins of functionalism, in its modern form, are bound up with the advances made within biology in the nineteenth century. If classical mechanics remained the ideal form of a matured science, biology, and more specifically evolutionary theory, became the more immediate inspiration among leading schools of social thought. Comte's works, although antedating Darwin, provided a cogent rationale for the proximity of the relation between biology and 'sociology', and his formulation of 'social statics' was a major influence upon the subsequent spread of functionalist notions, as worked out first by Herbert Spencer and later by Durkheim. The idea of social evolution, of course, played a basic part in the writings of all of these authors, as did biological analogies borrowed directly to explicate the 'anatomy and physiology' of social life.

Durkheim's ideas have been without doubt the most important single influence upon the development of functionalism in the present century, in spite of the fact that the only significant explicit discussion of 'functional explanation' offered by him occupies no more than a few short pages in *The Rules of Sociological Method*. The incorporation of these ideas within what emerged as a distinctive, although only loosely knit, school of 'structural-functionalism' in sociology, however, only came about through the dislocation of 'function' from 'evolution'. In Durkheim, the notion of social evolution had already become attenuated. Mechanical and organic solidarity were still treated against a broad evolutionary background, but took the form more of an abstract typological contrast than a connected flow of evolutionary change. The transfer of the concept of function to anthropology, through the agency of Radcliffe-Brown and Malinowski, was directly connected to the repudiation of evolutionary theories. In breaking with the nineteenth-century preoccupation with evolution, these authors reacted specifically against the tradition of speculative attempts to reconstruct the origins of social institutions such as religion, marriage, etc. But they also reacted against 'scissors-and-paste' ethnology of the sort which, in attempting to chart the stages in the evolution of society, assembled together examples from numerous different societies without regard to the social context in which they were embedded. 'Functionalism' (a name that Malinowski willingly applied to his theoretical views, but which Radcliffe-Brown disliked) had much to do with the origins of modern field-work in anthropology, the emphasis being placed upon studying institutions in relation to social totalities.

Functionalism re-entered sociology when it crossed the Atlantic. Through his teaching while at Chicago, Radcliffe-Brown contributed directly to its influence. But this was, of course, strongly reinforced by the works of Talcott Parsons. Although Parsons studied briefly under Malinowski while in Britain, the themes he developed, and continued to elaborate through the rest of his career, were closer to Radcliffe-Brown's views. The concept of 'structure', in the work of both authors, was conjoined to that of 'function'. Rather than Malinowski's 'instrumental functionalism', it was structural-functionalism which became for some three decades the pre-eminent, if never an unrivalled, stream of social theory within American sociology. Structural-functionalism provided an array of functionalist notions more coherent and detailed than anything achieved previously; most of its adherents argued that it is *the* theoretical basis identifying the distinctive tasks of social-scientific explanation. Many authors linked to functionalism in this modern form were to a greater or lesser degree influenced by Parsons. But it has become notorious that 'functionalism' is understood in a variety of ways by different authors, whether sympathetic or critical. Since Parsons's writings embraced many themes not immediately relevant to a discussion of functionalism, I shall not attempt to confront them directly here. Instead, I shall direct my attention solely to three major contributions from other authors: first, two relatively early sources, R.K. Merton's 'codification' of the tasks of functional explanation, and the subsequent critical emendation of this offered by Ernest Nagel.[1] Although first published in 1949, and thus antedating the main body of the functionalist controversy, for which it was an essential point of reference, Merton's essay was later revised and expanded. More important, it anticipated and in some degree attempted to meet criticisms of functionalism that later became focal to the debate: such as that functionalist schemes allow no mode of approaching problems of conflict, power and so on. Moreover, Merton's work was also of major importance in the reincorporation of functionalism within sociology, the thrust of his argument being that the ideas of Radcliffe-Brown, Malinowski and other anthropological authors provide a theoretical frame for sociology, but only if substantially amended so as to be able to encompass problems that are peculiarly acute in, even if not specific to, the more developed societies.

To these, I shall add an examination of a third piece of work: that of Stinchcombe.[2] This was not a contribution to the functionalism debate as such, but it did confront, in a detailed, sophisticated way, several of the same issues, and stood in direct line of descent from Merton.

Merton: functionalism systematized

The themes of Merton's account are very well known and I shall recapitulate only briefly those elements relevant to the arguments I shall develop later.

Merton begins by noting the very thing that became the despair of many participants in the functionalism controversy: the 'plenty and variety of functional analysis' (p. 10). But he advises against disillusion; this diversity makes a codification both possible and necessary. A systematizing of functional analysis has to connect theory and method: but it must also prove itself in the handling of empirical materials. The second of these is given some considerable attention by Merton, who attempts to provide extensive illustration of the fruits of the functionalist orientation – in this emphasis he differs from the more rarefied nature of many subsequent commentaries. The main features of Merton's discussion can be characterized as follows. To begin with, certain deficiencies in the pre-existing literature have to be clarified or remedied:

1 The term 'function' has to be precisely defined. It has various different lay uses, e.g., as equivalent to 'public gathering', as well as a technical sense in mathematics. Moreover, just as great a variety of lay terms are often used as synonymous with it: 'purpose' and 'consequence' among others. We must separate out notions that refer to 'subjective states' of actors from those that refer to the outcomes of action. 'Social function', Merton says, 'refers to *observable objective consequences*, and not to *subjective dispositions* (aims, motives, purposes)' (p. 14). What a person intends to

achieve may or may not coincide with the outcome of his or her action.

2 Several of the typical emphases of functionalism in anthropology have to be revised, or rejected altogether. The thesis that society always has a 'functional unity', or implicit harmony, which Merton associates with Radcliffe-Brown, has to be abandoned. Or at least, it cannot be taken as an axiom: the degree of intergration of a society has to be treated as empirically variable. The same hols for with the 'postulate of universal functionalism', expressed by Malinowski – the idea that every standardized social practice and cultural item has a function – by virtue of its persistence. Malinowski's assertion of the 'indispensability' of functional needs is also questioned. To claim that, for example, 'religion has certain indispensable functions in every society' hides a confusion: is it the institution of religion, as such, which is necessary to society, or is it the functions it is held to fulfil? Saying that the existence of society involves certain functional prerequisites is not the same as saying that certain particular institutions are indispensable, for the same functions may be performed by different institutions.

3 Merton is at some pains to reject the charge that functionalism is inherently 'conservative', a view which, according to him, cannot be sustained once the views noted in the previous paragraph are dispensed with. In documenting this, Merton seeks to show that a revised functionalist scheme, far from being intrinsically conservative – an assimilation of the existent and the inevitable – is fully compatible with the 'dialectical materialism' of Marx and Engels – a demonstration that numerous other authors after Merton also found it necessary to attempt.

Among the elements regarded by Merton as involved in such a revision, these are the most important:

4 Functions are defined as 'those observed consequences [of standardized practices or items] which make for the adaptation or adjustment of a given system' (p. 43). Function is contrasted to dysfunction, which refers to phenomena that act against the 'adaptation or adjustment' of the system.

5 Functional analysis involves the assessment of a 'net balance of an aggregate of consequences': a particular social practice may, for instance, be functional in some respects, or on certain

levels, for the system of which it is a part, and dysfunctional in others.

6 Manifest functions, being 'those objective consequences contributing to the adjustment or adaptation of the system which are intended and recognized by participants in the system' (p.43), have to be separated from latent functions, which are not intended and recognized.

7 Analysis of the functional requirements or prerequisites of social systems has to be complemented by recognition that there is a range of variation of functional alternatives. The possibilities of change that exist in any given case, however, are limited by 'structural constraints' deriving from 'the interdependence of the elements of a social structure' (p. 44).

Nagel: a critical emendation

Although Merton's essay was much discussed, few can have given it as thorough a review as that offered by Nagel, writing as a sympathetic critic concerned to relate Merton's views to concurrent developments in biological science. Nagel begins by drawing attention to a traditional point (noted, for example, by Comte, who regarded biology and sociology as 'synthetic' disciplines, in which there is a 'priority of entity over element', in contrast to the 'analytic' sciences of chemistry, physics, etc.): that functional notions are rare in sciences other than biology. The difference seems to depend upon the fact that biology studies entities that are self-regulating in respect of changes in their surroundings. Functional analysis applies to such entities, regarded as systems, but not to systems which lack self-regulating capabilities.

A main thread of Nagel's argument consists in an attempt to trace through ambiguities which Merton's account, although itself directed to a clarification of previous literature, in Nagel's view leaves unresolved. These concern, to begin with, the significance of 'subjective dispositions' in Merton's discussion. It is not clear, Nagel claims, why – in distinguishing a class of 'manifest functions' – Merton singles out actors' purposes and motives for

special attention. Why shouldn't we regard subjective orientations as merely a systemic variable like any other? If 'subjective
aim-in-view' is not introduced as such a variable, Merton's
distinction of manifest and latent functions is not necessary, since
it does not distinguish a type of function; if it is such a variable, on
the other hand, the distinction is one between substantive 'items',
in Merton's sense, not between types of function. Nagel apparently concludes that it is more useful to consider subjective states
as functional variables: one can then trace out the functional
consequences of an 'intended and recognized' outcome as potentially different from circumstances where the outcome is not
known to those involved. Merton's discussion of functional
consequences, Nagel holds, is itself ambiguous. The 'function' of
an item could refer simply to a characteristic of a system which it
serves to maintain; or to the totality of effects which it produces
that contribute to the 'adaptation or adjustment' of the system.
But this makes it difficult, perhaps impossible, to employ
Merton's notion of a 'net balance of functional consequences',
since there is no 'final' or 'decisive' baseline along which this can
be judged as a 'net balance'. Functions and dysfunctions are
relational, in respect of definite traits of the system which the
analyst is interested in explaining.

Nagel concludes by trying to show that Merton's formulations
of 'functional alternatives' and 'structural constraints' need elaboration. Merton fails to follow through an implication of his own
distinctions here. A 'functional alternative' might refer to an
alternative item which fulfils the same function as another – the
only sense which Merton considers – or it might refer to an
alternative *function*, which (perhaps in conjunction with others)
meets certain system 'needs'. The difference is consequential for
functional analyses of potential social change: 'structural constraint', if connected only to the first sense, is obviously likely to
be more narrowly conceived, and 'conservative', than if connected also to the second.

These points comprise what I take to be the critical import of
Nagel's discussion. It is perhaps as well to add, for any reader
who is unfamiliar with the essay itself, that Nagel accepts much of
Merton's analysis, and is concerned primarily to translate it into a
series of formalized propositions.

Stinchcombe: functionalism and theory construction

Stinchcombe's assessment of the logic of functional analysis occurs in the context of an 'eclectic' discussion of method, with functionalism being represented as one strategy of explanation among others: this is the only part of Stinchcombe's work that I shall refer to here.

Functional explanation, for Stinchcombe, is a type of causal explanation within 'multi-component' theoretical schemes. 'By a functional explanation', he says, 'we mean one in which the *consequences* of some behaviour or social arrangement are essential elements of the *causes* of that behaviour' (p. 80). Three causally related links are involved: a 'structure or a structure activity'; a 'homeostatic variable'; and 'tensions' disturbing the relation of the first two. An illustration is offered from evolutionary biology, concerning the activity of the liver in sustaining blood sugar at constant levels. There are wide variations, because of differences in food eaten, etc., in sugar content of blood entering the liver from the digestive system. Hence those animals or types of animal which develop effective livers tend to survive at the expense of those which do not. 'Tension' is a necessary element in this, according to Stinchcombe, since if digestive activity were constant, there would be no selective survival tendency of animals with 'functional livers' to survive. In this example, the storage of sugar represents the structural activity, the blood-sugar level the homeostatic variable, and variations in digestive demands the tension between the first two.

Functional analyses, Stinchcombe suggests, are appropriate in circumstances of equifinality. In closed systems, final states can in principle be explained in terms of their initial conditions. In biological or social systems, on the other hand, a uniform consequence can result from the recurrence of different types of activity. Thus social organizations normally 'try to pursue their goals in the face of uncertainty and variability of the environment', but they do this in different ways: by, for example, attempting to be flexible in response to external changes, by trying directly to control markets, by predictive planning, and so on. 'Such an equifinal pattern suggests a functional explanation

of organizational behaviour in terms of uncertainty reduction'
(p. 81).

Stinchcombe also takes up the themes of the 'conservative'
nature of functionalism, and its relation to Marxism. Like
Merton, he argues that the 'conservative cast of functional theory
is not logically necessary', although it is 'an inherent rhetorical
opportunity in the theory' (p. 91). Such opportunity derives from
the possibility of looking upon homeostatic variables as morally
desirable, and their upsetting as necessarily unfortunate. Functional analysis can be placed in the service of radicalism by
showing which particular structures operate to perpetuate
phenomena that are deemed morally undesirable, or which
operate to the advantage of sectional groups; 'as Marx realized,
some consequences are more consequential than others' (p. 99).

The appeal of functionalism

Before passing to a critical appraisal of these versions of functional analysis, we might ask what has drawn so many to
functionalist notions or approaches in the social sciences.

As far as the development of functionalism in the nineteenth
century is concerned, it is clear, as I have previously mentioned,
that functionalist notions gained popularity under the sway of
evolutionary biology. If the modern period of functionalism dates
from a break with evolutionism, there have been few functionalists who have abandoned the view that functional analysis in the
social sciences shares major logical uniformities with its counterpart in biology. In the three accounts summarized above, for
example, Merton draws upon the writings of Cannon, the
physiologist, while seeking 'not to backslide into accepting the
largely irrelevant analogies and homologies which have so long
fascinated the devotees of organismic sociology' (p. 40). Stinchcombe makes use of the writings of the nineteenth-century
physiologist Claude Bernard, whose works in fact had an important influence upon those of Cannon.

There are perhaps three main factors which have stimulated
the endeavour to connect the social sciences and biology. First,

the wish to demonstrate that there is a logical unity between the social and natural sciences, at least in so far as the latter deal with complex, 'open' systems rather than with closed systems or aggregate populations of elements. It is perhaps worth noting that the initiative has not come only from the sociological side of the fence. Cannon's writings, for example, contain attempts to extend his theories to the explanation of social institutions, using organic analogies very reminiscent of 'organicism' in nineteenth-century social theory. Second, obviously, the belief that it is fruitful, indeed necessary, to regard forms of social organization as integrated unities of interdependent parts. 'Interdependence' is of course variously conceived, but usually centres upon a notion of reciprocal effect: a modification which affects one part will tend to have repercussions on other parts, finally returning to influence the initial source of modification itself. In so far as this sustains equilibrium, homeostatic principles observed in physiology apply also to social systems. Third, the belief that social systems manifest a 'hidden teleology', operating through unintended consequences of social action. Merton's differentiation of manifest and latent functions makes explicit an integral feature of functionalist theory in the social sciences: that social institutions demonstrate a teleology which cannot be necessarily inferred from the purposes of the actors involved in them. In sociological functionalism, this *always* depends ultimately upon the thesis, or the assumption, that there are 'social needs' which have to be met for society to have a continuing existence. The teleological element in this is normally presumed to be similar to that operating in biological adaptation: 'needs' are defined in terms of the facilitation of 'survival value'.

There is a fourth factor, of a different type: that of ideological persuasion, a matter never far from the centre of the functionalism debate. It is not my aim to give detailed attention to this, although I shall want to revert briefly to it at a later stage. But one should point out that the conventional claim that functional notions are only contingently associated with 'conservatism' in politics is hardly borne out by their history in social thought. 'Conservatism' is not really an appropriate word to use in this connection; but from Comte to Spencer to Durkheim to Parsons the terminology of functionalism has appeared in conjunction with the reconciliation of progress with order. Such an observation of course, as Merton remarks, does not show that functionalism is logically tied to such views.

What I propose to do in the sections which follow is provide a *decodification* of functional analysis, an examination of certain fundamental weaknesses in functionalism in the concern, not to reject its emphases in favour of subjectivism, but to encompass them within a different theoretical scheme. To approach this task, concentrating principally on the three accounts I have singled out for special attention, I shall group the shortcomings of functionalism under the following headings: functionalism and intentional or purposive action, the explanatory content of functionalism, and the concepts of 'system' and 'structure'.

Functionalism and intentional action

First decoding: *functionalism is a teleological theory which, however, allows for only a limited and deficient explication of purposive human action.* Every major school of social theory incorporates an explicit or implicit treatment of intentional action. That often characteristic of functionalist schemes treats purposes as the 'internalization' of social values: a view that shows a direct line of continuity from Comte through Durkheim to its fullest elaboration in Parsons.

Nagel criticizes Merton's distinction between manifest and latent functions, which is essentially an attempt to separate out 'subjective' intent and 'objective' consequences, on the basis that 'it isn't evident why it ["subjective disposition"] should be listed under a special category in what is ostensibly a *general* paradigm of functional analysis' (p. 82). Stinchcombe apparently agrees with this because, while he does not refer to Nagel, he specifically regards 'motivation' as prototypical, although not exhaustive, of functional analysis. To say that someone 'wants' something, according to Stinchcombe, is to say that 'the consequences of behaviour are its principal cause' – for him the basic feature of functional explanation. Wanting, he claims, is equifinal by definition, although of course the reverse does not hold.

Now the difficulty of regarding 'subjective states' of wanting as a special instance of functions in general is precisely that which Merton established the differentiation of manifest and latent functions in order to avoid: that is, to distinguish the teleology of intentional action from the hidden teleology of its consequences. Stinchcombe is surely wrong to treat wanting as a case of a general class of situations in which 'conduct is caused by its consequences'. For in intending and wanting it is not the achieved *circumstance* which is the cause of the behaviour, but the desire for its realization. A person may want something, but not initiate any course of action to obtain it: and *per contra* a want may be realized by a concurrence of events that is quite independent of the conduct of the actor. More important, however, for functional analysis is the fact that a course of action undertaken with certain intentions, or with a particular motivation, may have outcomes quite different from those anticipated by the person undertaking it. The thesis that action has 'unintended and unrecognized consequences', as Merton makes clear, is a necessary element of any sort of even modestly sophisticated scheme of functional analysis in the social sciences, as contrasted with functional analysis in physiology.

None the less, Merton's own distinction between manifest and latent functions itself does not withstand close scrutiny. For he uses the terms 'unintended' consequences, on the one hand, and 'unrecognized' or 'unanticipated' consequences, on the other, as synonymous. But they are not synonymous. The difference is one of consequence for a theory of social action, but it is one which is glossed over in most schools of social theory that tend towards determinism. A useful example to take to illustrate the issue is Durkheim's formulation of the concept of suicide, and the part which it plays in his attempted explanation of the phenomenon. Durkheim defines suicide, famously, as 'all cases of death resulting directly or indirectly from a positive or negative act of the victim himself, which he knows will produce this result'.[3] What Durkheim does here is quite consciously – perhaps one should say intentionally – obliterate the difference between doing something knowing a particular outcome will come about, and doing something intending that a particular outcome will come about. Not to acknowledge a distinction between these inevitably tends to define as irrelevant to the causal explanation of action the intentions, reasons, motives, etc., with which people act. One may undertake a particular course of conduct knowing that a particular outcome may result, but either be indifferent to that outcome x because one is really after something else, y; or because one is prepared to seek to achieve x in spite of knowing that y, an undesirable outcome, may result. On the one hand, the accomplishment of self-destruction is what the actor wants and intends to achieve through his or her act; on the other, it is what he or she is prepared to accept, or risk, in order to accomplish some other end in view.

While Merton may accept that there is a difference between 'intending' and 'anticipating' that a consequence of action will occur, he makes nothing of it, since he brackets the terms together and uses them interchangeably. It is perhaps the fact that he does use *both* terms in this way, however, which makes the distinction between manifest and latent functions appear more novel in the pre-existing functionalist literature than in fact is the case. The differentiation between purpose and function, after all, had already been made strongly by Durkheim, in *The Rules of Sociological Method* as well as more substantively in his other works. But 'manifest function' means more than this, implying that not only (1) the person knows that the consequence she or he intends to bring about will come about, but also (2) she or he knows in what way that consequence is functional (or dysfunctional in the case of 'manifest dysfunctions') for a given social system. One should notice that, while bracketing 'intending' and 'anticipating' together so far as (1) is concerned, Merton's discussion is ambiguous in relation to (2). The same differentiations, however, apply. Does one have to undertake an action intending (and knowing) that the particular *function* should be a consequence, for a 'manifest function' to exist? The whole matter becomes further complicated if one attempts to connect it to Merton's concept of a 'net balance of functional consequences'. An actor may intend (and know about) only some of a ramified series of functional and dysfunctional consequences of what he or she does, thus possibly mingling all four potential combinations of the manifest/latent/functional/dysfunctional distinctions. There is yet one more ambiguity, and an important one. Merton does not specify *who* has to intend and know what the function of an item is for it to be a manifest function. Manifest functions, he merely says, are those intended and recognized 'by participants in the system' (p. 43) to which they relate. But which participants? One may say: those whose conduct produces the functional consequences in question. Perhaps this is what Merton means. But the circumstances may easily exist in which some participants in a social system know what the functional consequences of the behaviour of *others* are, and where those others themselves are ignorant of such consequences. The significance of such a situation is not hard to see: it is likely to contribute to, and express, the power of those who are in the know over those who are not.

All this shows that what initially appears as a neat, inclusive distinction, between manifest and latent functions, papers over various basic problems concerning the nature of intentional action and its implications for social theory. I shall take up some of these problems subsequently. What I have said so far, however, only bears on the manifest/latent distinction, not on the concept of 'function' itself, to which I shall now turn.

The explanatory content of functionalism

Second decoding: *functionalism is a social theory in which the teleology of the capital term, 'function', is either redundant or falsely applied.* The question, 'is functional analysis causal analysis?' is one that has frequently cropped up in the functionalism debate. The issue is connected to the traditional division drawn between 'statics' and 'dynamics', to use the terms Comte adopted from physical theory or, in the terminology of Radcliffe-Brown, 'synchronic' versus 'diachronic' studies. Durkheim was not alone in regarding such a differentiation as coterminous with that between function and cause. It is, of course, precisely the teleological flavour of the notion of function that is involved here: for how can a consequence of behaviour also be its cause? It might seem, therefore, that we have to reserve causal explanation, as Durkheim did, for historical accounts of the origins of things, where effects follow causes in linear sequence, treating functional explanation as distinct.

Such a view *prima facie* can be supported by the sort of physiological example favoured by functionalists. That is to say, it might be held that the functions of an organ in the body can be examined without much, or perhaps without any, reference to the causes which brought that organ into being. But this is a specious idea. A statement such as 'the function of the brain is to coordinate the nervous system' can in principle be transposed into causal statements about the typical effects of a definite range of events in the brain upon a range of events in the rest of the nervous system. The three versions of functionalism I have looked at above all seem to agree that 'function' can be rendered as 'functional effect' or 'functional consequence'. What is the difference, then, according to them, between functional explanation and causal explanation?

Stinchcombe provides the most explicit answer to this. Functional explanation is a particular *type* of causal explanation; and he has no hesitation about saying that it is an 'inverted' one in which the consequences of action are 'elements of its causes'. What this really turns out to refer to is the operation of a homeostatic process, explicated in terms of equifinality. Now Stinchcombe says that 'it isn't true that equifinal causal structures indicate wanting' (p. 82). This is consonant with his analysis because, for him, just as functional explanation is a subtype of causal explanation in general, so wanting is a subtype of functional explanation in general. This implies, although Stinchcombe does not say so, that 'wants', or the properties of actors, can be distinguished from 'system needs'. For homeostasis, if it is to be made the exemplar of functional analysis, has to be conjoined to a notion of system. A homeostatic process is essentially one of adjustment in which, through the operation of what Stinchcombe calls a 'causal loop', change in one element causes change in another, causing in turn a readjusting change in the first element. But such a phenomenon cannot be called 'functional' unless it is related in some way to the survival or continuity of a more inclusive system within which it exists. Otherwise the term 'function' itself is again redundant. A homeostatic process is merely a set of causes and effects unless it can be said to be operating with some 'end in view' or to fulfil some need.

I want to claim that the notion of system need, even in biology, always presupposes the existence of 'wants' or 'interests'; and that, in the social sciences, this has the result that the idea of system need – on which, as I have tried to show, the use of the concept of function depends – is characteristically an illegitimate or falsely applied one. Functional analysis in the setting of biology or physiology normally takes the form of showing that a given homeostatic mechanism in the body involves adjustments that contribute to the life of the organism as a being. This shows, I think, that the organism 'wants' or 'has an interest' in its continuing survival, and is why it sounds odd to apply the term 'function' to purely mechanical systems even though they may involve homeostatic processes. We may speak of the function of the mainspring of a watch, or of the carburettor in an engine, but these are man-made systems, where the element of need or interest exists as a latent human one. Social systems, unlike organisms, do not have any need or interest in their own survival, and the notion of 'need' is falsely applied if it is not acknowledged that system needs presuppose actors' wants. Many functionalists, of course, have recognized that system needs depend upon wants and some, like Malinowski, have made this the centrepoint of their analyses. But if there are no independent system needs, as we have seen, the notion of function is superfluous, for the only teleology that has to be involved is that of human actors themselves, together with the recognition that their acts have consequences other than those they intend, and that these consequences can involve homeostatic processes.

This leaves aside, however, a further way in which 'survival' constantly enters into functionalist theories, on the basis of analogies with evolutionary biology. It is not fortuitous that while the origins of modern structural-functionalism coincide with the abandonment of nineteenth-century evolutionary anthropology, some of its foremost exponents have recently returned to evolutionary models. I shall argue in the next section that functionalist interpretations of social change are closely bound to evolutionary conceptions. At this point I shall consider evolution only from the point of view of the possible significance of 'survival functions'. It is frequently proposed that, although it is inadvisable to claim that social systems have 'needs' as such, we can nevertheless assume that every society which has enjoyed a continuity of existence over time *must* have met certain exigencies. A correlate viewpoint holds that the introduction of particular social forms or institutions in certain societies, lacking in others, gives them 'adaptive advantages' and thus promotes their survival at the expense of those others.

This view might initially appear to be quite different from that emphasizing 'functional prerequisites', but it can be demonstrated that it is not. Upon examination, what are claimed as functional prerequisites turn out to fall into two types. First, there are those that are actually tautologous: that are logically implied in the conception of 'human society'. Two functional prerequisites distinguished by Aberle et al., for example, are those of 'shared cognitive orientations' and 'role differentiation and role assignment'. In every society, 'members must share a body of cognitive orientations' which, among other things, 'make stable, *meaningful*, and predictable the social situations in which they are engaged'; and in every society, there must be different roles that are regularly performed, 'otherwise everyone would be doing everything or nothing – a state of indeterminacy which is the antithesis of a society'.[4] But the authors have already defined 'society' in such a way as to make these conceptually necessary elements of it. A society is defined as a 'self-sufficient system of action', where 'action' is implicitly conceived of in the Parsonian sense as 'meaningful' conduct oriented by shared expectations, and 'system' as stably connected activities – exactly the characteristics later treated as if they were empirically independent. Second, there are factors which enhance the 'adaptive capacity' of societies: e.g., the development of modes of 'provision for adequate relationship to' the material environment, or 'the prescription of means for attaining the socially formulated goals of a society and its subsystems'.[5] Such elements still seem to hover perilously near to being logically involved in the authors' concept of 'society', but if we accept that they are separable, then they are no longer 'prerequisites', but 'adaptive advantages' which some societies are liable to develop more effectively than others. Take as an illustration the first of these. If this means nothing other than the provision for material production sufficient to keep the members of society alive, and to allow them to reproduce their numbers, it relapses into the former type of logical implication of the notion of society: for the authors have previously held that a society involves 'a self-sufficient system of action which is capable of existing longer than the life-space of an individual, the group being recruited at least in part by the sexual reproduction of the members'.[6] If it means more than this, on the other hand, it must involve reference to such characteristics as, for instance, the capacity of a society which has developed a particular technology to *dominate* its environment. But this will give it an 'adaptive advantage' over others.

The concepts of 'system' and 'structure'

Third decoding: *functionalism, or more specifically structural-functionalism, mistakenly assimilates the notions of system and structure.* Both the terms 'system' and 'structure' appear chronically in the literature of structural-functionalism. Neither, of course, is specific to it: 'system' is used in various branches of contemporary social and biological theory, as in so-called 'General Systems Theory'; 'structure' appears almost everywhere, but has also been used to designate a particular tradition of thought, 'structuralism'. Now if there is anything distinctive about the latter, it is that 'structure' is employed in an 'explanatory' way, in the sense that underlying or deep structures are held to explain surface appearances. This is not the sense of structure that is the characteristic usage in structural-functionalism, where the term usually refers to a discernible pattern in surface particulars: i.e., in social relations in general, or the organization of institutions within a global society. In structural-functionalism, it is 'function' rather than 'structure' that is called upon to play an explanatory role in directing our attention beyond surface appearances.

As structure is used in a diffuse way to refer to 'discernible pattern', it is not surprising that in the functionalist literature it is often used as more or less equivalent to 'system'. If a pattern represents an enduring arrangement of 'parts', then one only needs to inject 'functioning' into it for the 'structure' to become a system. Perusal of Merton's text, for example, shows that he often uses 'structure' and 'system' as interchangeable terms. Moreover, while he devotes a considerable segment of his discussion to trying to correct indiscriminate uses of 'function', he does not provide a comparable analysis of 'structure', the meaning of which is largely taken for granted in what he has to say.

Much the same is true of Stinchcombe's discussion. The term 'structure' appears throughout his book, but is not subjected to special analysis as function is; in the sections dealing with functional explanation, 'structure' is treated as synonymous with 'behaviour', 'pattern of behaviour', and 'structural activity'. Although structural-functionalist writers tend to assimilate structure and system in their actual usage, there is a distinction between the two which is frequently recognized by them in a formal way. It is essentially one that corresponds to that between anatomy and physiology in the study of an organism. If 'structure' refers to anatomical pattern, 'function' to how that pattern operates, then 'system' refers to the two taken conjointly. Merton perhaps implicitly accepts something of this sort. In the course of his attack on the 'postulate of functional unity', for example, he quotes (p. 16) from Radcliffe-Brown, who says that a social system is 'the total social structure of a society together with the totality of social usages, in which that structure appears and on which it depends for its continued existence'.[7] Merton does not, however, explicitly comment upon this.

Now the use of structure as 'anatomy' can perhaps be defended in biology, where, say, the skeleton, or organs such as heart and liver, are in a way 'visible' independently of their 'functioning'. Even here it may be difficult to suppose that one could describe what they are independently of what they do, and there is a sense in which they are continually 'in process': that is to say, continually changing, being built up, eroded away, etc. The distinction does not in fact apply at all in social life where 'patterns' only exist in so far as they are constantly *produced and reproduced* in human action. There is no place for the two terms 'structure' and 'system' as these are ordinarily applied in 'structural-functionalism': this is why, even where authors set out to employ such a distinction, they tend to collapse the one into the other. There can be 'structures' that 'function' in particular ways, but then there is no need or place for an independent concept of system; there can be 'systems' that 'function' in definite ways, but then the notion of structure is superfluous. For 'structure' means, in the usage of structural-functionalism, something akin to 'stable, patterned arrangement'. When this refers to social life, it cannot but refer to regularities that are reproduced in human action or interaction; that is, structure and function necessarily presuppose each other. 'Functioning structure' – organized, patterned elements in interaction – means nothing different from 'system', since the notion of interdependence of parts is clearly already there in the idea of stably reproduced patterns, as interconnected elements. Structure and function cannot here be treated as 'independently observable' phenomena, that can then be taken together as 'system'. What makes some sense when one considers a dead body, which is observed independently of its 'functioning', or an unwound watch, which can be observed when it is not working, makes no sense at all when applied to human society, which only exists *in* its 'functioning'. (To forestall misunderstanding, it should perhaps be said that nothing of importance hinges on the meaning of 'observe' here: one could easily substitute 'conceive of'.)

We need to salvage the concepts of both structure and system, although not that of function itself; but each of these terms has to be understood differently from their characteristic use in structural-functionalism. The notion of system which usually appears in structural-functionalist writings is inadequate not only because it is not clearly distinguishable from structure, but because of the particular way in which 'interdependence of parts' is typically conceived. Both Merton and Stinchcombe treat the latter as satisfactorily explicated on the basis of a homeostatic model borrowed from biology. Stinchcombe in particular makes the homeostatic process or causal loop integral to his definition of function. The use of the term 'system' and the not infrequent appearance of terms such as 'feedback' in functionalist writings make it seem that functionalism and systems theory are more or less the same: as if functionalism were simply an early anticipation of systems theory. But homeostasis is not the same as feedback proper. The former involves only the blind adjustment of system parts such that a part in which modification is initiated is 'readjusted' as an outcome of the process that it sets in motion. This is a more primitive process than is involved in feedback, which relates to the existence of self-regulating systems governed by cybernetic controls. Nagel is the only one of the three authors discussed previously to link his analysis specifically to the idea of self-regulation, but he once more in fact only concerns himself with homeostasis or 'compensating mechanisms' (p. 78).

Let us assume that Stinchcombe's formulation of homeostatic process as the operation of causal loops is adequate. Homeostasis then can be distinguished from self-regulation in systems, the latter involving the selective filtering of 'information' that is applied to control 'lower-level' mechanical processes. Homeostatic processes of the mutual adjustment of causally connected elements may or may not be cybernetically regulated in this sense. This distinction is an important one, which can be profitably applied in social analysis, and is largely neglected in the functionalist literature. But this does not mean that one can accept the framework of General Systems Theory, as it stands, as appropriate for the social sciences. Von Bertalanffy counterposes the 'mechanistic' views characteristic of nineteenth-century physical science with the twentieth-century perspective of systems theory. The former represented things as the 'aimless play' of atomic elements, without direction or *telos*. General Systems Theory, however, reintroduces teleology into natural science, and thereby closes the distance between nature and society.[8] But purposiveness, in human affairs, cannot be grasped in terms of a version of teleology which merely involves cybernetic control through the feedback of information. This is a point of quite fundamental importance, which will have to be further amplified subsequently when I return to questions posed earlier about intentions or purposes. For the moment let me assert that purposiveness in human action involves not just self-regulation, but self-consciousness or reflexivity. 'Purpose' in relation to human affairs is related in an integral way to the possessing of reasons for action, or to the rationalization of action in processes of self-reflection. In this respect it is quite different from whatever teleology is involved in self-regulating processes in nature.

A specific version of cybernetic information control was introduced into the social sciences by Parsons. Here it is assumed that hierarchies of control can be discerned in social systems, in which the controlling elements are values, with social, economic relations, etc., being regarded as the 'lower-level' processes subject to such governance. This has an obvious affiliation with Parsons's emphasis on 'shared values' in social cohesion. It is therefore subject to all the objections which a diversity of critics made about that theory. However that may be, 'values' cannot anyway serve as 'information regulators' in the sense which is demanded in systems theory: as control centres which process information so as to regulate feedback.

To summarize at this point: we can distinguish three types of circumstance relevant to the 'interdependence of parts', which are progressively more inclusive. These are, shortly expressed, regulation, self-regulation and reflexive self-regulation. The first, as a homeostatic process, involves a loop of causally interrelated elements; the second, a homeostatic process that is coordinated through a control apparatus; the third, the deliberate accomplishment of such coordination by actors in the pursuit of rationalized ends. An example of the first might be the 'vicious cycle' of circumstances whereby poverty, poor educational achievement and unemployment are interconnected, so that any attempt to modify, say, educational attainment tends to be defeated by the causal loop that interconnects the three states of affairs. In so far as, for instance, the state is an institution through which the relations between all three are processed and stabilized, there is a situation that approximates to the second type. The third circumstance only comes into being when people purposively control the processes involved in cognizance of the conditions under which they occur, thus subordinating the teleology of feedback to their own *telos*. Such might be the difference between the state in nineteenth-century capitalism, and the 'planning state' of modern times.

Let me now turn to the concept of structure. What I have said so far carries the implication that while one may, if one likes, continue to talk of social 'patterns', this should be taken to refer to the stable reproduction of systems of social interaction. If the notion of structure should not be used in this sense, where it is superfluous, how can it be otherwise conceptualized? A ready answer might seem to lie in the concept as employed in 'structuralism'. Although the latter term has been used in a diffuse variety of ways, 'structure' here refers to something like an underlying message or code explaining the surface appearance of myths, linguistic expressions, etc. The specific difficulty with this version of the concept of structure is that it dispenses with the active subject altogether. Although I have argued that functionalism is unable to develop a satisfactory treatment of intentional action, it certainly does not ignore it: Merton's distinction between manifest and latent functions is directed precisely to such an end. No correlate analysis appears in the structuralist literature, in which, if human subjects appear at all, it is typically only in such a guise as the nebulous shapes of Althusser's 'bearers' (*Träger*) of a mode of production. Many structuralists have made a virtue of necessity. Thus Lévi-Strauss, commenting on Ricoeur's characterization of his work as 'Kantianism with an absent subject', willingly accepted the designation.[9]

I shall offer no particular defence of the claim that any such approach to social theory is at best partial, and that action – and reflexivity – have to be regarded as central to any comprehensive attempt to provide a theoretical explanation of human social life. At the same time, it is of the first importance to avoid the relapse into subjectivism that abandoning the concept of structure would involve. How can we reconcile a notion of structure with the necessary centrality of the active subject? The answer lies in the introduction of a series of concepts that are not found either in functionalism or in structuralism, together with a reformulation of 'structure' itself. These other concepts are those of the *production and reproduction of society*; *structuration*; and the *duality of structure*. Once we finally drop, once and for all, misleading analogies with the visually easily represented 'anatomical structure' of organisms, we are able to realize the full import of the fact that social systems only exist in so far as they are continually created and recreated in every encounter, as the active accomplishment of subjects. Where this has been acknowledged theoretically in existing schools of social theory, it has only been at the expense of the recognition of a structural dimension – as in 'symbolic interactionism'. Let us at this juncture reconceptualize 'structure' as referring to generative rules and resources that are both applied in and constituted out of action. Under the heading 'generative rules' I group two analytically separate types of rules: semantic and moral. Semantic rules include those of syntax or grammar but also, equally importantly, the totality of largely implicit, taken-for-granted rules that structure everyday discourse and mutual understandings of action as 'meaningful'. Moral rules include any sort of rule (or formalized legal statute) generating evaluation of acts as 'right' or 'wrong'. By 'resources' I mean whatever possessions (material or otherwise) actors are able to bring to bear to facilitate the achievement of their purposes in the course of social interaction: that therefore serve as a medium for the use of *power*. Rules and resources must be regarded both as the media whereby social life is produced and reproduced as ongoing activity, and at the same time as produced and reproduced by such activity: this is the crucial sense of the 'duality of structure'. Structure is the generative source of social interaction but is reconstituted only in such interaction: in the same way as a spoken sentence is generated by syntactical rules and yet by virtue of this serves to participate in the reproduction of those rules.

To examine the structuration of a social system is to show how that system, through the application of generative rules and resources, is produced and reproduced in social interaction. Social systems, which are systems of social interaction, are not structures, although they necessarily *have* structures. There is no structure, in human social life, apart from the continuity of processes of structuration – unlike in the case of organisms where, in a certain way I have noted earlier, 'structure' can be considered independent of 'function'.

In this concluding part of this section, I want to revert to a brief consideration of functionalist accounts of social change. Critics of functionalism have often asserted that it cannot supply a theory of conflict, or of social change. This is quite clearly mistaken. If the 'postulate of functional unity' is rejected, as it is by Merton, and a central place is accorded to the concept of dysfunction as well as that of function, the result is a quite sophisticated approach to sources of social strain that may be important in stimulating change. But all I have earlier said of the concept of function also applies to that of dysfunction: if the first is redundant, so is the second. I shall shortly suggest a terminology for analysing sources of strain that can conceptually handle the sort of problems to which Merton applies the function/ dysfunction opposition, so rather than consider that in further detail here I shall turn to the prototypical functionalist account of change: the theory of social evolution. Merton's account belongs to the period when notions of social evolution, as a consequence of the emphases of Radcliffe-Brown and Malinowski, were temporarily under a cloud. Their later re-emergence, in the hands of Parsons and others, attests to their connection with functionalism generally.

The nature of the connection is not difficult to tease out, although obviously the versions of evolutionary theory adopted by such authors have differed considerably. There are perhaps two levels at which the implicit or explicit dependence on biological models has had clear consequences in functionalist theory in the social sciences. The first involves an analogy with the growth of the individual organism, rather than with evolution of species as a whole. In most complex organisms, such as the human body, growth involves progressive differentiation rather than intermittent, radical transformation. Hence *one* consequence has been that models of social change as involving the differentiation of system parts in progressive and continuous fashion have often been popular among functionalist authors, and the image of such progressive differentiation towards increasing complexity is *one* meaning that the term 'evolution' has had in the social sciences. However, the view of social change as progressive differentiation can readily go along with a broader treatment of evolution as involving discontinuities, on the basis of a parallel with the emergence of new species in biological evolution. Change equals differentiation except when interrupted by major phases of transformation which involve the appearance of new 'social species-types'. Now there are many objections which can be made against the use of evolutionary models in the social sciences, even where these do not involve assumptions of unilateral development. One is the difficulty of defining species-types: animal species have definite and easily identifiable characteristics, for the most part, and there are usually very large numbers of members of a species. In the case of human societies, distinctions between 'types' are much more difficult to draw with any precision; and no type has more than a limited number of known members. But I shall not be especially concerned with this kind of objection, which may or may not be conclusive if pursued in detail. Instead I want to concentrate upon the dependence of evolutionary models on the notion of 'adaptation' to an externally given 'environment', and the consequences of this for the type of theory of social change that tends to emerge. The idea of adaptation to environments is central to most models of evolution in the social sciences because, as with biological evolution, it is held that the survival, and thus overall development, of different forms of human society can be explained in terms of differential adaptive capacity to external exigencies. Just as problems arise in designating 'social species-types', there are difficulties here in giving any sort of precision to the key terms 'adaptation' and 'environment', since the latter does not always mean, in functionalist theories of evolution, 'physical environment'. Ignoring these also, I want rather to point to three ways in which, even if such difficulties could be satisfactorily resolved, evolutionary theory in the social sciences which involves the notion of adaptation is deficient. (In saying this I am leaving open the possibility that there may be evolutionary models that can be generated from non-functionalist schools of social thought.)

The three problems at issue are the following: (1) 'Adaptive success' in the struggle for survival is treated as the explanatory element in the theory of social change: the sources of stimulus to change thus tend to be regarded as exogenous. An evolutionary standpoint of this sort is hard to reconcile with, say, Merton's scheme of functions versus dysfunctions in a 'net balance of functional consequences', that is, with internally generated change that originates in clashes between classes or interest groups. (2) Evolution in the animal world operates blindly, as the outcome of 'successful' mutation. Such a model transferred to human society cannot cope with the distinctive characteristic of the latter: purposeful intervention in the course of social development in the attempt to control or direct it consciously. (3) A connected point: the relation of human society to its material environment is ill-conceived as one of mere adaptation. Animals, as Marx pointed out long ago, simply 'adapt' to the environment, accepting its exigencies; where animals produce, they do so mechanically, and their production does not constitute a significant intervention in nature. But human beings actively transform nature, and subordinate it to their own ends.

A recodification of basic concepts for social analysis

Having decodified 'functional explanation', let me recodify a series of basic concepts which might go beyond functionalism without abandoning the sorts of theoretical tasks which Kingsley

(Structural-)functionalist theory	Theory of structuration
Basic concepts: A System B Structure C Function/dysfunction D Manifest/latent functions	*Basic concepts:* A System B Structure C Structuration D Production and reproduction of society
Explication: A System = interdependence of action, conceived of as homeostatic causal loops	*Explication:* A System = interdependence of action, conceived of as (i) homeostatic causal loops; (ii) self-regulation through feedback; (iii) reflexive self-regulation
B Structure = stable pattern of action	B Structure = generative rules and resources
C Function = contribution of system 'part' in promoting integration of system Dysfunction = contribution of system 'part' in promoting disintegration of system	C Structuration = generation of systems of interaction through 'duality of structure'
D Manifest function = intended (anticipated) contribution of action to system integration Latent function = unintended (unanticipated) contribution of action to system integration Distinction also in principle applicable to dysfunction	D Production and reproduction of society = accomplishment of interaction under bounded conditions of the rationalization of action
	Additional concepts: E Social integration/system integration F Social conflict/system contradiction

Davis once claimed are so integral to sociology that it and functionalism are one and the same.[10]

Functionalism, and the broad-ranging traditions of social thought influenced by it, originated in a view of human social activity which has become so integral to 'sociology' – the very term coined by Comte himself – that one can see a definite plausibility in Davis's claim that the two are identical. This is a view which seeks to discover the causes of human action in features of social organization, and consequently persistently dismisses agents' intentions and reasons – in short, what I call the rationalization of action – as only weakly involved in explaining of what they do. In Comte, what is nominally a project directed to the attainment of human freedom, the escape from the mystifying bonds of religion, eventuates in the discovery of a new form of bondage: to the 'higher reason' of society itself. Thus Comte's 'sociology' rediscovered religion, having initially pro-claimed the arrival of human emancipation from its fetters. If the theological penumbra of functionalism, still clearly discernible in Durkheim, has been progressively stripped away in modern structural-functionalism, the residue of Comte's theme of 'progress with order' remains. In so far as it does remain, the thesis that functionalism is ideologically neutral, that it can be applied equally to 'conservative' or to 'radical' ends, is belied. Merton's account, it is clear enough, is one of the most liberal versions of functional-ism. His version of the 'structural constraints' on the possibilities of deliberately engineered social change is quite easily separated from functionalism as such – and in any case he does not offer a generic specification of what they are.

In place of the central concept of the social (functional) determination of action, the theory of structuration begins from the concepts of the production and reproduction of society. That is to say, social interaction is regarded as everywhere and in all circumstances a contingent accomplishment of actors: and as a skilled production which is sustained under conditions of the reflexive rationalization of action. The purposive component of human action has no counterpart in nature, since the teleology of human conduct is carried on within the context of a reflexive awareness of reasons that is intimately and integrally interwoven with 'moral responsibility' for activity. I have already pointed out that those schools of social theory which have recognized distinctive characteristics of human conduct, such as 'symbolic interactionism', have shirked analysis of structures – perhaps because the latter appear, in their connotation in functionalism, as basically 'constraining' influences on behaviour. Another way to put this is to say that symbolic interactionists have concerned themselves with the production of society, as a skilled accomplishment of actors, but not with its reproduction. The theory of structuration treats the reproduction of systems of interaction in terms of the duality of structure, whereby the structural generation of interaction is also the medium of its reproduction. This breaks completely with the abstract dichotomy of 'statics' and 'dynamics', or 'functional' versus 'historical' explanation, typical of functionalism. Change is regarded as inherent in every circumstance of the reproduction of a system of interaction, because every act of reproduction is *ipso facto* an act of production, in which society is created afresh in a novel set of circumstances. It also makes power an axial feature of all social interaction, since reproduction always involves the use of (generalized) resources which actors bring to any social encounter.

While the notion of function is redundant to the theory of structuration, that of 'social integration' can still be regarded as a basic one – together with the further one of 'system integration'. If the former concerns integration within systems of interaction, the latter concerns the integration *of*, or 'between', systems of interaction. The notion of integration needs to be given some attention. Integration should not be treated as, as such, equivalent to 'cohesion', the latter referring to the degree of 'systemness' of parts, as expressed in terms of any or all of the three levels of interdependence. Integration is most appropriately used to refer to the degree to which each part of a social system has direct ties or interchanges with every other part. The integration of social systems is always crucially connected to the distribution of power within them. This is easily clarified, at least on a conceptual plane. 'Ties' and 'interchanges' in the above sentence should not be regarded as mutually equivalent: that is to say, such ties normally involve unbalanced exchanges in terms of resources that are applied in interaction.

The separation of 'social integration' from 'system integration' bears directly upon difficulties that have long been associated with functionalism. These difficulties in substantial part stem from the tendency of such authors to focus upon the integration of the 'individual' in 'society' as the overriding problem for functional analysis, regarding 'society' as any and every form of social interaction from the single encounter up to the global social order. This has three consequences: (1) for these writers social integration, that is the conjunction of the behaviour of individual actors within reproduced systems of interaction, depends primarily upon the moral coordination of their acts. Since this is applied as a theorem to 'society' generally, it follows that the integration of the global order (system integration) itself depends upon a *consensus universel* – a notoriously suspect view that Merton certainly distances himself from. (2) As the emphasis is placed above all upon the integration of the 'individual' in 'society', via processes of moral socialization, there is great difficulty in dealing conceptually with sectional group interests and conflicts. The only theoretical avenue for explaining conflict is in terms of lack of moral regulation of individuals by the community as a whole: in other words, the theory of anomie. (3) Since the only 'interests' that tend to play any significant part in this type of perspective are those of either the 'individual' or 'society' (the latter being conceptualized as functional needs), little conceptual place is found either for *divergent* interpretations of 'normative elements' founded on clashes of group interests (such as class interests), or for adherence to moral obligations founded upon 'pragmatic acceptance' rather than 'internalized moral conviction'.

A distinction between social and system integration helps to overcome such shortcomings, because we can hold that modes of social integration are quite different from those of system integration. The theory of structuration suggests a treatment of social integration that contrasts rather profoundly with that characteristic of the 'normative functionalism' of Durkheim, Parsons and others. Such authors concentrate upon 'internalization', meaning basically the 'internalization of values', in explaining the reproduction of forms of interaction through purposive conduct: the values that provide the cohering moral consensus also figure as internalized, motivating elements in the personalities of the actors. The theory of structuration differs from this standpoint in two main ways: (1) the explanatory schema of 'internalization' is a deterministic one in which, for all Parsons's stress upon a 'voluntaristic' conception of action, interaction does not appear as negotiated and contingent. For this we substitute the view that interaction is a skilled accomplishment, reflexively negotiated against the backdrop of the rationalization of conduct. (2) In contrast to the thesis of 'internalization', which tends to operate with a gross notion of 'motivation' as the 'subjective component' of action, a differentiation is made between *motives*, *reasons* and *intentions or purposes* in action. Motives refer to wants (conscious or otherwise) involved in the impulsion of conduct. To suppose that this is all there is to the 'subjectivity' of action, however, is to ignore the reflexive monitoring of conduct that distinguishes specifically human behaviour from that of the animals. By the rationalization of action I mean the capability of all ('competent') human actors to control their activity through a chronic awareness of its conditions and consequences, thereby connecting wants to intentions, to what they actively seek to attain in interaction with others.

In social integration, the 'parts' are purposive actors. In system integration, the 'parts' are collectivities, or systems of social systems. The sense of 'part' is not easy to explicate in either of these cases, although I shall not deal in any detail with the issues involved, which have been much discussed in the literature on 'methodological individualism' and its critique. What I have to say here, however, and in what follows immediately, presupposes a definite stance on these issues. Those who have advocated methodological individualism, in one version or another, have frequently regarded functionalism as one of their major targets of critical attack. In so far as they object to notions such as 'system need', I regard their criticisms as entirely justified. In so far as they object to the use of notions such as 'collectivity' or equivalents altogether, or regard them as shorthand descriptions of individual action, their position is untenable. The structural components of social action are not properties of individuals, but of collectivities or social systems. This can be illuminated by reference to speech acts and language. Speech acts are always the situated products of particular actors, and presuppose, for example, knowledge of (ability to use) syntactical rules whereby those acts are generated; but those rules, as such, are properties of the language community. To avoid the reification potential in such phrases as 'properties of the collectivity', however, it is essential to stress that such properties exist only in and through their reproduction in concrete acts.

It should be clear that the distinction between social and system integration does not suppose that the first involves 'subjective' elements (purposes, etc.), while the second relates to the 'objective' consequences of action. We must also separate this differentiation from that between social conflict and system contradiction. In discussing social conflict, we should be careful to recognize the difference between 'conflict of interests', or 'division of interest', and active conflict or struggle. In referring to 'conflict', I mean the second of these. Conflict may involve the confrontation of either individuals or collectivities, but necessarily entails conscious struggle, in which such confrontation enters into the rationalization of conduct of at least one – normally both or all – of the parties concerned. It is not important here to say anything about the sources of social conflict, save to point out that conflict is not, as power is (the application of resources in purposive action), integral to every social relation. While all cases of conflict involve the use of power, the reverse does not hold.

Now we know that conflict in this sense is not the same as what Merton means by 'dysfunction', even though he gives the latter concept prominence in order to break with the 'postulate of functional unity' and to show that a functionalist schema can cope with the analysis of tensions and strains in society. 'Dysfunction' is not equivalent to 'conflict', of course, because the former is tied to the same explanatory exigency as that of function: system needs, or the adaptive success of the system. The idea of dysfunction is also treated by Merton as a basis for dealing conceptually with the complexity of the advanced societies: the object of functional analysis is to trace out a 'net balance of functional consequences' that stem from a given social item. This view initially seems an attractive one, especially when set against the 'normative functionalism' of Durkheim and Parsons. On closer examination, its weaknesses are apparent. The difficulty of applying the notion of a 'net aggregate of functional outcomes' is definitely a logical deficiency. But if this is abandoned, further problems ensue. Although it seems a straightforward pairing of concepts, the function/dysfunction relation is in fact asymmetrical in terms of the logic of functional explanation. Without the notion of system need, the homeostatic causal loop involved in 'function' does provide one (type of) explanation of why a social practice persists. Yet stripped of any connection with 'system need' or 'functional prerequisite', the notion of dysfunction explains nothing at all. That is to say, it does then become equivalent to conflict – or covers that as well as what I shall now characterize as system contradiction.

By 'system contradiction' I mean a disjunction between two or more 'principles of organization' or 'structural principles' which govern the connections between social systems within a larger collectivity. Two such structural principles might be, for example, those of the bonded allocation of labour characteristic of feudalism, and the free mobility of labour stimulated by emergent capitalist markets, the two coexisting within post-feudal society in Europe. Stated in this way, system contradiction sounds identical to 'functional incompatibility' within the language of functionalism. To make clear its distinctiveness from the latter, we must point out that the existence of a structural principle *always* presupposes an explicitly or implicitly acknowledged distribution of interests on the level of social integration. Once we have dropped any notion of system need, it is evident that there can be no talk of system contradiction without the presumption (on the part of the theorist) of identifiable division of interest (which in turn presupposes mutually exclusive wants) between actors or categories of actors. It is this and only this which makes structural principles such as those mentioned above contradictory: the example presumes that certain actors (entrepreneurs) have interests in promoting the free mobility of labour, while others (feudal landowners) do not. The important point is that the existence of system contradiction does not inevitably imply the occurrence of social conflict, as I have specified the latter notion; the connection is a contingent one.

This is a good point at which to return to the problem of purposive action. While functionalism, in its various versions, always involves reference to intentional action, which is contrasted to the hidden teleology of function, it has not produced an account of the *transformational capacity* of self-reflection within human affairs. The theory of structuration, however, presumes just such an account. The production and reproduction of society is everywhere and always a skilled creation of situated actors, grounded in the reflexive rationalization of action. Yet the rationalization of action is bounded. There are three basic respects in which we can explicate the aphorism that, 'while human beings make history', they do not do so universally 'under conditions of their own choosing': in respect of unacknowledged factors of motivation (repressed/unconscious wants); in respect of the structural conditions of action; and in respect of unintended consequences of action. The latter two are those which concern us here. For the structural conditions of action are constraining elements in human conduct only in so far as they are themselves unintended consequences, rather than the intended instrument of the realization of ends. This is why it is important to separate out the 'recognized' or 'anticipated' consequences of action from their 'intended' consequences. For human freedom consists, not in merely knowing the consequences of action, but in applying that knowledge in the context of the reflexive rationalization of conduct.

FIVE

'Britishness' and the Social Sciences

'As British as a good cup of tea'; 'as British as fish and chips'. Many of the social characteristics we take to be distinctively British don't stand up very well if subjected to scrutiny. Tea, after all, didn't originate in Britain and was only adopted as a regular drink in the nineteenth century. Chips were first thought of in France, and again only became united with fish as a working-class dish at some point in the nineteenth century.

As a social scientist looking at the Britishness of the social sciences, I have a natural inclination first of all to turn the question round a bit. What do the social sciences have to say to us about 'Britishness'? Britishness, pretty obviously, means one's identity in a nation: the British nation is, in the terms of the political theorist, Benedict Anderson, an 'imagined community'. 'Britain' was a retrospective invention, a set of symbols designed to create a unity where little really existed. 'Britishness' was a means, if you like, of papering over the cracks in a national state formed through conquest internally, and which came to stand at the apex of an empire externally.

No one is 'British' who doesn't also have another identity – as English, Scottish, Welsh or, in Northern Ireland, 'loyalist'; or, for a lengthy period, as Irish, Australian, South African and so forth. Britishness has always been an inherently ambiguous idea. When we ask, therefore, how British are the social sciences, we have to problematize the nature of Britishness itself. My thesis here will be that the history of the social sciences reflects the very tensionful nature of Britishness which it is also the business of the social sciences to analyse.

The early history of social science in Britain bears the mark of two waves of change which established the British state. Thomas Hobbes and John Locke, writing in the seventeenth century, are recognized internationally today as key founders of modern political science. Each in his different way responded to the issues involved in the consolidation of British governmental power – problems of political control, sovereignty and legitimacy. They wrote as Englishmen, confronting the processes of political centralization which produced the Act of Union.

Even at this early date, however, social and political thought in this country was deeply entwined with Continental influences – few if any scholars were wholly 'English' in their outlook. Hobbes, for example, made various visits to Paris, and was influenced by the ideas of a group of philosophers centred upon Marin Mersenne. The group included the celebrated author René Descartes, whose treatise *Discourse on Method* was a main influence upon the political theory which Hobbes went on to produce.

In the eighteenth century, the intellectual and practical centre of intellectual innovation shifted to the domain of industry. The political element remained important, but in the shape of political economy – or what was later simply called economics – the emphasis came to be placed on the conditions of industrial development. Here some of the key figures were Scottish – the most notable among them being Adam Ferguson, John Millar and Adam Smith. Their Scottishness was not incidental to their views; they wrote from the perspective of an advanced commercial society which had established itself on the Scottish lowlands. They weren't particularly concerned in their writings with Scotland as a distinctive political and cultural entity. Rather to the contrary: the vantage point of their Scottish location allowed them freely to generalize about new processes of economic development and economic organization which they believed would come to affect everyone. And so indeed they have done.

The other prime social sciences, anthropology and sociology, have different origins again – and rather later ones. Anthropology, in my estimation, for a century or more occupied a pivotal position in British intellectual culture. For anthropology is the science of otherness, of the alien; and in its global spread, the British Empire was of course constantly meeting with and seeking to domesticate otherness. Anthropology was far from being the lackey of imperialism. The great anthropologists of the nineteenth century, travellers and authors – such as James Frazer or Edward Tylor – mostly sought to defend and protect the authenticity of non-Western cultures against naive or hostile Anglo-Saxon parochialism. Yet – unlike their American counterparts – the anthropologists in Britain didn't study the 'internal colonialism' of their own state. In other words, they didn't study the Irish, the Scots or the Welsh; they focused their attention much farther away.

Like the other developing social sciences in the mid to late nineteenth century, anthropology in Britain was strongly influenced by both Continental and American streams of thought. Yet a distinctive British school – or schools – of anthropology certainly existed. Frazer and Tylor in particular worked out versions of evolutionary and comparative anthropology which both recognized the dazzling variety of different cultures and slotted them into a coherent pattern of interpretation.

Sociology – the study of the very type of society of which at that time Britain was the leading example, namely modern industrial society – was the absent partner at this intellectual feast. The subject did achieve some recognition in the late nineteenth century. But its most prominent representative at that date, Herbert Spencer, internationally feted in his own lifetime, turned out to be an ephemeral influence upon the culture of social science. Sociology remained for many years marginal to British intellectual life and didn't become well established as a university subject until long after the rest of the social sciences. Oxbridge was the litmus test here. As the dominant universities in Britain, Oxford and Cambridge have long exerted a far-reaching influence upon the intellectual and cultural life of the country. Unlike the other areas of social science, sociology didn't become a major part of the curriculum at Oxford or Cambridge until as late as the 1960s. The subject had a foothold in London University, at the London School of Economics. The distinctively British version of sociology, however, was that linked to Fabian socialism, and it didn't have much international influence.

The absence of an adventurous sociological imagination in British intellectual life was consequential. To put things baldly, until the period after World War II, the part played by sociology in the US and the major Continental countries was in Britain usurped by anthropology. British intellectual culture largely lacked the sense of self-reflection or self-critique which sociology elsewhere either fostered, or to which it actively contributed. It was fine to conduct investigations into the traits of alien peoples, but not to subject the core characteristics of British culture to the same scrutiny. Most investigations were confined to aliens in our own midst – for example, the urban poor.

Let us now bring what is inevitably a complex and tangled story – much more so than I have time to portray here – up to the World War II period. The postwar generation of British intellectuals included a diversity of internationally renowned social scientists – people whose theories and ideas decisively shaped their chosen fields of study. In economics the influence of J.M. Keynes (who died in 1946) was still strong – and of course was not only an intellectual force, but deeply affected political and economic practice in the UK and most other countries of the industrialized world. A cluster of economists who were either the direct pupils of Keynes – such as Joan Robinson or Richard Kahn – or strongly indebted to him, achieved positions of pre-eminence in the discipline. What came to be called 'Keynesianism' may or may not have been true to Keynes's own thought, but it placed a definite tradition of economic thinking at the head of economic theory and policy across a good deal of the world.

Were these economic thinkers distinctively British? Well, they were and they weren't. Robinson was English and so, in spite of his name, was Kahn. But other prominent economists of the time working in this country, such as Nikolas Kaldor or Thomas Balogh, were from abroad (Hungary). Pietro Sraffa, who for a while exerted a good deal of influence over certain sectors of the economics profession here, was Italian. In general, the early postwar period was one in which much of what was from one angle distinctively 'British', or 'English', was stamped by the impact of émigré thought and culture. Many who had fled from the Nazis in the 1930s came to maturity during the early period after the war, or their ideas were influential then. Some of those working mainly in philosophy – such as Ludwig Wittgenstein or Karl Popper – had a major impact upon the social sciences. But many of the most renowned social scientists were themselves émigrés, such as Bronislaw Malinowski in anthropology, who came to this country at an earlier point.

So far as the question of Britishness is concerned, Malinowski is an interesting and also an emblematic figure. Malinowski was born in 1884 in Cracow, in a region of Poland that was politically part of the Austro-Hungarian empire. He was of a highly cosmopolitan background, and spoke seven languages fluently. He spent two periods of time in the Trobriand Islands, in the South Pacific, which were then part of the British Empire. The writings he produced as a result were very widely read within anthropology itself, but some of his works and teachings also reached a public audience in the UK and US. Malinowski never wrote directly about the British – and he had his own personal struggles with his identity in his adopted society, in which he never felt fully accepted. At the same time, he saw himself as combating British insularity in the name of that very society, where citizenship was limited to Britain itself and to some of its white dominions.

Anthropology in Britain had a complex relation to the empire, but it was undoubtedly bound up inseparably with it. All the major British anthropologists in the post-World War II generation built their careers on the basis of studying colonized cultures. Along with economics, anthropology at this time could lay fair claim to be at the cutting-edge of the social sciences internationally. British anthropologists in fact made up a veritable galaxy of stars which no other country could match – although several were born in South Africa, not the UK. After Malinowski came such figures as E.E. Evans-Pritchard, Meyer Fortes, Audrey Richards, Edmund Leach, Gregory Bateson, Max Gluckman and Raymond Firth. Evans-Pritchard, Fortes and Richards all produced major studies based on work in British West Africa, while Leach studied India and what was then Ceylon.

Emigré intellectuals plus anthropologists: was this what Britishness in the social sciences effectively amounted to in the first two decades after World War II? To put it in a nutshell, I would say 'yes'. Dislocated, tensionful since its beginnings,

Britishness took on a new twist in the fading days of imperial power. The changing status of the country as regards its global empire found oblique expression in the flourishing of these areas of social science. The issue of what Britishness actually was, however, was hardly addressed – and, compared to these other social sciences, sociology in particular remained in the doldrums. Only one sociological thinker of any consequence internationally – T.H. Marshall – was produced by Britain in the early postwar period. And his work was concerned with social policy as much as, or more than, with sociology itself.

Over the past thirty years or so, however, the balance has shifted very considerably, and the composition of intellectual life, so far as the social sciences are concerned, has altered. Social science in Britain, I would say, has suffered from a relative decline overall in terms of its international status. So, probably, have most other branches of British intellectual culture, including the natural sciences, over this period. General relative decline in the social sciences has been accompanied by a new alignment of the various social science disciplines. Economics and anthropology don't rule the roost in the way in which once they did. The decline of anthropology has been steep. One would be hard put to it to name a single anthropologist working in British universities today of equal stature to the leading figures in the earlier generation. In some ways this isn't particularly surprising. There are no longer colonial domains for anthropologists to sally forth to; and in fact, the subject-matter of anthropology as a whole – that is, premodern or traditional societies – has virtually disappeared from the world as a result of the spread of industrialization.

Unlike anthropology, economics is flourishing numerically. Virtually all universities in the UK have economics departments, some of them very sizeable. Yet as measured by international standards, distinguished economists on a par with the previous generation seem few and far between. The centre of gravity in economics appears to have shifted decisively to the US. Economics in Britain is both the most insulated from the other social sciences and the most Americanized. Continental thought has made its impact, and there are various schools of institutional and so-called post-Keynesian economics. But the dominant outlook in economics in this country – the neo-classical approach – is the same as that which rules the roost in the US. This situation doesn't look set to change greatly in the immediate future. There are rumblings of discontent within economics in this country and elsewhere – some forms of economic theorizing are so abstract as to be utterly remote from the world of real economic affairs they are supposed to help illuminate. And economic thought in its orthodox guise doesn't appear to have been of much help in coping with problems of mass unemployment or expanding inequality. Given the failure of Marxist economics, however, the available alternatives to neo-classical perspectives seem at the moment limited in scope.

And so we come back to sociology and political theory, where the picture is rather different. Sociology, and to a lesser extent political theory and political science, had new beginnings in this country in the 1960s. Sociology, of course, was to many outside observers the wild child of the 1960s, born of the radical rhetoric and the collective ferment of the time. Students flocked to the newly born subject seeking truth in revolutionary confrontations with the existing state of affairs. It might seem that, after this brief flash of glory sociology has fallen away.

The reality is both more prosaic and more positive, as far as the history of sociology is concerned. For the discipline has made real strides since the endeavours of the 1960s. At that time, while there were of course indigenous traditions to draw upon, American influences were predominant. They remain important, but the history of sociology in Britain over the past thirty years has been the creation of new ideas which do have a certain Britishness about them.

Particularly as far as theoretical thinking is concerned, it is Continental thought, rather than American, which has had most impact on sociology in recent years. This is also true of the rest of the social sciences, with the exception of economics. The social sciences have always had quite strong connections with philosophy, and have been affected by, as well as contributing to, the controversies with which philosophers have struggled – questions of relativism, the nature of scientific explanation or the interpretation of language and symbolism. Structuralism, poststructuralism, hermeneutics and phenomenology – all of these varying intellectual traditions, which have Contintental origins, have made their mark in this country.

Each has had its uncritical admirers. But British sociologists and political theorists in this country have provided a sympathetic, yet critical and discerning audience. Over the years, among the distinctive traits of British intellectual culture are said to have been its pragmatism and its empiricism. British intellectuals are supposed by and large to have shunned generalizing theory and what sceptical Anglo-Saxon critics see as the rhetorical flights of fancy of some of their counterparts on the Continent. These observations aren't true of sociology in Britain today. British sociology has shown itself capable of creating an interesting mix of American and Continental traditions of thought, without succumbing to the blandishments of either. The subject has become a diverse one, and, like the other social sciences, could probably be said to lack an intellectual centre. On the other hand, in the work of an author such as John Goldthorpe, for example, one can see a formidable mixture of empirical rigour and theoretical innovation.

As in all other areas of intellectual culture, sociological thinking is becoming internationalized. The restless academic, swanning around the world to conferences on this, that and everything, is likely to find much the same topics and theories being discussed everywhere. Is the social world fragmenting? What are the likely consequences of the transformations in Eastern Europe? What's happening to the family, marriage and sexual life? Are we now living in a postmodern era? But British sociologists don't come to these things as questions asked by others. They have contributed a great deal to setting the agenda for these worldwide debates.

It won't do to end on too sanguine a note. Neither sociology in particular, nor the social sciences in general, are in good shape in Britain, and this isn't only because sources of funding for social research have diminished over recent years. It's also because the world has taken the social sciences by surprise. Few if any social observers, for example, anticipated the events of 1989 and after in the Soviet Union. Few predicted that the progressive expansion of the welfare state would be thrown into reverse. Speaking more positively, few supposed that a peaceful transition from apartheid could be made in South Africa, or that serious peace negotiations would be opened in the Middle East or in Northern Ireland.

The world has become a puzzling place and practising social scientists haven't thus far been much better than anyone else at casting light upon what is going on. What *is* going on is a complex process of globalization, which is deeply affecting both intellectual culture in Britain and the texture of British society itself. Social science and Britishness are consequently coming to interact in new ways. The fragile and contested nature of 'being British' used to reflect the ambiguities of empire, but now once more has come closer to home. In people's changing attitudes towards the monarchy, government and other national institutions, Britishness has become problematic all over again. Who is to say that it won't evaporate altogether? The challenge now for the social sciences is to confront our national identity, or identities, afresh, in the context of new social changes sweeping through our lives with unparalleled urgency.

SIX

The Future of Anthropology

Should we declare an end to anthropology, along with all those other endings so freely spoken about today? For nearly all the societies and cultures which were once the specialized 'field of study' of anthropology have now disappeared or become altered almost beyond recognition. Anthropology faces two sets of problems. Some are shared with the other social sciences. Together with all the social science disciplines, with the exception of economics, anthropology has felt the impact of postmodernism, the apparent collapse of foundationalism in epistemology, and the rise of a much more reflexively organized intellectual culture. Newspapers, magazines and TV deal in much the same sources and ideas now as do academic authors, but reach audiences of millions rather than a few hundreds or thousands.

In addition, however, anthropology has its own distinct litany of troubles, wearyingly familiar to anyone working in the subject. Here the question isn't only the disappearance of the exotic, the far-away places which were once so inaccessible. Anthropologists used to deal with individuals and groups who by and large didn't answer back. The anthropologist would go off to some distant corner of the world, carry out the obligatory field-work, and some while after return to write the whole thing up in the form of a monograph. The book would be lodged in a number of university libraries, most of them in Western countries, to be safely ignored save by a few specialists within the anthropological profession. In a world of developed reflexivity, this sort of situation rarely applies. Those who are the subjects of anthropological treatises are likely to read them, react to them and perhaps use them in local and even global political battles. Moreover, anthropology is widely seen as tainted by its association not just with the West, but specifically with colonialism. No doubt the connections between anthropology and colonialism were complex. One could hardly say, as some of the cruder attacks upon anthropology have maintained, that anthropologists were the complicit agents of colonial expansion and administration. Particularly where it turned against evolutionism, and the idea of the 'primitive', anthropology became in some part the defender of non-modern cultures in the face of the Western onslaught. Yet obviously anthropology did draw much of its sustenance from the colonial relation.

What justification, if any, is there for a continuing role for anthropology? If there is indeed such justification, what shape might the discipline henceforth assume – where would its distinctiveness lie?

There are various ways in which the autonomy of anthropology in the past has usually been understood. The specificity of anthropology might be seen in substantive, methodological or theoretical terms, or some sort of mixture of these. Substantively, the distinctiveness of anthropology, particularly in relation to sociology, was normally thought of as bound up with its concern with the non-modern. Sociology, by contrast, concerns itself with the nature and impact of modernity. Today, however, modernity is everywhere. Sociologists might see their province as primarily that of the First World while anthropologists concentrate upon the Third World. Yet as globalization develops apace, divisions between First and Third World societies crumble; and in any case the Third World is the creation of modernity rather than simply standing outside it. To persist with a substantive definition of anthropology as about non-modern societies and cultures would mean turning the subject into a version of museum studies. The anthropologist would be a sort of curator of an historical museum of humanity's past.

On a methodological level, the distinctiveness of anthropology has sometimes been supposed to lie in its devotion to intensive field-work – that is, to ethnography. Yet an argument could be made that intensive field-work was developed in sociology before anthropology. It is in any case a form of research method which is used across the social sciences rather than distinguishing any one of them. The mystique of field-work in anthropology was closely bound up with the idea that anthropology investigates the exotic; for the more alien a group or community appears, the more an immersion in its practices and customs is necessary to understand them. But with the dissolution of the esoteric, the claim that what is distinctive about anthropology is its method isn't a particularly convincing one.

That leaves theory. Like all academic subjects, anthropology has its own theoretical traditions. Sociologists and anthropologists might both lay claim to Durkheim, for example, but otherwise the intellectual ancestries to which they look tend to diverge. How much continuing intellectual mileage is there in the traditions of theory that have dominated anthropology? The answer would seem to be – only a limited amount. Evolutionary anthropology quite rightly finds few supporters in the present day. Versions of anthropological theory coming from later periods, including structural-functionalism and American cultural anthropology, are commonly recognized to have marked limitations. Each tended to picture the theoretical object of anthropology as the self-contained local community. Neither develops sophisticated conceptions of power, ideology or cultural domination.

A discipline which deals with an evaporating subject-matter, staking claim to a method which it shares with the rest of the social sciences anyway, and deficient in its core theoretical traditions – these things don't exactly add up to a defensible identity for anthropology. Yet things are by no means as bleak for anthropology as such an assessment seems to suggest. We couldn't just turn from anthropology towards sociology, because orthodox sociological traditions have as much difficulty in grasping the changes now transforming local and global social orders as do those coming from anthropology. Partly because of the differences in their areas of substantive concentration, anthropologists quite often have addressed questions which have passed sociology by; and some of these questions have now returned to full prominence. They include, for example, the resurgence of ethnicity, the seeming revival of 'tribalism' in one form or another, and the continuing importance of religion and ritual – among other issues. Anthropologists and sociologists in large part have to concentrate upon common areas of interest now. In discussing them, however, these two groups tend to draw upon at least partly different literatures; and the insights which can be brought to bear from contexts of anthropological thought might often prove to be at least as valuable as those coming from within sociology. A refusal to declare an end to anthropology, therefore, doesn't simply reflect the inertia inherent in an established academic enterprise. Anthropology *does* have a past which has to some degree to be lived down, but that past contains ideas that either remain as important as they ever were, or have actually become more significant today.

If anthropology is not a dead enterprise, how might it make its mark again, intellectually and practically? I don't see that anthropology in this respect is in a different position from the other social sciences. A number of issues must be faced. Should anthropology remodel itself in relation to the fall of epistemology and the arrival of postmodernism? How does, or should, the academic discourse of anthropology relate to other forms of knowledge-production in a world of heightened reflexivity? What implications do answers to these first two questions have for the practical connotations of anthropology?

Of some things we can be fairly sure. A new flowering of anthropological theory and research won't come about from succumbing to postmodernism, or from a prolonged preoccupation with the theory of knowledge. A newspaper article on contemporary social thought once gave the following definition of postmodernism: 'postmodernism: this word is meaningless: use it often.' The irony was apt. It is in fact a word we might do well to forget altogether, while acknowledging that some who have used it have directed our attention to important social changes and intellectual dilemmas. In my opinion, much of what passes for postmodernism suffers from its association with another 'post' – post-structuralism. Poststructuralism in the majority of its versions, I think, has a defective theory of meaning, and therefore of representation, which can be traced right back to the origins of structuralist linguistics in Saussure. Meaning is understood in relation to the play of signifiers, not – as it should be – in the context of practical experience. Although I won't elaborate the argument here, it seems to me that those who speak of a crisis of representation in anthropology, or who see anthropological work merely as a species of creative fiction, are the victims of such a false theory of meaning.

This point is closely connected to issues in epistemology. One should not confuse an intensifying of social reflexivity with the collapse of defensible knowledge-claims. Reflexivity is a social or institutional phenomenon; it doesn't, or shouldn't, refer to the particular position of the anthropological observer. A reflexive universe of social action, simply put, is one where nobody is outside. Everyone, more or less throughout the world, has to filter and react to many sources of incoming information about their life-circumstances. Such information is not simply part of the 'external world'; in their reactions to, and usages of, information, social agents construct, reconstruct and deconstruct the action environments which such information sought to describe or interpret in the first place.

In a reflexive world we are all knowledge-producers, and the phenomena of tribal groups making videos about their communities, or television journalists making sophisticated programmes drawing upon the same sorts of intellectual resources as academics do when they write their books, become commonplace. Can the professional academic compete in such circumstances? Is there, indeed, any role for the intellectual at all where the intellectual is at most one 'expert' among many others? Academics and other intellectuals will have to get used to the fact that their claims and findings are likely to be routinely interrogated by those outside the groves of academe. They can no longer act as high priests – the generous dispensers of arcane knowledge to a generally ignorant populace. These things, however, don't destroy the usefulness of the academic. The usual differences between academic specialists and lay people continue to obtain. Academic professionals normally engage with a subject-matter in a more thoroughgoing and catholic fashion; and the researches and theoretical innovations of the social sciences are necessary resources which wider forms of public reflection presume.

The practical connotations of anthropology are likely to depend more upon a rekindling of the anthropological imagination than upon a narrowing-down of the subject to limited social policy issues. I don't think this necessarily means that anthropology has to be an 'uncomfortable discipline'. Anthropology must be ready to contest unjust systems of domination, along the way seeking to decide what 'injustice' actually is, and be prepared to bring potentially controversial issues to light. Yet there is a limit to the unmasking of power, and there are problems and issues over which it is important to seek to build a collective, even global, consensus. Pre-established forms of anthropological enterprise, including the classic intensive study of the local social arena, may often be of practical importance. Numerous instances exist, in both the developed and less developed countries, where policies undertaken with the best of intentions have rebounded, or proved destructive, because they were based upon mistaken or inadequate knowledge of the groups at whom they were targeted. Anthropology today, nevertheless, must be deployed above all to get to grips with the extraordinary changes now transforming all our lives. What has practical relevance in anthropology depends not just, or even primarily, on finding 'technological' solutions to discrete problems, but rather on forging new perspectives, new ways of looking at things. Anthropology should contribute to the collective effort that the social sciences as a whole need to make to confront a social world which has changed almost out of recognition in a few short years. Perhaps then there will emerge a new generation of anthropological thinkers on a par with the old?

SEVEN

Four Myths in the History of Social Thought

In this discussion I shall place in question four prevalent interpretations of the history of social thought – interpretations which derive particularly from the exegesis of the writings of Emile Durkheim. These interpretations, I want to argue, while widely accepted, are either false or misleading. As popular myths centring upon the works of one of the most influential contributors to the formation of modern sociology, they have exerted a major effect upon assessments and evaluations of the past development of the subject.

They are the following: (1) The myth of the *problem of order*. According to this interpretation, the thought of certain authors whose work has been of outstanding importance to modern sociology – above all that of Durkheim – can be understood as an attempt to resolve an abstract 'problem of order' which has deep roots in Western social philosophy. (2) The myth of the *conservative origins of sociology*. This thesis holds that the most significant intellectual parameters underlying modern sociology – and here again the writings of Durkheim are singled out for special emphasis – derive from various forms of conservative ideology which came into being as a reaction against the changes produced by the 'two great revolutions' of the late eighteenth century in Europe: the French Revolution of 1789 and the Industrial Revolution. (3) What might be called the myth of the *great divide*: the conception that a decisive break occurred in the development of social thought with the writings of the generation of authors (stretching roughly from 1860 to 1920) to which

Durkheim belonged. According to this view, whereas the leading thinkers in the earlier part of the nineteenth century devoted themselves to creating grandiose, speculative theories of a 'pre-scientific' character, those of the subsequent generation abandoned these in favour of a more modest, scientific approach, rejecting philosophies of history. (4) The fourth myth has actually arisen from attempts to criticize the first one mentioned above – that of the problem of order. The problem of order, it is held, has occupied only one tradition of social thought; there is a counter-trend which takes as its starting point an endeavour to examine problems of conflict and change in society. According to this view – which shares most of the assumptions of that which it nominally sets out to criticize – the history of social thought since the turn of the nineteenth century can be usefully understood as involving a persisting debate between what has been called 'consensus', 'integration' or 'order' theory on the one hand (of which Durkheim is regarded as a leading exponent), and what has been termed 'conflict' or 'coercion' theory on the other (represented above all by Marx).

Like all myths, these four interpretations of the development of social thought contain elements of truth, and genuinely illuminate aspects of Durkheim's work in particular and the formation of modern sociology in general. But if each possesses a certain validity, each also constitutes a distortion. Again like all myths, these interpretations of the development of social thought are the result of the collective elaboration of many writers; in the analysis which follows, I shall confine myself to some of the more prominent expositions of these viewpoints.

The problem of order

The myth of the problem of order received its most forceful and authoritative formulation in the works of Talcott Parsons. It forms a major theme of what was perhaps the most influential study of the development of social theory ever produced – *The Structure of Social Action*, a study which has also helped to spread the myth of the great divide.[1] In the book, Parsons traces the origins of concern with the problem of order in Western social thought back to Hobbes's *Leviathan*. The 'Hobbesian problem of order', as Parsons presents it, is essentially very simple in character. According to Hobbes, the desires of individuals (in a state of nature) tend to be mutually incompatible. Hence they are involved in a war of all against all – or they would be, if it were not that they cede their natural liberty to a sovereign power in return for security against the potential assaults of others. Hobbes's solution to the problem of order was unsatisfactory, however, because it did not explain *why* people accept the sovereign authority, assuming it to be a matter of individual contract. None the less, Parsons argues, the essential components of Hobbes's solution remained largely unquestioned so long as utilitarianism retained a dominant position in social theory. Only near the end of the nineteenth century, when utilitarianism came under fire, did social thinkers manage to approach a satisfactory resolution of the Hobbesian problem – and Durkheim took the lead in this.

It is not possible to discuss, within a relatively small compass, all of the issues raised by Parsons's analysis. But it is dubious, first of all, how far Parsons's treatment of the problem of order, even in Hobbes, is acceptable. As Parsons formulates it, the 'Hobbesian problem' turns upon a contrast between 'individuals in nature' and 'individuals in society'. But although this has been traditionally ascribed to Hobbes, this statically conceived antinomy is foreign to Hobbes's own thinking, which is much more historically oriented. The significant question is how far the Hobbesian problem of order, in Parsons's exposition of it, helps to yield an accurate understanding of the main thrust of Durkheim's sociological interests.

In fact, Parsons's exposition of Durkheim's sociological concerns is misleading in various ways:

1 It is untrue to the intellectual influences which Durkheim sought to combat. The problem of order, Parsons makes clear, depends upon postulates implicit in utilitarian theory, whereby society is assumed to be the outcome of contractual relationships. He therefore takes the critique of utilitarianism to be virtually the only polemical foil of any importance in Durkheim's writings. But, although it is less overt, of equal consequence in Durkheim's thought is his critical evaluation of idealism, in two forms: first, 'holistic' idealism; and, second, Kantian philosophy.

2 This leads to a misrepresentation of the key themes of Durkheim's first and most basic work, *The Division of Labour in Society*. According to Parsons, there is a fundamental ambiguity in the study: while Durkheim argues that the Hobbesian resolution of the problem of order is inadequate, because there must be a 'non-contractual element in contract', he does not show what the relationship is between this 'non-contractual element' and the growth of organic solidarity. The replacement of mechanical by organic solidarity would seem to presuppose the eradication of the *conscience collective*; but this cannot be so if there still must be general consensual values which govern the formation of contracts. The 'ambiguity' identified by Parsons disappears if it is understood that *The Division of Labour* also involves a critique of the view that 'order' in society always presupposes the existence of strongly defined and precise moral codes of the sort characteristic of traditional societies. What Durkheim shows is that the emergence of organic solidarity entails the development of a different *form* of moral life ('moral individualism') to that characteristic of mechanical solidarity.

3 Since Parsons treats *The Division of Labour* as representative of an early, and transitory, phase in Durkheim's thought, his discussion tends to sever this work from Durkheim's later writings. Thus *The Elementary Forms of the Religious Life* is regarded simply as a subsequent, and more sophisticated, attempt to solve the problem of order. If, however, the evolutionary scheme set out in *The Division of Labour* is regarded not as a rather inadequate resolution of the problem of order, but as a framework within which the whole of Durkheim's subsequent writings have to be placed, then again quite a different picture emerges to that portrayed by Parsons. The guiding theme of Durkheim's sociology then becomes that of establishing the continuities and the *contrasts* between 'traditional' and 'modern' society. The theory developed in *The Elementary Forms* shows that even the apparently secular ideals embodied in moral individualism have a 'sacred' character: the decline of (theistic) religion does not entail the disappearance of the sacred, even though its content changes radically.

4 The institutional component of Durkheim's analysis becomes almost entirely lost to view. Much of Durkheim's writing concentrates upon the authority structure of the modern

state, contrasting this with the characteristics of the less-developed forms of society. What disappears from Parsons's discussion is Durkheim's consistent stress upon the fact that the moral revitalization of contemporary society, necessary to reduce anomie, can only take place given the occurrence of important institutional change. The 'anomic division of labour' can be alleviated only if the 'forced division of labour' is abolished: this demands that the class structure become systematically reorganized.

5 While Parsons himself does not discuss the political background to Durkheim's writings, his account of the latter's work has served to reinforce a not uncommon misinterpretation of the political grounding of Durkheim's sociology. According to this view, the parallel theme to the problem of order in Durkheim's sociological writings is his political commitment to re-establishing 'order' in French society in the wake of the disasters which attended the fall of the Second Republic. Yet if this is taken to mean a desire to reconstruct the society in the form which it took prior to 1871, it is quite a misconceived representation of Durkheim's political views. In common with other Republican intellectuals with whom he was closely affiliated (such as Jaurès), Durkheim saw the demise of the Second Republic as offering the possibility – and, indeed, showing the necessity – of implementing profound social and political changes in France: changes which had been heralded, but not concretely achieved, in the Revolution of 1789. These transformations he saw as the condition of attaining unity within the Third Republic.

'Order', of course, is a term with various possible connotations: but the perspective comprised in the 'Hobbesian problem of order' was one, in fact, which Durkheim rejected at the very outset of his intellectual career. Far from supplying the guiding theme of Durkheim's sociology, it was not, in the terms in which Parsons formulates it, a problem for Durkheim at all.

The conservative origins of sociology

The thesis that Durkheim's writings constitute a prolonged investigation of the problem of order has close connections to that which stresses his indebtedness to 'conservative' ideology. This thesis has been stated with greater and lesser degrees of subtlety. It is hardly necessary to discuss at any length the opinion that Durkheim was a conservative in his political views. Durkheim made very few forays into the sphere of practical politics, and the specific characteristics of his attitudes towards the concrete political issues of his day are impossible to evaluate. But the tendency of some commentators to connect Durkheim to right-wing nationalistic movements of his time is wholly incorrect. Durkheim's political affiliations were always with liberal Republicanism, and his participation in the Dreyfus affair on the side of Dreyfus's defenders gave unambiguous evidence of where his sympathies lay.

Most of those who emphasize Durkheim's heavy reliance upon ideological conservatism, however, have recognized his liberalism in politics. The argument is that, Durkheim's political liberalism notwithstanding, on the intellectual level he adopted the key conceptual theorems which formed part of the 'revolt' against the legacy of the eighteenth-century rationalist philosophers – as manifest in the writings of such authors as de Maistre, Bonald and Chateaubriand:

> The conservatives at the beginning of the nineteenth century form an Anti-Enlightenment. There isn't a work, not a major idea indeed, in the conservative renaissance that does not seek to refute ideas of the *philosophes*. Some, such as Chateaubriand, delighted in seeming occasionally to espouse one of the Enlighteners as the means of mounting attacks on another – usually on Voltaire, whose brilliant attacks on Christianity were vitriol for the deeply Christian conservatives. Even in Burke there are kind words occasionally where these will serve to promote a sense of inconsistency and division within the Enlightenment. But hatred of the Enlightenment and especially of Rousseau is fundamental in philosophical conservatism . . . And, at the end of the century, in the writings of the non-religious and politically liberal Durkheim we find ideas of French conservatism converted into some of the essential theories of his systematic sociology: the collective conscience, the functional character of institutions and ideas, intermediate associations, as well as his whole attack on individualism.[2]

In assessing this view, it is useful to separate two propositions which it embraces: the first concerns the intellectual origins of

Durkheim's thought, and the second relates to the theories embodied in Durkheim's sociology itself. For someone may lean heavily upon an intellectual source, but put the ideas comprised within it to a very different use to those which were current previously. It does not follow that, because a thinker uses notions taken from conservative social philosophy, his or her own theories will assume a conservative character. I shall argue, however, that it is mistaken to regard Durkheim as a conservative in either of these senses.

In his discussion of the significance of conservatism for the development of modern social thought, Nisbet distinguishes three main 'ideological currents' in the nineteenth century. Besides conservatism there were, vying for supremacy, the powerful influences of 'radicalism' and 'liberalism'. Each of these also helped to shape the emergent sociological perspectives of major thinkers in the nineteenth century: e.g., Marx ('radicalism') or John Stuart Mill and Spencer ('liberalism'). Even a cursory examination, however, shows that none of these currents of thought was nearly as clear-cut or distinct as Nisbet tends to imply. In the first place, 'conservatism' and the other labels which Nisbet affixes to the ideological framework of social thought are extremely broad in scope, and he lumps within them authors whose ideas were really quite widely divergent. Second, and perhaps more important in this regard, it is difficult to find any significant figure in nineteenth-century social thought whose ideas did not involve some sort of – more or less successful – synthesis of all three ideological currents. Marx is a case in point. It can hardly be denied that Marx was strongly influenced, and not just in a negative fashion, by 'conservatism', in the shape of Hegel's philosophy. But, of course, he sought to integrate this with ideas taken from each of the other two 'currents' – from political economy and 'radical' French social philosophy – while rejecting *all* of these as adequate representations of the social processes he sought to analyse. This is the relevance of the distinction mentioned above: what a thinker makes of received ideas is not simply contained in those ideas themselves – however much she or he may find it difficult to escape from the confines of inherited concepts and theories.

Durkheim's writings, while not as all-embracing in their intellectual indebtedness as those of Marx, embody ideas originating

in various prior traditions. Nisbet distinguishes only two intellectual sources of Durkheim's work: one methodological and the
other substantive:

> positivism (in its large sense – that of a methodology founded on
> the vigorous application of scientific values to the study of human
> nature and society) and conservatism . . . It was Durkheim's feat
> to translate into the hard methodology of science ideas and values
> that had made their first appearance in the polemics of Bonald,
> Maistre, Haller and others opposed to reason and rationalism, as
> well as to revolution and reform.[3]

But the principal sources of Durkheim's work are not so simply
classified. To begin with, Durkheim's debt to eighteenth-century
rationalism was not limited, as Nisbet states, to a methodological
spirit. In no small degree, Durkheim's writings, especially upon
state and politics, were shaped by a confrontation with Rousseau's
social philosophy – and this was not simply a negative influence.
The work of Saint-Simon and Comte, however, was evidently
much more important in helping to form the general outlines of
Durkheim's thought. It is certainly the case that Comte drew
upon the ideas of the conservative Catholic apologists. This is
especially true of the ideas expressed in the *Positive Polity*. But it
was Comte's *Positive Philosophy* which particularly influenced
Durkheim; and, in working out his substantive ideas concerning
the trend of development of modern society, Durkheim leaned
more heavily upon Saint-Simon than upon Comte's version of the
emergent hierocratic society as envisaged in the *Positive Polity*.
Evaluation of the significance of Saint-Simon as a precursor of
Durkheim's sociology is, of course, of some significance, since the
writings of Saint-Simon represent a common source of both
Comtean positivism and Marxian socialism. As will be indicated
below, Durkheim was by no means blind to the 'radical' aspects
of Saint-Simon's interpretation of industrial society, and he
incorporated parts of it into his own theory.

Durkheim's thought also has to be connected to more prox-
imate sources if the intellectual background to his works is to be
fully understood. Two sets of influences are particularly relevant
here. One is to be found in the writings of the older generation of
'academic socialists' in Germany. Early in his career, during the

course of a period of study in Germany, Durkheim became acquainted with the writings of authors such as Schmoller, Wagner and Schäffle, and he discussed their contributions in several lengthy articles.[4] While the precise extent of Durkheim's indebtedness to these thinkers is a matter of some debate, it is undoubtedly the case that certain of their ideas helped to filter his use of the legacy of French positivism. The 'science of morality' of which Durkheim set out to lay the foundation in *The Division of Labour* took its point of departure from certain of the ideas of the German reformist socialists. The second set of influences, rather more concealed, but of very profound importance in Durkheim's writings, derives from Kant and the French neo-Kantians, such as Renouvier. Indeed, if there is any single 'problem' underlying Durkheim's writings, rather than the 'Hobbesian problem of order' it is the 'Kantian problem' of the moral imperative. Kantian formulations constantly appear in Durkheim's works, even though they are not always explicitly acknowledged as such by him; and from the outset of his intellectual career he sought to effect a fruitful critique of these ideas by placing them within a social context, making particular use of Renouvier's conceptions.

If, therefore, conservatism, as defined by Nisbet and others, was an influence in Durkheim's intellectual heritage, this influence was much less unequivocal and direct than has been asserted. But how far is it true that the theoretical edifice which Durkheim fashioned from these various sources has an inherently conservative cast? It has been argued that Durkheim's sociology constitutes an all-out offensive against individualism: hence his stress upon the primacy of society over the individual and upon the need for authority. The error here lies in a failure to distinguish two senses of the term 'individualism'. Durkheim was not unremittingly hostile to all forms of individualism. He set out to criticize the 'individualism' which was entailed in the works of the English utilitarians, but he accepted, and undertook to study in a systematic fashion, that form of 'individualism' which he believed to be the necessary foundation of the organization of modern society. He sought to show precisely that the latter cannot be adequately understood given the ontological postulates of the former. The distinction between the two senses of individualism was explicitly recognized by Durkheim himself (although in his earlier writings he was not yet aware of its full implications). Individualism in the first sense, Durkheim identifies with 'the utilitarian egoism of Spencer and the economists': this must be rejected as comprising any sort of valid starting point for sociology. But individualism in the second sense is an altogether different matter; it is 'that of Kant and Rousseau, that of the idealists, that which the Declaration of the Rights of Man sought, more or less successfully, to give expression to'. This is *moral individualism*, something which, as he put it, has 'penetrated our institutions and customs, and which pervades our whole life'.[5] Individualism, in this sense, is a creation *of* society, an outcome of a long-term process of social development.

Many of the tensions and ambiguities in Durkheim's work, as well as much of what was distinctively original in his contributions, stem from his attempt to detach methodological from sociological individualism. Durkheim's array of conservative concepts, such as are supposedly involved in his use of 'society' (read: 'moral community'), '*conscience collective*', 'authority' and 'discipline', can only be adequately understood in these terms. Those who stress the conservative nature of Durkheim's thought, in common with those who emphasize the significance of the problem of order, have neglected the importance of the historical dimension in Durkheim's sociology. Consequently, Durkheim's functionalism is presented *in abstracto*; it appears as if these concepts are applied to reinforce a bluntly authoritarian theory of social control.

Thus it seems that Durkheim holds to a position very akin to that of Freud, according to which there is (as in the 'Hobbesian problem') an inherent antinomy between the individual and society, which necessarily entails that the existence of 'society' is tied to the repression of individual faculties and propensities. In fact, Durkheim's view is quite different to this. In traditional societies, individuals are subject to what Durkheim calls the 'tyranny of the group'. Not only is there little toleration of deviation from the moral codes embodied in the *conscience collective*, but there is only a low development of individual capabilities and faculties. The increasing complexity of society brings about both an extension of human freedoms and a growth in the richness of the individual personality. In such a situation, the forms of moral authority characteristic of traditional types of society become obsolete. Contrary to the conservative social thinkers, Durkheim consistently argued that there can be no reversion to the sort of moral discipline which pertained in previous times. 'The old gods are dead', and there can be no question of reviving them.

He certainly did not manage to resolve in a successful way all of the issues raised by his adoption of this standpoint. But the relevant aspects of his position are clear enough. In criticizing utilitarianism, he opted for the Kantian view that morality can never be reduced to the wants of the individual actor. Hence there is no form of moral phenomenon which does not have a 'constraining' aspect to it. But the important point is that constraint or obligation are not simply to be identified with repression. For moral conduct, according to Durkheim, never merely involves constraint alone: it also always has a positive valence. This is the basis of his attempted synthesis of utilitarianism and Kant's moral philosophy: moral conduct is founded neither upon desirability alone, nor upon duty alone, but upon a fusion of the two. In these terms, Durkheim sought to transcend the old philosophical dichotomies. While 'authority' and 'discipline' are components of all forms of social organization, it is mistaken, in Durkheim's view, to oppose them to 'freedom'. This is the very substance of Durkheim's sociological discussion of the development of individualism: moral individualism retains a constraining character, but acceptance of this form of moral authority is the very condition of escape from the 'slavish submission' characteristic of traditional types of society. 'Freedom' and 'authority', Durkheim asserts, have often been treated as if they were opposed: 'But this opposition is spurious. In fact these two terms imply, rather than exclude, each other. Freedom is the daughter of authority properly understood.'[6]

The great divide

The myth of the great divide has been elaborated in two quite opposing forms. The predominant version in Western academic sociology is that which I have mentioned previously in this chapter, which dismisses social thought prior to the last twenty-five years of the nineteenth century as pre-scientific in character. The contrast here is usually between 'philosophical' theories and 'scientific' or 'empirically founded' sociology. The other version of the myth of the great divide puts things in the reverse perspective, although the nature of the supposed contrast at issue is different. This is the view set out by some Marxists. The thesis here is that while Marx's writings established a scientific basis for social theory, the writings of the 1860–1920 generation of social thinkers represent little more than an ideological defence of bourgeois capitalism in the face of the threat of revolutionary socialism.

This latter version, which is only found in the cruder variants of Marxism, is hardly worth discussing in any detail. It is inconsistent with Marx's own standpoint: if bourgeois political economy was 'ideological', it nevertheless contained basic elements of validity. In order to understand the framework of Durkheim's sociology, it is undoubtedly important to examine the socio-political context in which he wrote – and it is certainly the case that there is a close relation between his political and sociological views, as I have tried to demonstrate above. But while this helps us to unravel the sources of some of his errors, it does not, in itself, show them to be such.

The other thesis is more complicated, and, so it might seem, more defensible. Durkheim is often regarded, especially by American sociologists, as the founder of empirical sociology – as the first writer to apply systematic empirical method to the examination of definite sociological issues. Suicide is taken as the model here. This view is manifestly false, however, and is written in ignorance of the prior history of empirical research in the nineteenth century. The systematic use of official statistics to examine, in a supposedly objective fashion, the distribution of 'moral phenomena' began much earlier in the century, under the tutelage of the 'moral statisticians' such as Quételet. It is not generally realized today, in fact, how far back the tradition of quantitative research into social phenomena can be traced. Durkheim drew upon a wealth of previous studies which had connected the distribution of suicide to social factors, and there was little that was particularly original either in the statistical method which he employed or in the empirical generalizations which he made use of in his study. (Thus, for example, the correlation between suicide rates and religious denomination was well demonstrated in previous research.) The originality of Durkheim's work lay much less in the methods which he used in *Suicide* than in the theory which he advanced; and the latter was worked out in the considerably broader context of the problems which occupied him in *The Division of Labour* and his other writings. (See Chapter 9.)

But it is clearly not enough to deal with the matter in these terms. The real question is how far Durkheim succeeded in separating 'sociology' from 'speculative philosophy'. Such was certainly the perspective within which he viewed his own work. Recognizing that Comte, in attempting to establish an autonomous science of sociology, conceived of himself as a 'positive scientist' of human conduct, Durkheim nevertheless denied the validity of that description. Comte was never able to free himself from the trappings of speculative philosophy. This is manifest, according to Durkheim, in the 'law of the three stages', which is imposed upon history rather than being derived from the empirical study of social development. The same is true of Spencer: Spencer 'did sociology as a philosopher', because 'he set out, not to study social facts in and for themselves, but to show how the evolutionary hypothesis may be verified in the social world'.[7]

Durkheim's own stress upon the partial character of scientific work, upon the laborious manner in which scientific advances are made, and upon the need to define in a precise way the subject-matter of sociology was conceived with the object of completing the break with philosophy which writers such as Comte and Spencer had advocated, but had failed to achieve. However, Durkheim's abstract statements on the issue can no more be simply admitted at their face value than can those of the authors whom he took to task. While it may be accepted that *Suicide* and perhaps even Durkheim's work on religion conform to the prescription that, in order to establish itself upon a 'scientific' basis, sociology must concern itself with restricted, clearly delimited problems, it is difficult to see how such a claim can be made for the theory developed in *The Division of Labour*. If it is not a 'philosophy of history', it is none the less of a sweeping and all-embracing character which is by no means completely alien to the sorts of scheme which previous nineteenth-century thinkers had produced. Moreover, Durkheim himself remarked that he found himself unable to escape from philosophical problems and constantly found himself reverting to them: 'Having begun from philosophy, I tend to return to it; or rather I have been quite naturally brought back to it by the nature of the questions which I met with on my route.'[8] To be sure, he tried to demonstrate that age-old philosophical questions could be seen in a new light by the application of a sociological perspective; but this was no more than had been claimed by various of his precursors, including Marx and Comte.

Durkheim also shared another concern with most prior social thinkers in the nineteenth century: the attempt to use 'scientific' observations to reach evaluative prescriptions. He frequently emphasized, of course, that sociology is a worthwhile endeavour only if it ultimately yields some practical application. But, far more than that, he tried to establish exactly how theory could be linked to practice – in his conception of the 'normal' and the 'pathological'. Few aspects of Durkheim's work have been more universally rejected than this one; yet none is more central to his thought. The role of the sociologist is to be like that of the clinician: to diagnose and to propose remedies for sicknesses of the body social. This is particularly important, Durkheim made clear, in situations of transition or 'crisis' in society, where new social forms are appearing, and others are becoming obsolete. In such circumstances, only sociological investigation can diagnose, in the flux of competing values and standards, what is of the past, and to be discarded, and what is the emergent pattern of the future. It is this task – that of identifying the roots of the 'modern crisis' – which Durkheim set himself in his sociology, and this takes up again the problems which Saint-Simon and Comte had set themselves a half century earlier.

Integration and coercion theory

The best-known exposition of integration and coercion theory is that originally offered by Dahrendorf. According to him, two conceptions of society have stood, since the beginnings of Western social philosophy, in opposition to one another. Each constitutes an answer to the problem of order, and each 'has grown in intensity' with the development of modern social thought:

> One of these, the *integration theory of society*, conceives of social structure in terms of a functionally integrated system held in equilibrium by certain patterned and recurrent processes. The other one, the *coercion theory of society*, views social structure as a form of organization held together by force and constraint and reaching continuously beyond itself in the sense of producing within itself the forces that maintain it in an unending process of change.[9]

The source of coercion theory, according to Dahrendorf, is to be found in the writings of Marx. In contrasting integration and coercion theory, he compares the works of Marx directly with those of Parsons, but many other writers have looked back to Durkheim as the main modern founder of integration theory. The differences which separate the views of Marx and Durkheim, it is held, rest upon divergent conceptions of the natural state of the individual. According to Horton and others, these are focused through the concepts of alienation and anomie respectively. Durkheim's model of the individual in a state of nature, it is held, owes most to Hobbes; Marx derived his from that portrayed by Rousseau. Whereas in the latter model the evils in the contemporary human condition are conceived to derive from the repressive effects of society – from which we must be liberated – in the former view these evils are seen as originating from the very opposite state of affairs: a lack of social regulation. The Marxian model inevitably concentrates upon coercion and power, at least as regards the character of existing societies, and, since it looks to future transformations, emphasizes change rather than order; the Durkheimian model concentrates upon consensus, and is essentially static in character.

It is worth distinguishing two partially separable issues here: the supposed divergencies between the work of Marx and Durkheim; and the role of coercion versus consensus in the more concrete analyses of the two thinkers.

The first of these is fairly easily disposed of. The conventional comparison of the conceptions of alienation and anomie in the writings of Marx and Durkheim is simply not true to the respective standpoints of either writer. The errors here certainly lie as much in the interpretation of Marx's thought as in that of Durkheim. Marx did *not* proceed in terms of an abstract contrast between 'the individual in nature' (non-alienated, free) and 'the individual in society' (alienated, unfree) in utilizing the conception of alienation. One does not become 'human', in Marx's terms, by escaping from society: as he perceived very early on in his career, this view is quite untenable, since most human faculties are developed through society. Both the eighteenth-century philosophers and the utilitarians began from the conception of the 'isolated individual': but the human individual is first and foremost a social being, and the very notion of the isolated individual is one which is created as part of the ideology of a specific form of society (and is itself an expression of alienated consciousness). Primitive beings are not in a condition of self-alienation, but in a condition of alienation from nature; as our mastery of nature grows, our alienation from nature becomes transcended – but only at the cost of alienation from ourselves. Expressed in less general terms: the technological progress created by capitalism has allowed us to conquer nature, but this very process has ramified and maximized our self-alienation. The point is that the two elements in the equation are both social in character: alienation refers not to a process whereby our natural needs are denied by our membership of society, but to one where socially generated capacities are denied by specific social forms.

The same is true of Durkheim's usage of the concept of anomie. It is obvious that the same two sides of the equation enter in here also: that is to say, that the condition of anomie also involves a dislocation between two sets of socially generated phenomena (needs and the possibilities of their realization). Like Marx, Durkheim stresses that most human faculties and needs are shaped by society. In a state of nature we would not be anomic, since, like the animals', our needs would be primarily organic, and hence adjusted to relatively fixed levels of satiation. 'All instinct is bounded because it responds to purely organic needs and because these organic needs are rigorously defined.'[10] Socialized individuals, however, are in quite a different position. Since our needs are socially created, it follows, according to Durkheim, that their *limits* must also be set by society. The problem of anomie rests not simply upon the social restraint of (given) needs, but upon the social penetration of both needs *and* means of satiation.

Neither Marx nor Durkheim managed to clarify all of the difficulties raised by his viewpoint, but it is an oversimplification to hold that, while the concept of alienation presupposes that individuals are in some sense naturally 'good', but are degraded by their membership of society, the concept of anomie presumes that people are naturally refractory to social organization, and must therefore be subject to restraint. The divergences between the concepts of alienation and anomie, in other words, depend upon differences in the respective analyses which Marx and Durkheim set out of the development of society from primitive to more complex forms. The question is how far these differences are accurately expressed in the opposition between integration and coercion theory. Dahrendorf separates Durkheim's integration theory from Marx's coercion theory by arguing that the first emphasizes 'consensus', the second 'power'; and the first neglects the importance of 'conflict' in society, the second accentuates it.

Now the Comtean term 'consensus' is one which Marx did not use, and would never have contemplated using. Durkheim makes use of it fairly often – although he much more frequently employs the phrases *'conscience collective'* or *'conscience commune'*. But it is important not to be misled by terminological differences here. The place of the concept 'ideology' in Marx's theory is not a wholly pejorative one. It is certainly true that 'ideology' refers to what Engels called 'false' consciousness, and that this is a conception which is completely absent from the notion of consensus. But while ideology is ontologically false it is not sociologically false. That is to say, moral ideas, as expressed, for example, in religious idea-systems, are of basic significance in stabilizing existing social systems, and in legitimating the class relationships which prevail within them. Marx's very hostility to religion, and his life-long attempt to effect a critique of political economy as a major element in the ideology of bourgeois society, only make sense if this point is recognized.

It is a familiar theme that, whereas Marx saw society as an unstable system of groups (classes) in conflict, Durkheim conceived of it as a unified whole – as an entity 'greater than the sum of its parts'; and that consequently he provided no analysis of the sources of social conflict. The misleading factor in this is the use of the blanket term 'society'. To judge the validity of the contrast, the only proper comparison is between Marx's and Durkheim's respective analyses of specific *forms* of society, and especially of that type of society which Marx called 'bourgeois society' or 'capitalism'. For if conflict, or class conflict, plays an essential part in Marx's analysis of extant societies, he did, after all, envisage the emergence of a type of society in which such conflict would disappear. Expressed in terms of this more tangible comparison, the contrast between integration and coercion theory again is inadequate as a mode of identifying the differences between the two thinkers. The differences lie not in the fact that one recognized the fact of class conflict in nineteenth-century Europe, while the other ignored it, but in their respective diagnoses of the origins of – and hence the remedies for – that conflict. Like Marx, Durkheim anticipated the emergence of a 'classless' society: but this was to be Saint-Simon's 'one-class' society, preserving a high degree of economic differentiation, rather than the Marxian form.

Marx regarded class conflict as the main motive-force in history, a theorem which Durkheim explicitly denied; and it can be argued, of course, that there is in Marx some sort of overall framework of a 'theory' of social change (in class societies) which is lacking in Durkheim's writings, apart from the fragment on the causes of the expansion of the division of labour in the book of that title. But this is not at all the same thing as to say that Durkheim was unconcerned with social change. What Dahrendorf says of integration theory, that it 'conceives of social structure in terms of a functionally integrated system held in equilibrium by certain patterned and recurrent processes', is sufficiently plastic to be as applicable to Marx's model of capitalism as to Durkheim's model of industrial society. Of course, the former is not a static, but an inherently mobile and temporary, equilibrium between the classes. Yet the same may be said of Durkheim's analysis of the 'transitional phase' between feudalism and industrialism. Moreover, Durkheim, like Marx, stressed that society is, in Dahrendorf's words, 'in an unending process of change', and that it is the task of the sociologist to chart the lines of development of society.

Myth and reality

The four myths in the history of social thought do not constitute a unitary conception of the development of sociology. Those who have accepted the myth of the conservative origins of sociology have not necessarily accepted the myth of the great divide; those who have promulgated the myth of the problem of order have not always accepted the dichotomy between integration and coercion theory. Nevertheless, as applied to the interpretation of Durkheim's writings, there are close connections between these various views.

The notion of the problem of order as Durkheim's overriding concern, and that of the conservative bent of his sociology, have fostered the idea that there is a clear discrepancy between Durkheim's political views and interests on the one hand, and the general character of his sociological writings on the other. This is explicitly stated by Nisbet: 'He (Durkheim) was a liberal by political choice and action, but his sociology constitutes a massive attack upon the philosophical foundations of liberalism . . . the substance of his thought is composed almost exclusively of perspectives and insights that have an umbilical relation to . . . early nineteenth-century conservatism.'[11] If this interpretation is rejected, the discrepancy evaporates; Durkheim's political liberalism finds its direct counterpart in his attempt, in his more general sociological analysis, to identify the characteristic authority structure of the modern nation-state.

I have said that each of the four myths possesses elements of validity. At this point we can attempt to unravel these.

We might begin with the question of 'conservatism'. The element of truth which links the sociology of Durkheim's generation to a conservative reaction to the 'two great Revolutions' can be more adequately understood only if this sociology is related to the social and political development of the major countries of Western Europe in the nineteenth century. This is a commonplace enough observation, but it is nevertheless a perspective which has been conspicuously absent from those accounts which have sought to show the indebtedness of sociology to conservatism. The 'conservatism' of Bonald and his contemporaries in

France was above all a response to the apparent consequences of
the events of 1789. As has been rightly written of Bonald,
'contemptuous of the urban communities and manufacture,
which he does not discuss, it is apparent that he wished to close
his eyes to contemporary economic realities . . . Bonald did not
write an economic treatise: he struggled against the Revolution.'[12] Throughout the nineteenth century, in France, social
thought continued to be dominated, in one way or another, by
the legacy of the 1789 Revolution. Now the occurrence of
the Revolution, of course, created shock-waves of anxiety and
fear among the ruling groups in both Britain and Germany,
and provided the overall backdrop to the most elaborate
theoretical system produced in the latter country: the philosophy
of Hegel. But while fear of revolution continued to haunt the
dominant strata in these two countries for decades, other trends
of development separated them quite decisively from the French
experience. In Britain, an accelerating rate of industrial development was accompanied by a unique process of the mutual
accommodation and interpenetration of the landed aristocracy
and the rising commercial and industrial elite. The result was a
society unmatched elsewhere for the relatively even tenor of its
development, and which produced neither a large-scale revolutionary socialist movement nor its counterpart, an aggressive,
irrationalist conservatism. In certain respects, Britain was strikingly 'conservative' in actuality; but this conservatism, especially
marked in the political sphere, proved to be compatible with
major and progressive changes in the social infrastructure. In his
famous lectures on *Law and Public Opinion in England*, Dicey
showed how this phenomenon could be indexed by the changing
nature of the legal system:

> France is the land of revolution, England is renowned for conser-
> vatism, but a glance at the legal history of each country suggests the
> existence of some error in the popular contrast between French
> mutability and English unchangeableness. In spite of revolutions at
> Paris, the fundamental provisions of the Code Napoléon have
> stood to a great extent unaltered since its publication in 1804, and
> before 1900 the Code had become invested with a sort of legal
> sanctity which secured it against sudden and sweeping change. In
> 1804 George the Third was on the throne, and English opinion was

then set dead against every legal or political change, yet there is
now hardly a part of the English statute-book which between 1804
and the present day has not been changed in form or in substance.[13]

Thus both the internal content of 'conservatism', and the interconnections between conservative ideology and social theory,
differed between the three leading European societies. In
Britain, utilitarianism, although of course undergoing significant
modifications from Bentham to Spencer, remained the dominant
form of social theory throughout most of the nineteenth century.
While it was eventually challenged by T.H. Green and the Oxford
philosophers, their critique remained embroiled in idealist metaphysics. In neither of the other countries did utilitarianism ever
enjoy anything like the same pre-eminence (even in its guise as
political economy). It has been a common tendency of British and
American writers, when discussing Continental social thought of
the nineteenth century, to exaggerate the significance of utilitarian
individualism. In France, it was from the beginning overshadowed
by the writings of the eighteenth-century philosophers; in Germany,
the strongly historical bent in philosophy and economics effectively
limited its penetration. The development of German society in the
nineteenth century was above all conditioned by three sets of
factors: the failure to effect a 'bourgeois revolution' in 1848, and the
consequently persisting domination of an autocratic, landowning
elite until well into the twentieth century; the fact that the
unification of Germany was accomplished under the hegemony of
Prussia, whose power was founded upon the position of this elite;
and the occurrence of a late, but very rapid, period of industrial
development whose effects were concentrated in the period
immediately following the unification of the country. These
factors created various streams of social thought, some largely
peculiar to Germany, involving odd fusions of 'conservative' and
'progressive' philosophies, as is found in the works of such
authors as Oldenberg, Wagner and Schäffle. 'Conservatism' here,
however, means primarily a nostalgic and romantic attachment to
the (idealized) pre-industrial village community.

The history of France in the nineteenth century, as Dicey's
remark aptly indicates, was one of a superficial political volatility
which masked a deeply engrained set of social and economic

divisions which either survived or were themselves engendered by the 1789 Revolution. The most revolutionary nation in Europe turned out to be anything but revolutionary in terms of actually creating the bourgeois society which was proclaimed in its slogans. 'Conservatism' in France was always linked to Catholicism and to the claims of embattled but militantly tenacious landowners, rentiers – and independent peasantry. While for the German thinkers of Max Weber's generation the overwhelming problem was that of the antecedents and consequences of 'capitalism' (analysed here primarily in terms of the destruction of traditional values by the spread of the 'rationalization' of culture), in France the debate was centred upon the problem of 'individualism' in the face of the claims of Catholic hierocracy. Durkheim's theory of the state was conceived as an attempt to resolve the 'legacy of the Revolution': the distance between the ideals of freedom and equality of opportunity heralded in 1789, and the reality of continuing stagnation in the social infrastructure. In France, since the turn of the nineteenth century, Durkheim remarked, 'Change follows on change with unparalleled speed. . . . At the same time, these surface changes mark an habitual stagnation . . . all these surface changes that go on in various directions cancel each other out.'[14] This phenomenon is to be explained in terms of the lack of differentiation between state and society. In these circumstances, the state is not independent enough to take firm action in initiating and realizing policies; it is simply swayed by the changeable moods of the mass. What must be established, Durkheim concluded, was a form of the state strong enough to resist the volatile whims of the mass (which, if allowed to hold sway, simply secure the rule of an underlying 'relentless traditionalism'), but which does not lose touch with the will of the majority and thereby create a coercive autocracy.

This is effectively a theory of the Republican state such as Durkheim saw emerging, and endeavoured to help to create, in the wake of the disaster of the war of 1870 and the Commune. The modern state is not opposed to, but is to be the principal agency of, the advancement of the moral individualism embodied in the ideals of the Revolution of the eighteenth century. As Durkheim sought to show in *The Division of Labour*, 'moral individualism' and 'utilitarianism' are not to be identified with each other. While in 1893 he believed it necessary to devote a lengthy section of the above work to a critical repudiation of utilitarianism, particularly in its Spencerian version, by 1898 he was clear that 'the practical philosophy of Spencer . . . hardly has any supporters any longer', and that there was little need to 'combat an enemy which is in the process of quietly dying a natural death'.[15] Moral individualism is a creation of society – and, more specifically, of the collective effervescence of the 1789 Revolution and its immediate aftermath – and hence derives its force from the authority of society; as such it is quite distinct from the 'egoism' of the 'isolated' or 'pre-social' individual of utilitarian theory.

In these terms, Durkheim attempted to distance his position from three streams of thought – 'individualism' (in the form of utilitarianism), revolutionary 'socialism', *and* 'conservatism'. *The Division of Labour* already exposes the essential flaw in the conservatism of the Catholic apologists: moral individualism is the emergent form of moral ideal in modern society, and there can be no return to the sort of moral order characteristic of previous ages (even in the guise of the hierocratic society of Comte's *Positive Polity*). But Durkheim drew upon important elements of this tradition of thought, just as he did upon each of the others. He owed certain of his key concepts to this source, as Marx owed certain of his to Hegel; but, like Marx, he attempted to apply them in such a way as to effect a critique of the very stream of thought from which they originally derived. Durkheim's work, in other words, originates in an attempt to synthesize, and thereby to transcend, each of these three traditions of thought bequeathed from the earlier part of the nineteenth century; and thus is most appropriately regarded as an attempt to rethink the foundations of liberalism in circumstances in which the liberal individualism developed in the British 'case' (i.e. utilitarianism) was manifestly inappropriate.

Durkheim's sociology can no more be adequately understood, therefore, merely as a critique of utilitarianism than as a critique of revolutionary socialism. The main problematic issue was not of 'order', but, if this term is to be used at all, of the reconciliation of 'order' and 'change'. Durkheim accepted what he took to be the essential component of socialism: the need for the regulation of unfettered market relationships. But he rejected, of course, both the possibility of radically restructuring society through revolutionary means, and the correlate assumption that class conflict was the medium whereby this could be achieved; on the abstract level, he denied that the major tenets of socialism have any necessary connection with class conflict. The theory of anomie, plainly, is of primary significance in Durkheim's rejection of both utilitarianism and socialism. But the remedy for anomie, he made clear, does not consist in the reapplication of traditional forms of moral discipline – as is suggested in conservative thought. Anomie, in other words, is a social condition which is contingent upon the transitional character of the contemporary age: it results from the fact that the changes necessary to complete the institutionalization of moral individualism have not yet come to fruition. This is the general theoretical counterpart of his more concrete interpretation of the factors retarding the development of a fully fledged 'bourgeois society' in France in the first three-quarters of the nineteenth century.

If it is not useful to treat Durkheim's concerns as deriving from an overwhelming interest in the problem of order, there can hardly be said to be much validity in applying this notion to Marx, and holding that 'order' here stems from the application of 'coercion'. The notion of 'order' is an ambiguous one, and can cover such a number of potentially quite distinct sets of circumstances (absence of conflict, absence of change, prevalence of mutually compatible cultural norms, etc.) that little is to be gained from using the term unless it refers to the more narrowly defined 'Hobbesian problem' implied in at least some versions of utilitarianism. From the very first stages of his intellectual career, Marx rejected utilitarianism, regarding it as an ideological expression masking the social relationships inherent in the capitalist division of labour.

Durkheim's sociology was founded in an endeavour to examine the conditions under which France could become a fully developed 'bourgeois society'. But this was more than a defence of a given *status quo* in the face of the threat of revolutionary socialism. If concern with the 'social question' was one major factor helping to shape Durkheim's thought, of no less importance was his anxiety to rebut the resurgence of conservative forces within the social structure. Like his famous contemporary in Germany, Max Weber, through taking over ideas from both socialism and conservatism, and by recombining them within a new framework, Durkheim sought to provide a systematic rationale for a bourgeois state which necessarily had to diverge from the 'classical' principles of liberalism, i.e., those which had developed in the very different context of Britain. Since the framework of development in Germany was itself very different from that of France – and the position of the liberal bourgeoisie much weaker – Weber's attempted synthesis was quite divergent from that created by Durkheim.

Durkheim's formula for the emergence of an autonomous discipline of sociology was connected in a very immediate fashion with his attempt to assess and combine ideas contained in both socialist and conservative traditions of thought, and was quite consciously worked out by him with such an objective in view. According to Durkheim, the major intellectual precondition for the establishment of a scientific sociology was the sloughing-off of the speculative philosophy which still remained an important part of the writings of prior thinkers such as Saint-Simon and Comte. But the most significant residue of speculative philosophy in the works of these authors, according to Durkheim, was of two related kinds, each closely connected with the very social impulses which generated sociology itself. The first was the impulse towards social reform or social reorganization; the other, that towards a revitalization of religion. The former finds its most characteristic expression in the doctrines of socialism, the latter in the conservative call for a religious revival. Throughout the first three-quarters of the nineteenth century, Durkheim argued, but particularly in times of social upheaval, the impetus to these three sets of ideas – socialism, religion and sociology – appears. In the works of Saint-Simon these are found in almost inextricable confusion. Comte went beyond Saint-Simon, not only in giving 'sociology' its name (which Durkheim thought to be a 'rather barbaric neologism'), but also in making a substantive contribution towards the separation of this new discipline from the other forms of thought in which it was embedded; but he failed to make this separation complete, and in the latter part of his career largely sacrificed his sociology to the religious impulse.

Durkheim's stress upon the need for drawing a very clear delimitation of the subject-matter of sociology, its aims and objectives, thus has to be understood in terms of what he perceived as the pressure to dissolve sociology within the more directly practical impulsions involved in socialism and religious revivalism. Only an autonomous, firmly established, science of sociology can actually discern and analyse what socialism and revivalism share in common and can thereby accurately diagnose the solutions to the social problems to which each gives expression. For while socialism, especially Marxist socialism, claims to be scientific, the propositions it embodies, springing from a pressing awareness of the need for social reorganization, go far beyond what can be said to be empirically verified, or even verifiable. Hence Durkheim's frequent emphasis upon the necessarily modest and cautious nature of sociological investigation, and his attempt to preserve the 'positive' character of Comte's sociology in a new form. In spite – or, as this analysis has tried to demonstrate, because of – its restricted and scientific character, sociology really holds the key to the practical understanding of the 'modern crisis'.

Durkheim was thus led to establish a precise definition of the field of sociology, and to insist upon the limitation of sociological investigations to restricted and clearly bounded problems. But the very ambitiousness of the context which led him to construct this new sociological perspective placed sociology in an impossibly paradoxical situation; for no 'neutral', circumscribed discipline of sociology could come to grips with the problems which stimulated Durkheim's writings, and most of his works range very much more broadly than is consistent with his own methodological doctrine. In terms of the separation of sociology from ('speculative') social philosophy, Durkheim's writings hardly mark the clear-cut line of demarcation claimed by their author. It seems, in fact, to have been a characteristic of each successive generation of social thinkers throughout the nineteenth century to hold that, whereas the works of their forerunners were speculative or ideological, or both, their own writings were grounded in empirical reality and thus scientific in character. This was said by Saint-Simon of the eighteenth-century philosophers; by Comte and Marx of Saint-Simon (among others); and by Durkheim of all of these.

What validity remains, then, in the notion of the great divide? A full discussion of the issue would demand assessing how far, in sociology, intellectual advance comparable to that found in the natural sciences is possible. The sociological programme which Durkheim set himself made it possible for him to illuminate a variety of diverse problems in sociology and social philosophy. But this is not the same as breaking with the general frames of thought and analysis which guided his precursors. There are perhaps two respects in which Durkheim's sociology marks a new point of departure from the social thought of his predecessors. The first concerns his abandonment of unilinear evolutionism and his use of materials drawn from cultures outside Europe. Each of the previous thinkers whose works formed an important part of Durkheim's intellectual horizon was mainly bounded by the European experience; indeed, their very willingness to set out 'universal' schemes bears witness to this. Although Durkheim did not abandon evolutionism altogether, his use of anthropological studies within a comparative framework marks the beginning of the modern era in Western social thought, and made possible the variety of researches carried out under the aegis of the *Année sociologique* school by scholars originating in numerous different disciplines. The very success and prestige of this group was indicative of the progress made in the effective institutionaliza- tion of sociology as a recognized academic discipline. This is the second, and perhaps the most basic, element of validity in the notion of the great divide. It is significant that it was Durkheim's sociology, rather than other potential competitors' (e.g., that of Le Play and his followers), which was the most eminently successful in this respect. For Durkheim's writings offered a unique combination of a firmly made claim to scientific respect- ability with a persuasive explication of the problems facing the retarded emergence of a mature industrial state.

EIGHT

Auguste Comte and Positivism

There can be few works whose form and style seem to contrast as radically with their author's temperament and experiences during their writing as Comte's *Cours de philosophie positive*. The first volume of the *Cours* was written in 1830; Comte completed five more in just over a decade subsequent to that date. The six volumes offer an encyclopedic conspectus of the development of the sciences, beginning with mathematics, moving through physics, chemistry and biology, and culminating, in the final three works, in an exposition of the nascent science of 'social physics'.

The tone of the work is sober, its style ponderous, its theme the evolution of social and intellectual order. Its author, however, the erstwhile protégé of Saint-Simon, led a life only slightly less bizarre and disrupted than that of his mentor. From 1817 Comte worked in close but increasingly acrimonious association with Saint-Simon, which ended in a public quarrel in 1824 (producing a chronic controversy over the true originality of Comte's *Cours*, which he claimed owed nothing to that 'depraved juggler' Saint-Simon). The history of Comte's life from that date onwards was one of bitter wrangling with a succession of other scholars, a despairing and frustrated search for academic employment and academic recognition in France, punctuated by periods of madness. He met and married a woman who had previously been on the official police register as a prostitute; at the ceremony, which Comte's mother insisted he undertake, an attendant from the psychiatric hospital was on guard, and the groom harangued the priest throughout the ritual. The union was from the beginning a strained one, with intermittent separations and a final parting in 1824; Comte's violent rages were not infrequently vented physically against his wife.

None of this emotional misery emerges in the *Cours*, which is a testament to the equilibrium of nature and of society. It is unquestionably one of the greatest works of the period, helping to place Comte alongside Marx as a dominant figure in nineteenth-century social thought. From their influence come the two opposed yet intermingled traditions that to the present day serve as a continuing focus of debate in the social sciences. Comte's writings, as filtered through those of Durkheim a generation later, connect directly with modern functionalism, for many years the leading perspective in orthodox sociology, anthropology and political theory; Marxism has long served as the main vehicle of critical opposition to this orthodoxy. However fundamental their differences, Comte and Marx shared the preoccupations of the nineteenth century with the crises unleashed by political revolution and the advent of industrialism; and each looked to the triumphs of natural science in seeking to develop the social understanding that would allow human beings successfully to harness the forces thus released to their own self-betterment. For Comte and Marx alike, the development of such self-understanding appears as a logical extension of the success of natural science, in which the demystifying of the physical world for the first time makes possible, and indeed necessary, a scientific understanding of the sources of human conduct itself.

Comte's 'hierarchy of the sciences', documented in massive detail in his *Cours*, expressed this in much blunter fashion than anything that appears in Marx. The relation between the sciences is shown to be hierarchical in both an analytical and a historical sense, the latter being explained in terms of the famous 'law of the three stages' of intellectual development. Analytically, Comte makes clear, the sciences form a hierarchy of decreasing generality but increasing complexity; each science logically depends upon the ones below it in the hierarchy, and yet at the same time deals with an emergent order of properties that cannot be reduced to those with which the other sciences are concerned. Thus biology, for example, presupposes the laws of physics and chemistry in so far as all organisms are physical entities which obey the laws governing the composition of matter; on the other hand, the behaviour of organisms, as complex beings, cannot be simply and directly derived from those laws.

The logical relation between the sciences, according to Comte, helps us to understand their progressive formation as separate disciplines in the intellectual evolution of humankind. The sciences which develop first – mathematics and then physics – are those dealing with the most general laws in nature, that govern phenomena most removed from human involvement and control. From there, science penetrates more and more closely to human-kind, producing finally in social physics a science of human conduct itself. The process is not achieved without struggle; scientific understanding lies at the end of the progression of intellectual life through the theological and metaphysical stages which characterize all branches of thought. The 'theological stage', in which the universe is comprehended as determined by the agency of spiritual beings, reaches its apex in Christianity with its recognition of one all-powerful deity: this stage, 'l'état fictif' as Comte calls it, is 'le point de départ nécessaire de l'intelligence humaine'.

The metaphysical phase replaces those moving spirits with abstract forces and entities, thereby clearing the ground for the advent of science, 'l'état fixe et définitif' of human thought. The enunciation of the law of the three stages, Comte says, is enough 'pour que la justesse en soit immédiatement vérifiée par tous ceux qui ont quelque connaissance approfondie de l'histoire générale des sciences'. (Comte later claimed to have achieved personal verification of the law of the three stages in his periods of insanity, which he had experienced, he said, as a regression from positivism to metaphysics to theology on the level of his own personality, in his recovery retracing these stages forwards again.)

The task of the *Cours* is not only to analyse the transmutation of human thought by science, but essentially to *complete* it. For, Comte made clear, human understanding of ourselves is still in its pre-scientific phase:

> Tout se réduit donc à une simple question de fait: la philosophie positive, qui, dans les deux derniers siècles a pris graduellement une si grande extension, embrasse-t-elle aujourd'hui tous les

ordres de phénomènes? Il est évident que cela n'est point, et que, par conséquent, il reste encore une grande opération scientifique à exécuter pour donner à la philosophie positive ce caractère d'universalité indispensable à sa constitution définitive . . . Maintenant que l'esprit humain a fondé la physique céleste, la physique terrestre, soit mécanique, soit chimique; la physique organique, soit végétale, soit animale, il lui reste à terminer le système des sciences en fondant la *physique sociale*. Tel est aujourd'hui sous plusieurs rapports capitaux, le plus grand et le plus pressant besoin de notre intelligence.

Social physics was above all to be directed to practical ends. If it is true that the strange extravagances of the immanent social future envisaged in the *Système de politique positive* are absent from Comte's earlier work, it is still the case that the main elements of his political programme already appear there. These are stated with greater clarity, in fact, in the *Cours* than they are in the later work. The overriding theme is the necessity of reconciling order and progress. As Comte saw it, his insistence on the conjunction of these two social conditions separated positive philosophy from both the 'revolutionary metaphysics' that had provided the inspiration for the events of 1789, and the political theory of the 'retrograde school' of Catholic conservatism, which had been formed as a reaction against the turmoil ensuing from the Revolution. The latter school wanted order, but was against progress; the former sought progress at the expense of order. As a consequence, Comte argued, the two ideas seem disconnected, even antithetical: 'On ne peut se dissimuler qu'un esprit essentiellement rétrograde a constamment dirigé toutes les grandes tentatives en faveur de l'ordre, et que les principaux efforts entrepris pour le progrès ont toujours été conduits par les doctrines radicalement anarchiques.' For the 'order' desired by the Catholic apologists was nothing but a reversion to feudal hierocracy; while the 'progress' aspired to by the revolutionaries was nothing less than a subversion of any form of government as such. The sort of society which Comte foresaw as guaranteeing both order and progress none the less placed a heavy enough emphasis upon the sorts of features that bulk large in the works of the 'retrograde school' – moral consensus, authority, and an antagonism to the 'chimera of equality' – even if stripped of their specific association with Catholicism.

The man who coined the neologism 'positive philosophy' also introduced that of 'sociology' – abandoning 'social physics' in order to separate his own enterprise from that of Quételet, who had independently applied the term to his studies of social statistics, which Comte looked upon with some scorn. In envisaging sociology as a science of society which would make possible the same kind of control over the social world that had been achieved over the material world, Comte portrayed the new science as a natural outgrowth of the progression of human rationalism. His most important precursors in the formation of sociology, according to Comte, were Montesquieu and Condorcet. The distinctive contribution of the works of these authors, Comte asserted, is the emphasis on social life as 'aussi nécessairement assujettis à d'invariables lois naturelles que tous les autres phénomènes quelconques'. For Comte, recognition that social phenomena are subject to the operation of invariable laws is not at all incompatible with freedom of action or moral dignity: for the first depends on discovering and utilizing social laws, while the second is enhanced by the authority of rational self-knowledge, freeing us from 'l'automatisme social, passivement dirigé par la suprématie absolue et arbitraire, soit de la Providence, soit du législateur humain'.

Notwithstanding his lack of immediate influence in France (a bibliography published in 1828 by Quérard listed him as having died the year before), Comte did achieve a considerable following for positivism overseas, in other European countries, the USA and Latin America. In Britain, the *Cours* acquired a notable admirer in John Stuart Mill. Many such followers were alienated, however, by the drift of Comte's thought in the later part of his career, as expressed in his *Système de politique positive*, which appeared over the years from 1851 to 1854, and which Mill called 'this melancholy decadence of a great intellect'. If the *Cours* bore little of the imprint of Comte's personal life, the subsequent work was expressly intertwined with it in a way which Comte's rationalistic disciples found both shocking and vulgar. Following his final separation from his wife, Comte formed an attachment to Clothilde de Vaux, a young woman deserted by her husband; after she died of consumption Comte gave over the rest of his life to a worship of her memory. The cool rationalism of the *Cours* gave way to a passionate advocacy of the Religion of

Humanity, the Church of Positivism, whose rituals were elaborately set out by its appointed High Priest.

As a social movement, which Comte had all along sought to make it, positivism died with the withering of the groups of followers who remained to celebrate the Festival of Humanity held in London in 1881. The influence of Comte's writings, however, derives not from their practical issue but, as far as modern social science is concerned, from their reworking in Durkheim's version of sociological method. Durkheim had little use for the grandiosity of Comte's later pronouncements; but he was much influenced by the earlier. Durkheim held more or less the same view of Comte as the latter expressed of Montesquieu and Condorcet: that while Comte had set out an acceptable general plan for establishing a science of society, he had failed to advance very far in putting that plan into practice. As Mill remarked: 'M. Comte, at bottom, was not so solicitous about completeness of proof as becomes a positive philosopher.' The 'law of the three stages', according to Durkheim, is proclaimed as by fiat, not corroborated empirically; and Comte's writings are still embroiled in that very style of philosophy of history that Comte claimed to have transcended.

This having been said, in setting out his own methodological scheme for sociology, Durkheim drew heavily upon Comte's *Cours*, and several of the major emphases in the latter reappear in *The Rules of Sociological Method*: the plea for a 'natural science of society', and the insistence that 'social facts' can be studied with the same objectivity as occurrences in nature; the differentiation of functional from historical analysis which, as a distinction between 'statics' and 'dynamics', plays such a basic role in the *Cours*; and even the belief that the science of sociology can rationally distinguish what contributes to moral order, and is thereby socially 'healthy', from that which is disintegrative and 'pathological'.

Comte invented the term 'positive philosophy' as a direct counterweight to the 'negative' criticism fostered by revolutionary political theory. In the *Cours*, the lengthy analysis of the development of the sciences is presented as a necessary preamble to his practical programme via the thesis that the progressive yet orderly evolution of science provides a model for a parallel evolution of society as a whole. What would Comte say to the modern philosophy of science which, in the writings of Bachelard, Kuhn and others, has supplanted evolution with revolution in the very heart of natural science itself? The transformation is a profound one, but aptly expresses the distance of the contemporary world from both that which Comte knew and that which he confidently foresaw for the future.

It would not be correct to rank Comte among the more ingenuously optimistic philosophers of progress in the nineteenth century: he was too much preoccupied with the possibility of 'moral anarchy' for that. Comte's *Cours* is none the less a monumental declaration of faith in science, in each of several respects: as providing a moral philosophy that would supplant that of feudalism without dissolving the moral order altogether; as supplying the only possible criteria of truth, measured against which those claimed by religion and metaphysics appear as mere sham; and as providing the singular means in the form of social science whereby human beings both understand and rationally control the conditions of their own existence.

In the present day, none of these remains feasible, as Comte held them. We might well still agree that science, or at any rate the rationalizing influences among which science ranks as pre-eminent, dissolve traditional forms of religion and morality. But few would maintain any longer that, in and of itself, science can generate a moral ethos that is able to replace what has been destroyed: an expanded scientific understanding of the world has not produced the solutions to the moral crisis that Comte diagnosed. Positivism, in the sense relevant to the second claim, reached its high-point in the twentieth century in the writings of the Vienna Circle in the 1920s and 1930s. But in this radical form it was short-lived; since that time positivism in philosophy has been increasingly on the defensive, so much so indeed that the term itself has become almost one of abuse.

For both Comte and Durkheim (as well as for Marx), sociology was conceived on a par with the natural sciences, as *revelatory* or demystifying. Sociology is to strip away the illusions and habitual prejudices that have prevented human beings from understanding the sources of their own behaviour, just as the progress of natural science has eradicated such illusions about the physical world. But this is itself an illusion, in the way in which it was formulated by Comte and Durkheim at any rate – and, indeed, as it continues to survive within sociology today. This is not only because the sorts of 'invariant laws', whose discovery Comte anticipated, and of which he believed his law of the three stages to be one, have not come to light in sociology, damaging as this surely is for the programme that he mapped out for the positive science of society.

The point is that sociology stands in a different relation to the 'prejudices' of habit or common sense from that of the natural sciences. To the natural scientist, lay beliefs about nature may or may not be correct: no particular consequence follows, and all common sense is in principle corrigible in the light of the progress of scientific knowledge. (See chapter 3.) Lay resistance to the findings of the natural sciences, where it occurs, takes the form of a rejection of claims which undermine cherished beliefs – e.g., that the sun moves round the earth rather than vice versa. But if this is not unknown in sociology, another lay response is at least equally common: the 'findings' of the social sciences are regarded with suspicion not because they question common-sense beliefs, but on the contrary because they only reiterate, in pretentiously technical language, what everyone already knows anyway. What finds no place in Comte's version of a natural science of society, or in those of others subsequently influenced by him or advocating the same type of standpoint, is that, even without the assistance of sociology, human beings are already the creators of their social world, knowledgeable agents whose skills in making sense of the conduct of others are an integral element of the existence of society as such. The conditions under which sociological research can play a revelatory role are more difficult to establish than in the case of natural science, and cannot be understood within the framework of the logic of social science such as that offered in the intellectual tradition stemming from Comte and Durkheim. It is a mark of its influence that modes of social theorizing in which human beings are presented merely as objects to themselves, as merely acted upon, should have survived so long.

NINE

The Suicide Problem in French Sociology

It is not always recognized today how far Durkheim's *Suicide* was indebted to the works of earlier authors on the topic. Suicide was the subject of extended debate even in the eighteenth century. Most eighteenth-century works on suicide were concerned with the moral implications of the suicidal act, but towards the end of the century writers began to turn their attention to the apparently rapidly rising suicide rates in Europe, and out of this a more statistical concern with the determinants of suicide began to develop.

One of the earliest comprehensive investigations of suicide was made by Falret in his *De l'hypocondrie et du suicide* (1822). Falret examined at some length both 'internal causes' of suicidal tendencies in the individual, which he attributed principally to certain forms of inherited mental disorder, and 'external causes' producing variations in suicide rates between different groups. *De l'hypocondrie et du suicide* was followed by a proliferation of works on suicide by French, German and Italian writers. Perhaps the most influential of these were those by Guerry (1833), Lisle (1856) and Legoyt (1881) in France, Quételet (1835, 1848) in Belgium, Wagner (1864) and Masaryk (1881) in Germany, and Morselli (1879) and Ferri (1883) in Italy.[1] There were many others. In terms of sheer bulk of material, suicide was probably one of the most discussed social issues of the nineteenth century. By the time at which Durkheim wrote, a substantial number of empirical correlations had been established linking suicide rates with a range of social factors. Later writers confirmed Falret's contention that suicide rates tend to rise during periods of rapid social change and in times of economic depression, and that rates vary positively with socio-economic position, being highest in professional and liberal occupations, and lowest among the chronically poor. The fact that suicide rates are higher in urban localities than in rural areas was extensively documented. Some writers claimed to have shown that suicide rates co-vary with crime rates, but are inversely related to rates of homicide. Wagner was perhaps the first to identify clearly a direct relationship between rates of suicide and the religious denominations of Protestantism and Catholicism, but this was quickly substantiated by later investigation. It was widely shown that suicide rates vary by sex, age and marital status; as well as by time of the year, day of the week, and hour of the day.

Some writers gave prominence to racial and climatic factors in accounting for differential suicide rates. Most, however, questioned this type of explanation, and looked instead to social causes. Quételet placed great emphasis, as Durkheim later did, on the relative stability of suicide rates from year to year in comparison with other demographic data,[2] attempting to interpret differences between suicide rates in terms of variations in the 'moral density' of society. Many writers attributed the general rise in suicide rates to the dissolution of the traditional social order and the transition to industrial civilization, with its concomitants of increasing 'rationality' and individualism – an explanation close to that later elaborated by Durkheim.

Most of the early nineteenth-century investigations of suicide took for granted a close relationship between suicide and mental disorder. The notion that suicide derived from 'miserable insanity'[3] was clearly in part a survival of the belief that suicide is of diabolical inspiration, a view which, under the impress of the church, held sway until some way through the eighteenth century. The theory that suicide is always associated with some form of mental disorder was, however, given its most definitive formulation in Esquirol's classic *Maladies mentales* (1838). 'Suicide', asserted Esquirol, 'shows all the characteristics of mental disorders of which it is in fact only a symptom.'[4] In this view, since suicide is always symptomatic of mental illness, it is to the causes of the latter that the student of suicide must turn in order to explain the phenomenon. The nature and distribution of mental disorder in any population determine the distribution of suicide in that population.

The question of how far, and in what ways, suicide is related to mental disorder became a major problem occupying writers on suicide during the latter half of the nineteenth century, and was discussed at some length by Durkheim.

The originality and vitality of Durkheim's work did not lie in the empirical correlations contained in *Suicide*: all of these had been previously documented by other writers. Durkheim took a great deal of material directly from the works of Legoyt, Morselli and Wagner, and used Öttingen's *Die Moralstatistik* extensively as a source of data. Where Durkheim's work differed decisively was in the attempt to explain previous findings in terms of a coherent sociological theory. Previous writers had used a crude statistical methodology to show relationships between suicide rates and a variety of factors: Durkheim developed this technique in order to support a systematic sociological explanation of differential suicide rates. He was by no means the first to propose that suicide rates should be explained sociologically, but no writer before Durkheim had presented a consistent framework of sociological theory which could bring together the major empirical correlations which had already been established.

The basic contention made by Durkheim in *Suicide* is that problems relating to the analysis of suicide rates can be separated in a clear-cut fashion from those relating to the psychology of the individual suicide. The suicide rate of a society or community 'is not simply a sum of independent units, a collective total, but is itself a new fact *sui generis*, with its own unity, individuality and consequently its own nature'.[5] The factors governing the distribution of suicide are 'obviously quite distinct' from those determining which *particular* individuals in a group kill themselves. Having rejected inherited insanity, psychological imitation, race and various 'cosmic' factors as possible determinants of the distribution of suicide, Durkheim located these determinants in aspects of social structure, distinguishing three main types of suicide: egoistic, anomic and altruistic. Strictly speaking, these are not types of suicide, but types of social structure producing high rates of suicide. Egoism refers to a low level of 'integration' in social structure; anomie to a dearth of regulative norms in society.

Egoistic and anomic suicide are the predominant types in modern society.

Durkheim used the analysis of suicide explicitly as a platform for the vindication of his sociological method. He did not limit himself, moreover, to offering a sociological analysis of suicide rates, but tended to argue that the role of psychology in the explanation of suicide was a subordinate one. In a general way Durkheim's polemic was aimed against Tarde and other 'reductionist' schools of social thought. More specifically, however, Durkheim's argument was also directed at Esquirol and other representatives of the view that suicide rates could be explained directly in terms of the distribution of mental disorder.

The publication of *Suicide* stimulated divergent reactions in France. Durkheim's immediate disciples were prepared to adopt the text as a model of sociological method. Others, particularly in the field of psychology, were equally ready to reject entirely the claims for sociology advanced in the book. Most psychologists and psychiatrists continued to be heavily influenced by the 'psychiatric thesis', stemming from the position established by Esquirol, in relation to suicide. This thesis entailed the following propositions: (1) suicide is always the product of some psychopathological condition; (2) the causes of suicide must thus be sought in the causes of the relevant types of mental disorder; (3) these causes are biological rather than social; (4) sociology can therefore make little if any contribution to the analysis of suicide.

The foundations were thus laid for a controversy which, although part of a broader conflict between Durkheim's advocacy of sociology as an autonomous discipline and the resistance of its detractors, did not become fully developed until the period following World War I, after the death of Durkheim himself.

The first major assault on Durkheim's position was launched in 1924 by de Fleury, a psychiatrist, in his *L'Angoisse humaine*.[6] Following broadly the theoretical standpoint established by Esquirol, and supporting his argument with case-history material, de Fleury reiterated that suicide is always derivative of mental disorder, the causes of which are biopsychological rather than social. Suicidal tendencies, he concluded, are found mainly in persons suffering from cyclical depressive disorder (cyclothymia). This type of affective disorder, stated de Fleury, depends upon

inherited characteristics of temperament: the disposition to suicide is biologically 'built into' such individuals. The tendency to
states of morbid depression, moreover, according to de Fleury,
develops largely independently of the objective circumstances of
the individual. It is of little consequence, therefore, whether the
individual is integrated into a group or not. While fluctuations in
suicide rates can possibly be linked in a very crude way to social
or economic changes, their role in the aetiology of suicide is even
then only a secondary one: such changes may only serve to
partially 'cluster' the suicides of individuals who would in any
case kill themselves at a later date. The state of morbid anxiety
into which depressive individuals periodically lapse, wrote de
Fleury, 'is, in the immense majority of cases, the only cause of
suicide'.[7]

In 1930 Halbwachs published *Les Causes du suicide*, a work
intended to review, in the light of later statistics, the conclusions
reached by Durkheim thirty years earlier.[8] Halbwachs claimed
confirmation in detail of Durkheim's generalizations relating
suicide rates to family structure and religious denomination.
However, he emphasized that it is illegitimate to use, as Durkheim did, statistical relationships of this sort independently as if
each had a separate significance. The influence of family life, for
instance, argued Halbwachs, cannot be detached from 'a much
broader social milieu'.[9] The same is true of the religious factor. In
France, for example, the more strongly Catholic groups tend to
be also the most conservative and 'traditional', and have a
strongly integrated family structure. It is not possible to separate
the specifically religious practices from the broader community of
which they are one part. According to Halbwachs, several of the
factors which Durkheim isolated as producing a high suicide rate
combine in the characteristics of modern urban life. Halbwachs
provided an extensive, comparative analysis of suicide rates in
urban and rural areas indicating that, in general, rates are highest
in large towns. Reviewing Durkheim's propositions regarding
suicide and social change through an examination of the relationship between fluctuations in the business index and suicide in
Germany during the period 1880–1914, Halbwachs confirmed
that suicide rates do tend to rise during economic crises. The
increment in the rate does not, however, take place only at the
lowest point of a trough, but is spread over the whole phase of the

depression. Durkheim's thesis that rates of suicide rise during periods of marked economic prosperity was not substantiated: on the contrary, during such periods suicide rates tend to decline.

Although his statistical analysis is generally supportive of Durkheim's, Halbwachs rejected the typology of egoism and anomie proposed by Durkheim. In Halbwachs's own theory, suicide is attributed to the 'social isolation' of the suicidal individual. Suicide rates are high in social structures promoting the detachment of individuals from stable relationships with others – as is the case, according to Halbwachs, in urban communities. Halbwachs discussed in some detail the psychiatric thesis advanced by de Fleury. According to Halbwachs, only a minority of suicides are associated with a recognizable form of mental disorder, and these, he claimed, are not incompatible with his theory. 'Normal' suicides in Halbwachs's view may become detached from relationships with others as a consequence of many factors, which include many of the 'motives' popularly offered for suicide – such as failure in business, unrequited love, chronic illness, etc. But 'pathological' suicides also derive from the social isolation of the suicidal individual: it is precisely those mental disorders producing 'a failure of adaptation between the individual and his *milieu*'[10] which culminate in suicide. In both 'normal' and 'pathological' suicides, Halbwachs concluded, the 'true' cause of the suicide is a social *lacuna* which surrounds the individual suicide. In reaching this conclusion, although questioning Durkheim's analysis in several respects, Halbwachs reaffirmed the validity of the sociological approach to suicide: suicide is primarily a social phenomenon.

Those who were favourable to the psychiatric thesis found Halbwachs's arguments unconvincing. Courbon, for example, reviewing Halbwachs's book, accused the latter of an incompetent assessment of the relevance of psychopathology to suicide. Courbon repeated that suicide derives universally from pathological anxiety and depression and that these are 'through their purely biological nature' as completely independent of social factors as are colour of eyes or reaction time.[11] In his *Psychologie pathologique du suicide* (1932), Delmas summed up the views of the psychiatric school on the question of suicide, and made an explicit attempt to destroy the sociological standpoint of Durkheim and Halbwachs.[12] Social factors cannot possibly play a significant role in the aetiology of suicide, argued Delmas, since suicide takes place in such small proportion to any population. It sounds impressive to say that one country A has a suicide rate of 450 (per million) per year, while another country B has a rate of only 50. But invert these proportions, and we have a comparison of the following order: 999,550 (per million) per year *do not* commit suicide in country A, while 999,950 do not commit suicide in country B. The proportional difference between those who do not commit suicide is very small indeed. How could we say that there exist general social factors which 'protect' 999,950 in every million in country B, whereas only 999,550 are 'protected' in country A?

Using the same psychiatric classification as de Fleury, Delmas repeated that the 'fundamental cause' of suicide is pathological depression; and that the tendency to depressive states develops largely independently of the external situation of the individual. Endogenous changes, according to Delmas, produce with advancing age more profound and protracted states of melancholic anxiety: this, he claimed, rather than any changes in the social position of the ageing individual, is the major factor behind the common observation that suicide rates tend to rise with increasing age. The same can be said, he concluded, of other apparent direct causal relationships between suicide and social phenomena. If suicide rates are higher among unmarried than among married people, it is because depressives tend not to marry. It is the endogenous process of depression which is aetiologically crucial; the vast majority of suicides 'are exclusively the result of a biopsychological mechanism into which nothing social enters'.[13]

In *Le Suicide* (1933) Blondel finally attempted to reconcile the *thèse psychiatrique* with the *thèse sociologique*.[14] According to Blondel, in 'normal' suicides the social situation of the suicidal individual is a crucial determinant; the depressive personality, however, is born with a constitutional tendency towards pathological depression, and this is the 'deep-lying cause' of his suicide. Although the role of social factors in the aetiology of cyclothymic suicides is less central than in 'normal' suicides, in both cases there is nevertheless an interaction between the social and the non-social. This view was endorsed by several other writers. Dombrowski, for example, in his *Les Conditions psychologiques du suicide* (1929), had stressed that the controversy could only be resolved by examining the interplay between psychological and social factors. Psychopathological states, he suggested, produce in certain individuals a *Minderwertigkeit* which promotes a 'disharmony' in social relationships, thus leading to the social isolation of the individual emphasized by Halbwachs as the 'true' cause of suicide.[15]

Little further progress in the resolution of the controversy was made before the intervention of World War II, and after the war suicide did not receive the same amount of attention as a test problem in French sociology. This was due to a pronounced shift in the predominant character of French social thought generally. Until the period immediately preceding World War II, sociology in France remained firmly set in the theoretical cast moulded by Durkheim. Although some of Durkheim's most able followers were killed in World War I, several of the prominent figures (such as Halbwachs) survived and dominated the sociological scene up to 1940.

In the late 1930s, however, particularly under the leadership of Gurvitch, theoretical sociology in France began to come increasingly under the influence of German phenomenology. In his *Essais de sociologie* (1939) Gurvitch propounded a detailed series of criticisms of the fundamental tenets of Durkheim's sociology, attempting to expose certain of the major theoretical questions with which Durkheim had concerned himself as 'pseudo-problems' – problems falsely posed.[16] One such 'pseudo-problem' involves the debate over 'society' and 'the individual'. Both Durkheim and Tarde, Gurvitch emphasized, while engaging in a protracted polemic with each other, made a false opposition between society and the individual; there is, in fact, a constant 'reciprocity' between the 'individual' and the 'social'. In an article published in 1952, Bastide took up again the suicide controversy within the framework laid down by Gurvitch, arguing that the controversy hinged upon the same mistaken conception of the relationship between society and the individual.[17] The psychiatric thesis states that suicide is an 'individual' matter, since it depends mainly upon 'internal' biopsychological mechanisms, and that consequently the study of suicide is a psychological rather than a sociological matter. But this argument only has any weight if we accept the ontological realism of a dichotomy between society and the individual. To admit that psychology can properly contribute to the analysis of suicide does not mean that suicide, in certain aspects – particularly as a demographic phenomenon – cannot be studied sociologically; conversely, to accept that social factors play a role in the aetiology of suicide does not entail the exclusion of other factors as having causative force.

The suicide controversy in French sociology is of interest not only because of the direct content of the argument. Tracing the origins of the dispute allows some insight into the historical 'depth' which an intellectual controversy may have: the issues involved in the debate were already set out, and not in a radically different guise, in the early nineteenth-century literature on suicide. Through the agency of Durkheim, however, the analysis of suicide became a critical issue in the struggle to establish sociology as a recognized academic discipline in France. This was, of course, largely due to Durkheim's own stage-management; as Lévi-Strauss remarks, 'the clash occurred on the ground Durkheim had himself chosen: the problem of suicide'.[18]

Durkheim's interest in suicide as a research problem was a direct development from his concerns in *The Division of Labour*. But two other factors lay behind his selection of suicide as a topic for a comprehensive investigation. First, the very volume of work which had already been carried out by previous writers provided an abundant source of data which could be used to develop a systematic sociological analysis of suicide. Second, suicide appears to be wholly 'an individual action affecting the individual only'.[19] The demonstration of the relevance of Durkheim's sociological method to the analysis of an apparently purely 'individual' phenomenon had a particular significance in the context of the dispute with Tarde over the nature of social reality. *Suicide* supposedly represents a vindication of Durkheim's thesis that social facts can be studied as 'realities external to the individual' as against Tarde's position that the subject-matter of sociology consists in 'the sum of consciousness in individuals'.[20] The unfolding of the subsequent suicide controversy cannot be fully understood apart from the broader dispute between Durkheim and Tarde. As Gurvitch showed, the Durkheim–Tarde debate depended in part upon a largely fruitless argument about the primacy of the 'social' over the 'individual'. The degree of interdisciplinary rivalry which developed in the suicide controversy reflected a general acceptance of the same misconceived ontological dichotomy.

The major substantive issue separating the *thèse sociologique* from the *thèse psychiatrique* concerns the 'pathological' nature of suicide. In one sense this question is easily resolved; since suicide is in all societies statistically a rare phenomenon, considered in terms of deviation from the majority, suicide is necessarily an 'abnormal' act. But the real problems are the extent to which suicide must be explained in terms of factors producing recognized forms of mental disorder (itself now recognized as a problematic notion) and the relationship of *these* to social influences. There is no systematic evidence to support the contention that suicide is universally associated with identifiable forms of mental illness. It is probable that most suicides are preceded by some form of depression: but only in a minority of cases is this part of a recurrent pathological depressive disorder. Moreover, only a small proportion of individuals suffering from depressive disorder actually attempt or commit suicide. Empirically, therefore, the *thèse psychiatrique* has not been borne out by later research.

The question of the relationship between suicide and mental disorder served, however, as a cloak for the real theoretical problem in the French suicide controversy: the relevance of sociology to the explanation of suicide. As has been indicated, the dispute depended at least partly upon a misconception shared by both sides and integral to the Durkheim–Tarde debate: that suicide is 'fundamentally' either a 'social' or an 'individual' phenomenon. It would be facile, however, to dismiss the core of the dispute as a 'pseudo-problem'. The relationship between social and psychological factors in the aetiology of suicide is a focal problem in suicide theory, and one which bears directly upon the analysis of other phenomena which can be construed in terms of rates (e.g., homicide, crime and delinquency, or divorce).

It was Delmas's contention that, since suicide is statistically infrequent in relation to the total population of a society, social factors cannot play a significant role in its aetiology. The only necessary implication of this argument, in fact, is that sociology cannot furnish a *complete* explanation of suicide, since only a small proportion of those in, for example, a loosely integrated community actually kill themselves. Yet to pose the question

'Why are suicide rates *so small*?' does allow a clearer insight into the error of Durkheim's thesis that the explanation of incidence, as a psychological problem, can be conceptually and methodologically separated from the sociological analysis of suicide rates. In Durkheim's conception, optimally integrated social structures 'protect' their component individuals against suicide; in loosely integrated structures, or in states of anomie, the members of the group are less 'protected'. In the former conditions, suicide rates will be low; in the latter, rates will correspondingly increase. The question of why individual A commits suicide – why A is a suicidal personality – while B, in an identical social situation, does not, is, according to Durkheim, a psychological matter, and not relevant to the explanation of rates: in an economic depression, for example, it will be A, rather than B, who commits suicide. However, to ask 'Why are rates so small?', which is clearly a central question in the aetiology of any rate, is to ask 'Why are most of the population Bs rather than As?' Such a question, the answer to which depends upon an understanding of the factors producing suicidal propensities in the individual, is directly relevant to an explanatory assessment of suicide rates. The factors governing the distribution of suicide in a community cannot therefore be usefully considered in isolation from those determining why individual A commits suicide while individual B does not, i.e., apart from the study of suicidal personality. Durkheim's position is given a spurious plausibility by the assimilation of an ideographic question (why did this *particular* individual A commit suicide?) to the more important general psychological problem (why does a particular *type* of individual commit suicide?). The answer to the first question depends partly upon the investigation of strictly idiosyncratic factors in the particular suicide's life-history; the answer to the second question entails a generalized psychological theory of suicidal personality.

TEN

Reason Without Revolution?: Habermas's *Theory of Communicative Action*

Appropriately enough for an author concerned with the expansion of the public sphere and the fostering of debate, Habermas's writings have from the beginning of his career attracted widespread attention. Habermas has been a public figure in German life since his early association with – and disassociation from – the student movement of the late 1960s. His work has drawn sharp, even bitter, criticism from both right and left, for Habermas's writings are not easy to place, intellectually or politically. His thinking has been shaped in considerable degree by the controversies in which he has been involved. The accusation which Habermas directed against certain sections of the student movement – 'left fascism' – has reverberated through his subsequent intellectual career. His preoccupation with isolating the conditions of rational decision-making, and with specifying the conditions under which a consensus, governed purely by the 'force of the better argument', can be brought about, evidently in some part represents a protracted attempt to come to terms with the implications of this notorious remark. Successive confrontations with Popper, Gadamer, Luhmann and others have also left a deep imprint on his thought.

But it would clearly be wrong to regard Habermas primarily as a polemicist. He is a systematic thinker who has consistently sought to come to terms with a number of basic issues in philosophy and social theory. Habermas's writings range over an extraordinary variety of topics, and it would be easy to see in this a diffuse eclecticism. Certainly he does incorporate into his own theories ideas taken from a variety of apparently incompatible approaches. Anyone who has the least bit of sympathy with Habermas's overall project, however, must recognize that he employs such ideas in an innovative and disciplined fashion.

Habermas's work can be divided, broadly speaking, into two main phases. The first culminated in the publication of *Erkenntnis und Interesse* (*Knowledge and Human Interests*) in 1968. Although the views Habermas expressed therein have been influential in the social sciences and philosophy, the book also received a barrage of critical attacks. This critical onslaught undoubtedly did indicate some serious shortcomings in the work, and in Habermas's standpoint more generally. He sought to advance a novel conception of critical theory, on the basis of the constitution of knowledge through interests. But the 'interest in emancipation' seemed to exist only as a moment in the conjunction of the other two knowledge-constitutive interests. Habermas's later work can be seen as an attempt to give flesh to the emancipatory potential of social analysis. This endeavour led Habermas away from the framework adopted in *Erkenntnis und Interesse*. It seems apparent that Habermas would now regard the attempt to found critical theory upon epistemology as misleading if not actually mistaken. Epistemology, he insisted in *Erkenntnis und Interesse*, is possible only as social theory: social theory which examines the conditions under which, in Habermas's words, 'reason that becomes transparent to itself' is disclosed. However, if the traditional search for a transcendental basis of knowledge – a 'first philosophy' – is to be abandoned, why approach critical theory through the theory of knowledge at all? Habermas today holds that his excursion into epistemology was something of a detour in his endeavour to ground critical theory: the more direct route is through the embedding of reason in *language* in general, and in *communication* in particular.

Habermas's *Theorie des kommunikativen Handelns* (*Theory of Communicative Action*) is a synthetic statement and an elaboration of the ideas developed in this second phase of his writings. The theory of communicative action, Habermas asserts, is neither a metatheory nor a continuation of the theory of knowledge by other means. The analysis of communicative action allows us to connect three levels of rationality relevant to social analysis. One concerns rationality as debated in hermeneutics and Anglo-

American analytical philosophy, related particularly to issues of relativism. If divergent cultures or forms of life have their own inner criteria of rationality, in what sense is it possible to make comparisons of them – and subject them to critique – in terms of universal standards? Another concerns the rationality of action: how are we to grasp the distinctively meaningful character of human conduct? This touches upon questions of the significance of *Verstehen*, and of the role of the social sciences in claiming superior explanations to those which actors themselves already are able to provide as 'reasons' for their behaviour. Finally, Habermas is concerned with the social expansion of rationality as the rationalization of society characteristic of the modern West. Here is where he makes particular appeal to the writings of Max Weber, seeking to reformulate the conception of reification that links Weber to the early Lukács and to the Frankfurt School.

In defending an overall conception of rationality in each of these domains, Habermas evidently has a strong sense of swimming against the stream. He proposes universal criteria of reason at a time when relativistic styles of thought have become fashionable in various areas of intellectual discourse – as, for example, in post-structuralism. He wants to offer a vindication of Enlightenment and modernity when for many these have become effectively discredited. The rise of neo-conservatism is particularly important here. *Theorie des kommunikativen Handelns* is written at a characteristically Habermasian level of high abstraction; but there is also a directly political motif that runs through the book. Both neo-conservatives, who place primacy upon the achievement of economic growth through the revival of market forces, and the ecological critics of growth turn against the heritage of Western rationalism. Habermas is critical of both standpoints, while seeking to understand why they have come to the fore in the current era. In an interview, he says that his 'real motive' in writing the book was to make clear how 'the critique of reification', of rationalization, can be reformulated to offer a theoretical explanation for the decay of the 'welfare-state compromise' on the one hand, and on the other the critical potential embodied in new movements – without discarding the project of modernity or relapsing into post- or antimodernism.

Philosophy, Habermas argues, has always had as its main task reflection upon reason. But contemporary philosophy has become a diverse array of specialisms, no longer seeking to provide a unified world-view. This situation is partly a result of the collapse of attempts to found a 'first philosophy': all attempts to provide indubitable foundations for philosophical reason have broken down. Habermas accepts some of the implications of this. Philosophy can no longer hope to develop the sorts of grand metaphysical scheme that were sought after by Kant and Hegel. A new relation therefore has to be established, and is already becoming established, between philosophy and both the natural and social sciences. The procedure of 'rational reconstruction' Habermas takes as a key element here – the process of reconstructing what can be regarded, after the event, as the rational content of a field of research or subject area. He takes Piaget's developmental psychology as a type-case. Piaget reconstructs psychological development not just as a sequence of stages, but as so many steps in the expansion of the rational competence of the individual.

How should we use the term 'rational'? Rationality has less to do with knowledge as such, Habermas asserts, than with the manner in which knowledge is used. If we consider the circumstances in which we speak of something as 'rational', we see it refers either to persons or to symbolic expressions which embody knowledge. To say that someone acts rationally, or that a statement is rational, is to say that the action or statement can be criticized or defended by the person or persons involved, so that they are able to justify or 'ground' it. We cannot, as empiricism does, limit the grounds of rational acts or expressions to knowledge of the object-world. We must complement 'cognitive-instrumental rationality' with a conception of 'communicative rationality'. 'Dieser Begriff *kommunikativer Rationalität*', Habermas says, 'führt Konnotationen mit sich, die letztlich zurückgehen auf die zentrale Erfahrung der zwanglos einigenden, konsensstiftenden Kraft argumentativer Rede, in der verschiedene Teilnehmer ihre zunächst nur subjektiven Auffassungen überwinden und sich dank der Gemeinsamkeit vernünftig motivierter Überzeugungen gleichzeitig der Einheit der objektiven Welt und der Intersubjektivität ihres Lebenszusammenhangs vergewissern.'

Rationality *presumes* communication, because something is rational
only if it meets the conditions necessary to forge an understanding with at least one other person.

It is easy to see where this line of thought leads Habermas. He
has often made the case that human language involves a number
of 'validity claims' that are ordinarily implicitly made by
speakers, but which can be made explicit. When I say something
to someone else, I implicitly make the following claims: that what
I say is intelligible; that its propositional content is true; that I am
justified in saying it; and that I speak sincerely, without intent to
deceive. All of these claims are contingent or fallible, and all
except the first can be criticized and grounded by the offering of
reasons. When validity claims are rendered explicit, and when
their grounding is assessed purely in terms of how far good
reasons can be offered for them (rather than by constraint or
force), there exists what Habermas calls a process of 'argumentation'. Argumentation, as he puts it, is a 'court of appeal' of the
rationality inherent in everyday communication: it makes possible the continuation of communicative action when disputes
arise, without recourse to duress. It follows that the notion of
communicative rationality can best be explicated through an
examination of the general properties of argumentation. There is
more than an echo of Popper in this – a mark, perhaps, of what
Habermas has learned through argumentation. Reason, for
Habermas as for Popper becomes primarily a phenomenon of
methodical criticism: 'by identifying our mistakes', Habermas
proposes, 'we can correct our failed attempts'.

The idea of communicative rationality is the basis upon which
Habermas counters the tendencies towards relativism characteristic of much recent philosophical literature. In this context he
discusses the nature of myths in traditional cultures and the
relation between myth and science, in conjunction with the
controversies to which Peter Winch's writings have given rise.
Myths, Habermas argues, are concretized modes of thought,
which integrate many different aspects of life within a single
intellectual domain. They express the organization of societies
which have not generated separate intellectual domains, or
arenas of discourse, within which argumentation may be carried
on. Here we reach one of Habermas's main – and, one might add,
most questionable – proposals. The development of arenas of

discourse, which he tries to trace through the emergence of the 'world religions', and the subsequent differentiation of science, morality and art in modern culture, signify a general evolution towards an expansion of rationality. The more we are able rationally to ground the conduct of our lives in the three main spheres of existence – relations with the material world, with others, and in the expressive realm of aesthetics – the more advanced our form of society can be said to be.

The modern world for Habermas *is* more enlightened than the primitive. In his evolutionary theory, Habermas tries to demonstrate that this still has some connection with Marx's materialist conception of history. Since in the more traditional cultures the productive forces are undeveloped, social life tends to be dominated by the hazards of nature. The need arises to check the 'flood of contingencies'. These cannot be checked in fact, so they are interpreted away, in myth. Myths merge the worlds of nature and culture and attribute to elements in nature powers superior to those of human beings. Myths are anthropomorphic, since they draw into the network of human relations features of nature; and they reify culture by treating it as the operation of autonomous forces. They suffer, Habermas avows, from a 'double illusion'. He says this 'is certainly not well analysed', referring presumably to pre-existing discussions. But the same judgement could be made of his own treatment of myth, which is cursory in the extreme.

He does, however, give some considerable attention to Winch's philosophical analysis of traditional cultures, which of course rests primarily upon Evans-Pritchard's celebrated portrayal of Zande sorcery. Habermas argues that the latter's own interpretation of the activities of the Zande is superior to that offered by Winch. For Evans-Pritchard shows that a hermeneutic sensitivity is necessary if Zande beliefs and practices are to be understood adequately. But this does not lead him towards relativism; on the contrary, he is at pains to point out that Zande thought is deficient as compared to the canons of the testing of validity claims embodied in Western science. We can compare different cultures, or world-views, in respect of their 'cognitive adequacy' – which is to say, in terms of the defensible validity claims that they incorporate. Here Habermas leans rather heavily upon the views of Robin Horton. Traditional cultures, he accepts with Horton, usually involve closed world-views, refractory to change; modern culture, by contrast, is more open to modification in the light of learning experiences.

Piaget's conception of learning as stages of cognitive development can help us illuminate what such openness to learning implies. The three main phases of social evolution – the mythical, religious-metaphysical and modern (shades of Comte!) – correspond to the differentiation of cognitive capacities which Piaget identifies. Habermas is careful at this point to re-emphasize the significance of the procedure of rational reconstruction. The point, I take it, is not that each individual, in a modern culture, recapitulates the development of human societies as a whole. It is that there are several, increasingly extensive and intensive, modalities of the organization of rational thought and action. Cognitive development for Piaget is associated with a 'decentring' process. The decentring of cognition leads the child away from primitive egocentrism, towards the differentiation of the capacity for coping with the external world, the social world and the world of 'inner subjectivity' – the three dimensions to which Habermas's types of validity-claim correspond.

At this point, Habermas introduces the concept of the life-world (*Lebenswelt*). The life-world, as is suggested in phenomenology, is the taken-for-granted universe of daily social activity. It is the saturation of communicative action by tradition and established ways of doing things. The life-world is a pre-interpreted set of forms of life within which everyday conduct unfolds. It 'stores up the interpretative work of many preceding generations'. The weight of tradition in the life-world acts as a counterbalance to the intrinsic possibilities of disagreement which communication raises. The process of social evolution, involving the decentring of world-views and the consolidation of the three dimensions of discourse, alters the character of the life-world. The more advanced the decentring process, the less the achievement of consensus is guaranteed by pre-established beliefs or codes of behaviour. The expansion of rationality thus presumes a diminution of the hold of the life-world. Looking to one of the sources of Piaget's own thought – the work of Durkheim – Habermas reinterprets the transition from mechanical to organic solidarity in these terms. The writings of Durkheim and G.H. Mead he sees as complementing – one another in helping to distinguish the mechanisms of coordination of the life-world from the integration of social systems:

> Ob man mit Mead von Grundbegriffen der sozialen Interaktion oder mit Durkheim von Grundbegriffen der kollektiven Repräsentation ausgeht, in beiden Fällen wird die Gesellschaft aus der Teilnehmerperspektive handelnder Subjekte als *Lebenswelt einer sozialen Gruppe* konzipiert. Demgegenüber kann die Gesellschaft aus der Beobachterperspektive eines Unbeteiligten nur als ein *System von Handlungen* begriffen werden, wobei diesen Handlungen, je nach ihrem Beitrag zur Erhaltung des Systembestandes, ein funktionaler Stellenwert zukommt.

Habermas also seeks to forge here a direct connection with the writings of Max Weber. The formation of differentiated world-views, as these become separate from the life-world, consolidates the rational conduct of life as long as certain conditions are met. They must make concepts available for formulating validity claims for the three dimensions of reality (which Habermas also explicitly connects with Popper's 'three worlds'). Cultural traditions must allow reflective criticism which makes it possible to subject belief claims embodied in customary ways of life to descriptive evaluation. There have to be institutional mechanisms which coordinate learning processes over time and feed back new knowledge into the life-world. This implies the differentiation of science, law and art as the primary spheres relating to the 'three worlds'. Such a differentiation in turn presupposes the institutionalization of purposive-rational action, i.e., action which is oriented towards the achievement of specific goals, and which can hence be assessed in terms of its technical effectiveness. Max Weber, Habermas says, has helped us understand how important the differentiation of cultural spheres, and the formation of institutional forms geared to purposive-rational action, are to modernization. The two main spheres in which purposive-rational action becomes institutionalized, and the basis of system integration, are the economy and the state. Money is the dominant 'circulating medium' (Parsons) in the former, power in the latter.

I shall pass over here the complicated typologies of action and modes of discourse which Habermas offers, as well as his attempt to connect these with speech-act theory. His typologies are as difficult to disentangle as ever, but I do not think they add much to what he has written before. More novel is his extensive critical analysis of Weber; his discussion of the relation between Weber's concept of rationalization and the notion of reification as employed by Lukács and others; plus the attempt to relate all this to features of Parsons's social theory.

Weber helped to popularize the idea of *Verstehen* in the social sciences as well as connecting the rationality of action with the rationalization of culture. The notion of purposive-rational action plays a major role in Weber's characterization of the understanding of human conduct. Purposive-rational action can be assessed in terms of how far, given the goals an actor has, it meets criteria that are strategically 'adequate'. Although Weber used this form of assessment as the pre-eminent standard of rationality against which elements of irrationality of action can be discerned, for Habermas of course it is only one aspect of rational conduct. Normatively regulated action (corresponding to the social world) and expressive, or what Habermas also calls, following Goffman, 'dramaturgical action' (corresponding to the 'inner' world of subjectivity), also have standards of rationality. The notion of *Verstehen* as utilized by Weber needs to be modified in a two-fold sense. Grasping these additional dimensions of the rationality of action is especially relevant to elucidating why people act as they do. But the 'meaning' of action cannot be reduced to actors' intentions and reasons for the action. Here modern hermeneutics, and the philosophy of the later Wittgenstein, are much more important than the schools of thought from which Weber drew. To understand the meaning of action involves being able in principle to participate in the form of life in which that action is incorporated. However, Habermas emphasizes again, this cannot be done without, at least implicitly, assessing the validity claims raised within that form of life. Thus understanding cannot be severed from the rational evaluation of action.

Discussion of metatheoretical and methodological problems of rationality, Habermas asserts, helps drive home that concern with rationality is intrinsic to the practice of the social sciences; it is not something imposed by philosophers from the outside. Since world-views *already* embody validity claims and, in differential degree, modes of their discursive redemption, these first two aspects of rationality are inherently bound up with the third: the rationalization of culture. In examining modes of approach to rationalization, Habermas attempts 'a reconstruction of the history of theory' from Weber to Parsons, seeking to disclose how the social sciences have developed conceptual strategies for analysing the nature of modernity. He acknowledges that this is at best an elliptical approach to the questions at issue, but seems to regard it as an important first step.

According to Habermas, Weber is particularly significant for the problems he wishes to analyse because, unlike the other classical social theorists, Weber broke both with the philosophy of history and with evolutionism in its orthodox, quasi-Darwinian, sense – while at the same time conceiving of Western modernization 'as a result of a universal-historical process of rationalization'. As in his conception of *Verstehen*, Weber allocated to the expansion of purposive-rationality the key part in the historical process of the rationalization of Western culture. He therefore did not capture other aspects in which learning processes have taken place; but his writings do nevertheless contain useful categories for describing them.

Weber mentions many phenomena as involved in the rationalization of Western culture, including science, law, political and economic administration, art, literature and music. What gives a unity to the trends affecting this diverse array? Weber's own use of the term 'rationalization' was rather confused. The main element underlying Weber's various discussions of rationalization, according to Habermas, is the convergence of modes of activity based upon universalistic principle. The rationalized ethics associated with modern law, for example, treat norms as conventions – not as binding imperatives of tradition – governed by decisions based upon generalizable principles rather than arbitrary assessments. In Habermas's interpretation of Weber (which is certainly questionable on this and other points), rationalization is also a process of differentiation – the emergence of three 'value spheres', each with its own logic. These are the cognitive, moral and expressive elements of cultural rationalization, and can be analysed on an institutional level in terms of the three-fold typology Parsons develops of society, culture and personality.

One of Weber's most distinctive concerns, of course, was to contrast occidental rationalization with the directions of development of other civilizations. As Habermas points out, however, he did not formulate clearly in what ways the development of modernity in the West is more than one possible form of society among others. If 'rationalization' means the ordering of life according to universalizable principles, in what sense are those principles universally valid? Weber's answer is ambiguous. We know Habermas's standpoint: there are indeed universally valid procedural forms of rationality. In so far as the West has moved towards the 'postconventional' stage of institutionalized learning processes, rationalization of the Western type equals increasing rationality of belief and conduct.

From Weber to Parsons . . . but of course Habermas does not seek to retrace the path of orthodox sociology. In between Weber and Parsons come Lukács and the Frankfurt School; and Habermas approaches his analysis of Parsonian thought via a 'critique of functionalist reason'. The connections between Weber's interpretation of rationalization, Lukács's discussion of reification, and the critique of instrumental reason formulated by Horkheimer and Adorno are clear. They all agree that an expanding rationalization underlies the overall trend of development of Western society. In spite of placing different emphases upon the character of rationalization, these writers hold, like Weber, that the primacy accorded to purposive-rational action in modern culture produces both a loss of moral meaning in day-to-day life, and a diminution of freedom. Obviously Weber does not counterpose instrumental reason, as 'subjective reason', to 'objective reason' as Horkheimer and Adorno do; and he does not, like Lukács, equate rationalization with a reified social world which in principle can be radically transformed. But neither Lukács nor the Frankfurt School are able satisfactorily to free themselves from the limitations of Weber's standpoint. Lukács hoped to restore the missing philosophical dimension to Marxism by disclosing that rationalization, as described by Weber, involves an undialectical account of bourgeois culture. But this led him to relapse into an abstract 'objective idealism' which was in fact something of a retrograde step in philosophy rather than an advance. Horkheimer and Adorno only partly avoided this tendency, and were prone restlessly to shuffle back and forth between the poles of objective and subjective reason. Neither they nor Lukács were able to show how rationalization or reification are connected to the deformation of the communicative basis of interpersonal relationships. Thus, while retaining a necessary critical edge to social analysis, they lagged behind the advances already made by G.H. Mead on the other side of the Atlantic. For Mead made the transition from a philosophy of consciousness to a philosophy of language, centred upon symbolic interaction.

In Habermas's eyes there is something of an epistemological break between what he regards as the termination of the philosophy of consciousness – or of 'the subject' – and the emergence of communicative analysis. The theory of communicative rationality does not posit a self-sufficient subject, confronting an object-world, but instead begins from the notion of a symbolically structured life-world, in which human reflexivity is constituted. To accept this, and to pursue its implications for social theory, demands, however, departing from some of Mead's emphases. Mead did not investigate the conditions of reproduction of the social world. As Parsons and other functionalist sociologists have consistently asserted, the conditions of societal reproduction involve imperatives over and beyond those directly involved in communicative interaction. The integration of the conduct of the participant members of societies also involves the coordination of divergent interest groups in the face of various specifiable system imperatives. This observation is essential for Habermas's reformulation of the concept of reification. The problematic of reification, he says, should not be associated, as it was by Lukács and the Frankfurt School, with the conception of rationalization (or purposive-rational action) as such. Instead, reification should be connected to ways in which the 'functional conditions of system reproduction' in modern societies impinge upon and undermine the rational foundation of communicative action in the life-world. A critical appropriation of Parsons's work, Habermas claims, allows us to formulate an approach to reification, thus understood, in terms of the mechanisms of social and system integration.

As Habermas recognizes, there is a certain parallel between the synthesis of classical social theory upon which Parsons built his work and his own enterprise. From his earliest writings, Habermas points out, Parsons was preoccupied with the relation between human action on the one side, and the constitution of social systems on the other. Although many interpreters of Parsons have tended to accentuate one of these at the expense of the other, Habermas insists that they are of equivalent import-ance. We can express them in terms of the social integration/ system integration distinction. In the one instance, in the continu-ity of the life-world, we are concerned with the coordination of action orientations; in the other, with functional conditions of system properties ordered along a broader scale of time and space. According to Parsons, norms and values are constitutive of social integration, but not of system integration, which depends upon more 'impersonal' mechanisms. Habermas accepts this general standpoint, while proffering a range of criticisms of Parsons's own formulation of it. Parsons's conceptualization of action, he argues, is too restricted, and particularly in Parsons's later writings tends to be swamped by a concentration upon system functions; and the account of modernity which Parsons developed paints too much of a consensual picture, neglecting the fundamental tensions which have come to exist in contemporary society. While these criticisms are not novel, the mode in which Habermas seeks to draw upon Parsons's ideas is important (if still questionable).

According to Habermas, Parsons's concept of action – or, rather, the mode in which he sought to build such a concept into his theoretical scheme – represses the hermeneutic dimension of social analysis. Parsons failed to see that the social researcher must be able 'to go on' in the forms of life involved in the everyday world in order to describe and to account for the nature of those forms of life in a satisfactory fashion. Recognizing this implies seeing that the differentiation of social and system integration has a methodological aspect to it. Social integration necessarily has reference to participants' own concepts, whereas system integration can be described in other terms; the 'transla-tion' from one to the other involves a shift in methodological orientation on the part of the social analyst. Of course, this view continues the line of argument Habermas set out in previous writings in respect of systems theory. Systems analysis is certainly not illegitimate in social theory; but, on the other hand, it cannot lay claim to providing an overall framework for the explication of social conduct, as functionalists suppose. The integration of a society involves the constant renewal of a compromise between two forms of imperatives. The conditions for the integration of the life-world are bound up with the renewal of the validity claims (*Geltungsbasis*) underlying the structure of a definite world-view. The conditions for the functional integration of society have to do with the modes in which the life-world is related to a surrounding environment which is only partly controlled through the communicative action of human beings. Such a compromise can only be reached through the institutionalization and internalization of value-orientations (as Parsons also thought). If these do not conform to the functional demands of system reproduction, social cohesion is only preserved if such functional demands remain latent. In these circumstances the illusory nature of the validity claims on which the value-orientations are based may remain opaque. The result is systematically distorted communication.

For Parsons, language, in common with power and money, is represented as a medium of societal integration. According to Habermas, however, language has to be excluded from this role since it is implicated in all social activity; Parsons is able to represent language as one medium of integration among others because he obscures the linguistic foundation of the hermeneutic properties of the life-world. However, we can make good use of the Parsonian treatment of power and money as the media of the extension and coordination of purposive-rational action. A high degree of rationalization, produced by the evolutionary movement towards modernity, is the necessary basis upon which money (in the economy) and power (in the polity) become differentiated as 'steering media'. Each presupposes the institutionalization of positive law and the separation of the household – which it is one of Weber's main achievements to have emphasized. As differentiated spheres of system integration, the economy and the polity remain grounded in the life-world, from which they draw normative support and value-commitment. At the same time, they presume the specialized development of processes of the formation of consensus through communicative action. This in turn involves not only institutional differentiation but the development of personality structures capable of participating in postconventional discursive will-formation.

From Parsons . . . back to Weber and to Marx. In the concluding sections of his analysis, Habermas tries to focus these ideas upon a diagnosis of the pathological aspects of modernity. It follows from Habermas's overall view that the rationalization of communicative action must be analytically separated from the formation of the purposive-rational institutional sectors of economy and polity. This in turn means revising key notions in both Weber and Marx, since neither recognizes this distinction in the mode Habermas formulates it. For Habermas, the disentangling of steering mechanisms from the life-world is not as such pathological, but intrinsic to modernization. Such differentiation therefore necessarily has to be distinguished from conditions – which Habermas thinks have come to the fore in recent times – under which the communicative basis of the life-world is drained of the very supports which the economy and polity demand. This can be described as a process of the 'internal colonization' of the life-world, a destruction of tradition which threatens the very continuance of the reproduction of society as a whole.

The tensions and conflicts which dominate in modernized societies today have to be distinguished from those characteristic of earlier phases of development. The disembedding of steering processes from the life-world in post-medieval times provoked various kinds of protest movements, as the peasantry were forced into the towns and as the centralized state came into being. In the nineteenth and early twentieth centuries, the labour movement became the focus of resistance in the face of further economic and political differentiation. Marx showed how the transformation of concrete into abstract labour was the condition of the coordination of modern production. This was one of the very mechanisms distinguishing the economy as a separate institutional sphere. Labour movements may be seen as partially successful attempts to correct an imbalance between life-world and steering mechanisms deriving from the harsh dislocations effected by rapid capitalist development. But a parallel process of 'abstraction' also occurs in political life with the further modernization of the state. This is in fact the type case of the colonization of the life-world, since the public sphere comes to be more and more 'technicized' in the contemporary period.

Here we return to the question of reification. In Marx's writings, this notion is tied diffusely to the process of economic abstraction whereby 'living labour' is subordinated to the rule of impersonal economic mechanisms. In some part this is again a necessary element of modernization and cannot be regarded as pathological. The latter is the case, however, where monetary mechanisms have penetrated too far into the communicatively ordered life-world. The reification of 'communicatively structured spheres of action' is thus not first and foremost a phenomenon of class divisions. Here Habermas leans very definitely towards Weber and away from Marx. Against the hopes of revolutionary transformation which Marx anticipated would be achieved through class struggle,

> hat Max Webers Prognose, 'dass die Abschaffung des Privatkapitalismus . . . keineswegs ein Zerbrechen des stählernen Gehäuses der modernen gewerblichen Arbeit bedeuten würde,' recht behalten. Der Marxische Irrtum geht letztlich auf jene dialektische Verklammerung von System- und Lebensweltanalyse zurück, die eine hinreichend scharfe Trennung zwischen dem in der Moderne ausgebildeten *Niveau der Systemdifferenzierung* und den *klassenspezifischen Formen seiner Institutionalisierung* nicht zulässt. Marx hat den Versuchungen des Hegelschen Totalitätsdenkens nicht widerstanden und die Einheit von System und Lebenswelt dialektisch als ein 'unwahres Ganzes' konstruiert. Sonst hätte er sich nicht darüber täuschen können, dass *jede* moderne Gesellschaft, gleichviel wie ihre Klassenstruktur beschaffen ist, einen hohen Grad an struktureller Differenzierung aufweisen muss . . . Marx fehlen Kriterien, anhand deren er die Zerstörung traditionaler Lebensformen von der Verdinglichung posttraditionaler Lebenswelten unterscheiden könnte.

Marx's analysis, Habermas says, repeating a theme of his earlier writings, is most relevant to the early phases of the development of capitalist societies. In these phases, the economic mechanisms Marx identified do tend to be important. However, there is not one steering mechanism (the economy) in modern societies, but two; and the second, the administrative apparatus of power, was not satisfactorily grasped by Marx. Partly for this reason, orthodox Marxism is not able to illuminate some of the key phenomena of late capitalism, in which state intervention is increasingly extensive, and in which mass democracy and welfare reforms room large.

The conjunction of these phenomena in late capitalism, Habermas affirms, produces a new type of 'class non-specific reification' – although its effects are distributed unequally within the class system. His analysis of this is complex, and I shall not attempt to summarize it here. Basically, the theme is that the colonization of the life-world has destroyed traditional bases of communicative action, without replacing them with the forms of postconventional rationality that are required to couple the life-world to the range of activities controlled by expanding economic and political steering mechanisms. The colonization of the life-world has a double implication. Within the life-world itself, reification has the consequence of loss of meaning or anomie, with the range of associated problems which this produces within personality structures. From the perspective of the steering mechanisms, the result is a set of motivational and legitimation deficits. Whereas in his previous work Habermas saw 'motivation crises' as, in a certain sense at least, more deeply embedded than 'legitimation crises', it now appears that these connect directly to each of the steering mechanisms, and are of equivalent potential importance. Lack of motivational input creates problems for the maintenance of economic organization, while a diminution in legitimation threatens the stability of the political order.

The tasks of critical theory today, Habermas concludes, have to be integrated with this appraisal of the institutional form of, and the tensions inherent within, late capitalism. New conflicts, and new social movements, have developed which diverge from the older types of class struggle centred upon production relationships and the welfare state. Such conflicts concern no longer primarily the distribution of material goods, but rather cultural reproduction and socialization, and do not follow the established bargaining mechanisms associated with the unions or political parties. Since they are an expression of the reification of the communicative order of the life-world, it follows that these tensions cannot be alleviated through further economic development, or technical improvements in the administrative apparatus of government. The new conflicts, and associated social movements, derive from problems that can be resolved only through a reconquest of the life-world by communicative reason, and by concomitant transmutations in the normative order of daily life. How far do such tendencies contain an emancipatory promise which might in a significant way transform existing social institutions? Habermas hedges his bets; but he is inclined to see the new social movements as primarily defensive, concerned with protecting the life-world against further colonization. Ecological and anti-nuclear movements are of this kind, since they are characteristically linked with the impetus to defend the natural environment against despoliation, and to recreate communal relationships of various forms. Whatever the potential for specific movements, however, Habermas affirms strongly that the 'stitching' between system and life-world is likely to continue in the near future to be their point of origin. The theory of communicative action, he contends, helps us to understand why this is so, and can be placed in the service of indicating the pressure-points at which real change might be achieved; it replaces the older type of critical theory, founded upon now untenable philosophical positions.

Theorie des kommunikativen Handelns displays the same mixture of appealing and frustrating features that marks most of Habermas's other writings. However much one might cavil at its length, it is impossible not to be impressed with the encyclopedic range of Habermas's discussion. Who else could one think of, among those writing on social theory today, who could cover – apparently without effort – such a diversity of classical and current traditions of thought, connecting these with abstract issues of philosophy on the one side, and contemporary political concerns on the other? As a synthesis of Habermas's own thought, this work brings out the unity of the theoretical standpoint which he has worked out over the past decade or so. It contains at the same time a veritable treasure-trove of critical commentary on the works of others. Yet it *is* much too long. Habermas's style does not become any more limpid over the years, and the reader has to do a lot of work trying to puzzle out the relation between some of the main arguments. Habermas has a passion for tables and classifications even where these seem to obscure the process of rational argumentation rather than further it. One table contains no fewer than thirty-two categories! A consequence of this taxonomic fervour is that Habermas's writing has something of a puritanical formalism. Often where one would like to see *evidence* presented to support a view that is proposed, a table is offered instead – as if the way to overcome potential objections is to pulverize them into conceptual fragments.

Habermas's writings have been so consistently subjected to scrutiny by friend and foe alike that it is probably hard to discover any aspects of them where the critical ground has not already been well dug over. Rather than attempting to raise any critical points that are especially new, I will indicate where to me some of the main interest of Habermas's ideas lies, and where it seems to be questionable or open to attack. In offering such an appraisal, however, I shall schizophrenically divide myself into two. Since Habermas's work has a systematic character, it invites the reader to be inside or outside. Habermas has many followers, who try to work within his system, offering relatively minor modifications of it; and just as many opponents, who reject much of his enterprise. My inclination, I suppose, is to side more with the second group than with the first, but for the rest of this chapter I shall try to throw out fodder to both. On the left-hand side of the page I will mention the queries/problems/comments that are likely to occur to the sympathetic critic. On the right-hand side, I shall list those which – to borrow Marx's term – a 'critical critic' might ask of Habermas. (This tactic allows me both to have a table of my own, and to formalize a kind of discursive argumentation.)

Sympathetic Critic

1   I have followed the course of your writings from your earliest work up to the present time. Early on, I was led to believe that knowledge is grounded in interest, and that three types of knowledge-constitutive interests could be distinguished. This was an attractive notion, which I adopted with some enthusiasm. It seemed to help with the critique of hermeneutics and the critique of ideology. But having read your most recent work, I feel somewhat puzzled and even rather let down. Am I still to believe that knowledge is founded upon interest? And if so, how exactly do the three knowledge-constitutive interests relate to the three 'worlds', and three types of validity claim, which you now distinguish? You say that working through the theory of knowledge was a roundabout way of approaching the problems that most concern you, but

Critical Critic

1   There seem to me to be some quite radical, and unresolved, discrepancies between your earlier and your later work. The idea that knowledge is grounded in interest was a very bold claim, and the main basis upon which the distinctiveness of your views was founded. To give up this idea is surely to undermine some of the major claims you made – about the 'one-sided' character of hermeneutics, for example, in your debate with Gadamer.

(a) In your new work you seem clearly to admit the 'claim to universality' of hermeneutics for which Gadamer argued. For you accept that there is a necessary hermeneutic moment in the description of social activity, involving the capability of the observer to 'go on' in the form of life which is to be analysed or accounted for.

what exactly is the implication of this? I can see how two of the knowledge-constitutive interests seem to correspond to two of the 'worlds', but what of the third? This is a plea for enlightenment!

(b) In your earlier writings you made space for nomological explanation, drawing upon some of the elements of logical empiricism. You made a distinction between various types of science: the 'historical-hermeneutic' and the 'empirical-analytical'. What has happened to these sciences now? What role do nomological accounts play in the social sciences? These questions have become very obscure. Perhaps this is simply because you multiply classifications so much that it is difficult to see how they relate to one another. But I doubt that this is the only, or even the main, factor involved.

(c) If, as you now say, there are three 'worlds' connecting types of validity claim that can be discursively justified, surely you have moved towards a sort of neo-Kantian view which your earlier work was specifically concerned to avoid . . . or are you even flirting with some version of realism?

2 In treating 'reason' as 'rationality' you explicitly adopt the view that reason is wholly procedural – it refers to modes of justifying statements, or the belief propositions that underlie action. I think I can discern the influence of your interchange with Albert and Popper in the formulation of this standpoint. Because for Popper also, rationality (in the shape of scientific rationality) is also purely procedural. What makes something 'scientific' has nothing to do with its content, or its origins, but depends wholly upon the procedures that can be followed to test it. Popper's view, like yours, derives from the acknowledgement that there can no longer be a 'first philosophy' – that all knowledge is built upon shifting foundations. But Popper does insist upon a clear criterion or criteria (falsifiability, and connected attributes) which can

2 You claim to be defending 'reason' – as 'rationality' – while disavowing the idea of a 'first philosophy'. But I do not find your mode of defence plausible; and even if it could be satisfactorily sustained, it is so empty of content that it seems to leave unresolved all the main problems raised by relativism.

(a) I do not see why your approach should be free of the self-destructive tendency of rationality. Once we admit the principle of the critical evaluation of beliefs, how can anything be exempt? The tactic followed by the logical empiricists in defence of the Verification Principle, by Popper and by yourself – of declaring that your conception is procedural rather than substantive – is hardly convincing. Reason which concerns procedures of rational argumentation still needs to be defended by procedures of be put to use in seeking actually to differentiate among different theories or propositions. He also holds to a version of the correspondence theory of truth, anchored in the notion of verisimilitude. I am not at all convinced by Popperianism, but it does seem to provide what you have not thus far developed, and what Popper does offer – a means of distinguishing among validity claims relevant to the object-world. It is one thing to say that there are modes of argumentation presumed in the use of language. This is an idea I find convincing. But how do such modes of argumentation work in respect of real issues? Nearly all the material you present is of a formal nature, categorizing 'levels' of argumentation and so on. In discussing Winch, Evans-Pritchard and poison oracles you show persuasively that relativism can't be sustained. But you do not indicate – unless I have missed it – what criteria are to be used in assessing specific validity claims. How exactly would we show that the Zande are wrong to believe in poison oracles?

This sort of problem relates to a feeling of disquiet I have about your theory of truth. Truth for you concerns the way in which statements about the object-world can be warranted. But what counts as the 'evidence' that can warrant assertions? Since you say little about referential problems, we are left largely in the dark about this. There seems to be a definite need for further development of your ideas here.

rational argumentation. Your approach therefore does not seem to cope with issues of relativism any more effectively than those based upon some kind of version of a 'first philosophy'.

(b) Truth cannot be identified with the warrantability of assertions. I take it that the aim of your discourse theory of truth is to show that specifying the truth conditions of an assertion logically involves explaining what it means to justify, in argumentation, the claim that those truth conditions are met. But the theory actually presumes this, it does not demonstrate it. No amount of warrants I – or an indefinite community of future observers – bring to bear upon a statement prevents the possibility that the statement is none the less false. Whatever the difficulties with Popper's position, it does have the merit of admitting this possibility, because Popper does distinguish between the modes of investigation we can develop, as rational enquirers, and 'truth' as correspondence.

(c) Suppose your theory of truth were acceptable. It would still leave unresolved virtually all the major questions raised by the postpositivist philosophy of science and by the relativism debates. You distinguish between 'truth', as a concept referring to modes of establishing consensus in argumentation, and statements having referential properties in respect to the object-world. But once 'truth' has been made a procedural notion, a theory of truth no longer copes with questions of *how* one generates 'evidence', *what* counts as 'evidence', and in what *sense* propositions are 'testable'.

(d) The same point could be made in regard to what you call 'practical discourse'. After all, whatever problems – and they of course are formidable enough – may exist concerning evidence about the material world, the difficulties involved in justifying normative claims are even harder to resolve. But your discussion of the character of practical discourse appears no less formal than that of theoretical-empirical discourse.

(e) You claim a connection between language, rationality and a counterfactually posited ideal speech situation. I have never found this convincing. Is it anything other than the last gasp of a critical theory which, dissatisfied with the uncertainties of immanent critique, and suspicious of philosophical anthropology, pins its hopes upon the 'linguistic turn'? Is not language more aptly regarded, with Wittgenstein, as *all* the things that can be done in and through language? 'Our first sentence', you once wrote, 'expresses unequivocally the intention of universal and unconstrained consensus.' Why not say that our first gesture of recognition of another person promises a universal solidarity of human beings? Or perhaps the idea could be extended even further – to Lévi-Strauss's complicitous glance from a cat?

3 The conjunctions you draw between evolutionary theory, the psychology of cognitive development, and the method of rational reconstruction are evidently essential to your thesis that communicative reason isn't just Western reason. I accept your contention that history has to be separated from evolutionary theory, just as empirical psychology is not the same as the reconstruction of levels of competence. At the same time, I am a bit worried by how much reliance you place upon Piaget and Kohlberg, both of whose views have, after all, been subject to serious critical attack. Some of the parallels you discern between the development of reasoning in the cognition of the individual and the social evolution of the species seem

3 I have never understood how you are able to make such confident – and sweeping – use of Piaget and Kohlberg. Despite its brilliance, the empirical base of Piaget's work has always been weak, especially when generalized out of a Western context; and the studies on the basis of which Kohlberg claims that his stages of competence are universal are at best sketchy. Surely it is at least somewhat suspicious that the highest forms of human reason turn out to duplicate the ideals of the Western Enlightenment! If, again, you had begun with Lévi-Strauss rather than Piaget, you would surely have been led to very different conclusions. The fact that you discuss Lévi-Strauss only very cursorily reinforces the uncomfortable feeling I

almost too neat and tidy. I was somewhat surprised to see that the section of your book concerned with myths in oral cultures amounts to only a few pages. If you are going to demonstrate that oral cultures – and agrarian civilizations – operate at a lower stage of rationality than Western or modernized culture, surely a more detailed treatment is called for?

have that you tend to choose theories that *prima facie* fit with the general framework of your ideas – as if indicating how they can be fitted together is enough to validate them.

On the whole I think it was a healthy shift when social theory turned against evolutionism. Evolutionary theories have always been difficult to disentangle from ethnocentrism, and especially from Europocentricism. Although you hedge the concept of evolution with numerous qualifications and you are very careful to consider the connotations of ethnocentrism, I am not at all convinced that you avoid them. Let us follow the proposal I mentioned above, and relate your arguments to Lévi-Strauss rather than Piaget. There are three respects in which you treat oral cultures as inferior to civilizations, and particularly to the modernized West. Oral cultures involve closed world-views; fail to distinguish the three 'worlds' you see as integral to rationality; and are founded upon pre-conventional norms. A Lévi-Straussian viewpoint might agree, with some reservations, with such a categorization. But it would see these as involving forms of life that are every bit as 'rational' as those introduced by the 'hot' cultures of civilization. Oral cultures are not made up of individuals who have not yet undergone the 'learning processes' that bring enlightenment. On the contrary, the introduction of writing and the other paraphernalia of civilization is an unlearning process – a process of cultural destruction. The division we make between nature and culture is one that dissolves the intimacy with nature which is one of the richest forms of human experience. Finally, norms which are founded upon debate and discussion, it might be argued, are not just new forms of tradition. They mark the undermining of tradition –

the security of time-honoured practices – as such.

4   One of your most important accomplishments, in my opinion, is in respect of the critical reception of systems theory. You have forcibly emphasized that systems theory is caught up in the technicization of politics, and have demonstrated that the seemingly neutral application of means–ends thinking may become ideological. Your analysis of 'technique as ideology' is one of the most brilliant parts of your writings. At the same time, you have made it clear that systems theory, and the functionalist style of thought that tends to be associated with it, cannot be rejected out of hand. Thus you have adopted some systems-theoretical concepts into your own work, and in this book you have further clarified how such concepts relate to phenomena of the life-world. I am particularly impressed by the manner in which you apply the notions of system and life-world to the elucidation of the nature of modernity. Some questions still puzzle me a little. One of these concerns power. You now adopt a position, following Parsons, according to which the polity is the medium of the organization of political power. Since the polity is defined in terms of a specific institutional application of purposive-rational action, this seems to narrow down the concept of power rather considerably. How then would you connect the critique of ideology to the critique of domination today – since you seemingly previously employed 'power' in a much broader way?

4   I am unhappy with your distinction between system and life-world – as I was with the differentiation between 'labour' and 'interaction' which appeared prominently in your earlier work. If, as you say, the separation between system and life-world is methodological, how can it also operate as a substantive distinction within modernized societies? Moreover, your use of systems theory, of notions such as 'steering mechanisms' and so on, seems to do scant justice to the active struggles of individuals and groups out of which history is made. The sense of contingency in history, which is so strong in the writings of Max Weber, seems absent from your own work. You are critical of 'functionalist reason', but not critical enough.

5   You have brought the ideas of Max Weber much more into the centre of your work than was previously the case. I find your adaption and critique of Weber's concept of rationalization

5   Too much Weber! Too little Marx! Anyone who draws as heavily upon Weber as you do is likely also to be drawn into Weberian conclusions – whatever disclaimers they might make.

both intriguing and compelling. You have shown that Weber's work, in at least certain basic respects, is more important in diagnosing the traits of the type of society in which we live today than Marx's writings are. At the same time, by exposing some of the limitations of Weber's own analysis of modernization, you make it clear how the type of critique Marx advocated can be kept alive. Your theory of the colonization of the life-world provides a new basis for analysing the tensions, and the sources of opposition, characteristic of modern societies. All the same, I wonder if your analysis might lead to somewhat paradoxical conclusions. Aspects of the life-world have to be defended against the encroachments of political and economic steering mechanisms. But how can such a defence be achieved without transforming those mechanisms themselves? I am not sure just what sorts of transformation you think are possible, and how whatever possibilities you see might bear upon ideals of socialism as they have been conceived of in the past.

You criticize Weber for confining rationalization primarily to the expansion of purposive-rationality, but you are forced to agree that this type of rationality does dominate modern culture. Your diagnosis of the origins, and likely future, of current social movements looks remarkably similar to that Weber might have made – except that you want to speak of 'pathologies', and keep to a more optimistic outlook about the possibilities for social change. I cannot see what justifies your optimism. Weber did, after all, expect there to be protest movements directed against the prevalence of rationalization; and he expected that these would commonly take the form of religious revivalism or what have come to be called 'countercultural' movements. But he did not believe that these could be successful in turning back the tide of rationalization, with its oppressive consequences. In spite of all you have to say about frustrated validity claims, and about the colonization of the life-world, I cannot see that your analysis leads to a different substantive conclusion.

Let me at this stage put myself back together again. The fact that Habermas's work prompts so many questions – numerous others could of course also be raised – is indicative of its extraordinary intellectual power and scope. *Theorie des kommunikativen Handelns* represents a formidable achievement, and all of us working in social theory will be using it as a resource years after most of the current literature in the social sciences has been forgotten.

ELEVEN

Literature and Society:
Raymond Williams

C.P. Snow once provoked a storm of controversy by arguing that a chasm had opened up between the natural sciences and the humanities. But one could perhaps claim that this in fact understated the case. In so far as academic disciplines are concerned, at the time at which Snow wrote there were actually three broad areas largely sealed off from one another: for to these two separate constituencies of knowledge one should add the social sciences. Although the dominant tradition in the social sciences was one that set out to ape natural science, few sociologists either knew much about natural science or were well read in the literature of the philosophy of science. Fewer still paid any attention to aesthetics or literary criticism: the suggestion that these might have some bearing on problems of sociology, or vice versa, would have been received with scorn or incomprehension. All this has now changed. Social theory has become the meeting ground of the philosophy of science and poetics; at the same time, these influences have transformed, and have themselves been changed by, new conceptions of the character and goals of social analysis.

Marxist writings were involved in these transformations, although the discussions were by no means dominated by Marxist authors. 'Marxism', of course, included a variety of differing epistemological, theoretical and practical viewpoints. Some of these viewpoints, such as those associated with the input of phenomenology or structuralism, emanated from intellectual schools that were previously virtually unknown in Britain.

Britain in any case classically lacked a strong tradition of Marxist thought. One of the main contributions of the *New Left Review*, after Perry Anderson assumed the editorship, was to promote a sophisticated forum for the development of Marxist debate in Britain. Under Anderson's leadership, the *New Left Review* followed a definite 'house line': the presence of Althusser and of those substantially influenced by him loomed large. None the less there is no doubt that the journal played a part in furthering the goal of integrating the UK more directly into the diversity of Continental social and political theory. By the same token, it tended to operate in a rather rarefied and arcane intellectual atmosphere, and some did not welcome initiation into the 'mysteries of Paris'. The influence of Althusser and his students, not only as promoted by the *New Left Review*, but also as expressed in a different form in the writings of Hindess, Hirst and others, was violently attacked by E.P. Thompson in *The Poverty of Theory*.

The perspectives and style of the contemporary *New Left Review* were not at all to the taste of some of the 'older generation' of socialists who were connected with the earlier years of the evolution of the journal, originally formed from a merger of the *Universities and Left Review* and *New Reasoner*. All was not sectarian bitterness, however. Raymond Williams was one of the most distinguished of those in the 'older genera- tion' associated with the initial founding of the *New Left Review*, and continued to publish in its pages. One of the results was the work *Politics and Letters*, a dialogue between Williams and three members of the editorial board of the *New Left Review*, Perry Anderson, Anthony Barnett and Francis Mulhern.[1] Williams was interviewed by these three – presumably collectively, although this is not indicated and the separate questioners are not identified – over a period of some months.

The road Raymond Williams travelled in his career ran from a working-class background in Pandy, on the Welsh borders, to Jesus College, Cambridge. This was his personal long revolution, and in the course of the interviews it became apparent how closely his writings were bound to his own experiences. In being forced to confront his own biography, and his own bibliography, Williams did not attempt to force his intellectual career into a framework of recent construction. Rather, with the candour and modesty of a man slightly surprised about his own success, he admitted to major limitations in various sectors of his work, and talked freely of the chance factors that affected the direction of his life.

Williams came from a family with strong Labour Party affiliations, and moved in socialist circles from his early years through to his studies as an undergraduate in Cambridge – interrupted by World War II, and resumed afterwards. Rather than creating a source of tension or dissonance for the working-class boy 'making it' to Cambridge, Williams's socialist connections and interests provided a cushion against the potentially disruptive experience of moving between two very different milieux. His parents strongly believed in the desirability of education and were a source of consistent support; the Socialist Club in Cambridge offered a network of friends within the university.

As an undergraduate prior to the war, Williams joined the Communist Party, but not with the consciousness that he was abandoning reformist politics in favour of an actively militant stance. He spoke of the atmosphere of the Socialist Club as a 'confident culture', and this was obviously in both a personal and political sense very important to him. It left untouched the formal pattern of university work, since political activities were mostly kept separate from the university as an organization. It was very different from the climate of the late 1960s: not only because of the direct clashes with the university administration in which radical students were involved in the second period, but because of the 'intense divisiveness' among different groups on the left at the later time.

Williams did not stay in the Communist Party after being called up to serve in the war. His leaving was not brought about in a calculated fashion; he merely allowed his membership of the party to lapse. By the time he returned to Cambridge after the war, in which he served in an anti-tank unit and participated in the Normandy landings, he was no longer a part of this 'confident culture'. A period of disillusion and self-doubt was combined with a drive to take up academic work 'quite fanatically'.

The influence of Leavis was by that time beginning to make itself felt, and certain of his ideas attracted Williams strongly. From that time onwards, Williams became preoccupied with 'culture' in its various senses. Three elements of Leavis's views seemed to Williams to lend themselves to the formulation of a 'cultural politics' very distant in other respects from Leavis's position. One was the radical nature of Leavis's attacks upon academic literary criticism and contemporary standards of journalism. Another was the discovery of practical criticism: a discovery Williams found 'intoxicating' at the time, but towards which he later maintained a more reserved attitude. Just as important as these was Leavis's emphasis upon the significance of education, which Williams of course interpreted in his fashion, but which accorded with his own experience.

Williams shortly afterwards acquired a job teaching literature for the Workers' Educational Association in Oxford – a job which he found discouraging in some ways, but which also influenced his academic work in a direct fashion. He remained teaching in adult education before moving to a lectureship in Cambridge in 1961. Cambridge, one is tempted to say, always reclaims its own.

Culture and Society and *The Long Revolution* were the books that made Williams famous, but the second was very much an extension of certain basic ideas established in the earlier book. Each actively contributed to the long revolution which they diagnosed, in the sense that they reached a very broad audience.

In *Culture and Society*, Williams suggested that it was both possible and necessary to move towards what he called 'a new general theory of culture'. The main theme of the book was that both the notion of culture and the term itself, in recognizably modern usage, came into currency in England during the period of the Industrial Revolution. The connection, Williams tried to demonstrate, was not a fortuitous one, and he attempted to chart the progress of the idea through the works of a variety of authors from the opening of the nineteenth century through to the mid-twentieth century. The book introduced a number of other 'key words' which he showed came into use, or were substantially modified, in the period of the Industrial Revolution: 'industry', 'democracy', 'class' and 'art'. He had intended to include an appendix which would detail no fewer than sixty such key terms; by the dictate of the publisher this was removed from the published version, and only appeared some twenty years later, in 1976, as a separate book, *Keywords*. Yet the keyest of Williams's key words remained 'culture', which, he argued in *Culture and*

Society and *The Long Revolution*, expressed two related sets of processes. The emergence of the term marked an acknowledgement of the separation of a particular sphere of moral and intellectual concerns from the driving force of the new society, industrialism.

But the development of the concept of culture also provided what he called 'a court of human appeal . . . a mitigating and rallying alternative' to the experience of industrial production. As he made clear in *The Long Revolution*, the idea of culture was a response to political change as well as to economic change, more specifically to the development of democratic ideals. There is no easy and obvious correlation, he pointed out, between industrialization and democracy. Economic growth and political transformation, he thought, had been fairly well documented by previous writers. Such documentation had, however, to be related to a 'third revolution', the expansion of culture in its interrelation with economic and political development: this was the analysis he set out to provide in *The Long Revolution*.

The book, like its predecessor, provoked some considerable controversy, as their author had meant them to do. Many critics objected especially to the strongly defined 'sociological' components of Williams's analyses, as expressed in the relating of intellectual or literary culture to the 'structures of sentiment' of the culture of the common people.

The works counterpose 'industry', rather than 'capitalism', to culture, and do not adequately either explore the dislocations between different sectors of cultural life, or situate them within the context of class divisions. Cultural development appears as something of a separate and abstracted process – an emphasis which derived in some part, but certainly not completely, from the presumption that economic and political transformations had already been relatively well chronicled and the problem was to 'add on' the third dimension of culture.

Williams's subsequent writing career was a very productive one, and although in one sense he ranged over a considerable span of subjects, his work can none the less be readily seen as comprising a single overall project. He did not deviate from the goals of analysing and furthering the long revolution towards a 'participatory socialism', and of developing methods of cultural diagnosis and critique relevant to that goal. This continuity is evident enough in *Communications* and his book on *Television*. But both his novels and his more specialized discussions of drama and literary criticism relate closely to his other writings.

There are of course again strong biographical elements in Williams's novels, but their theme is not simply the description of personal experience: it is the relating of such experience to broad-based movements of social change. Just as in *The Long Revolution* he protested against the equation of working-class culture with a few 'proletarian novels', so in *Border Country* he wanted to avoid an account of an encapsulated working-class community separated from the rest of the world. The novel differs from the characteristic tone of much British fiction of the 1950s – the individual escaping, for better or worse, from the grip of a working-class upbringing; there is a greater emphasis upon the changes that the community itself undergoes. The transition between the personal and the public, the intersection between private experience or feeling and 'structures of sentiment', come through as predominant features of Williams's concerns, and ones with which he continually struggled.

It is prominent also in his works on drama. As an undergraduate he wrote a long essay on Ibsen, later partially incorporated in *Drama from Ibsen to Eliot*. Ibsen early on crystallized certain of Williams's own feelings at a time when he had lost some of the certitude he had previously enjoyed. But in Ibsen the combating of despair is treated as a subjective project, and it took some while before Williams managed to recognize in full the need to amend this view of 'individual liberation' in the light of a conception of 'social liberation'.

The position expressed in the book, he later came to realize more clearly, was an 'inherently unstable' one for this among other reasons. His discovery of Brecht enabled him to modify his earlier view. Williams did not see Brecht merely as a 'political dramatist'. Brecht transcended one of the main confines of naturalistic drama by refusing to treat events 'off-stage' as unexplicated determinants of the on-stage drama; not, however, by substituting politics for naturalism, but by making the actual dramatic actions embody the presence of erstwhile 'outside' history.

There seem to me to be many unresolved difficulties in Williams's work. Among these one might mention particularly his long-standing emphasis upon the concept of culture as the key word that opens more latches than any other; the pronounced concentration of his writings upon British sources and British history; and a series of latent 'hermeneutic problems', or problems of language, meaning and epistemology, especially manifest in *Keywords*. The first two of these points can be bracketed with one another. In fastening upon the notion of culture, Williams was able to open up new horizons for social history. *Culture and Society* and *The Long Revolution* were outstanding contributions, works whose contemporary relevance is far from exhausted.

At the same time, the centrality Williams accorded to 'culture' proved to be a double-edged sword. It created dilemmas that I do not think he was able to resolve satisfactorily in his subsequent writings. These dilemmas are various, but they stem in some degree from promoting the idea of 'culture' and demoting the idea of 'society'; and from the essentially conservative context from which he took the notion, although he tried to turn it to radical advantage. Even in *Keywords*, when discussing the origins of modern uses of 'culture', Williams underplayed the significance of its derivation from *Kultur* and from German Romanticism. He agreed with his *New Left Review* critics that it was a mistake to have written *Culture and Society* as if British thought developed in isolation from the Continent, and made it apparent that of his earlier works this was the one he felt least affinity with later. None the less, he continued to centre his writings on the concept of culture.

Both the German Romantics and their English admirers or counterparts on the conservative side – up to and including Eliot – juxtaposed culture and industry or technology. In seeking to radicalize their thought, Williams continued the same juxtaposition. But it is just this polarity which obscures the founding of modern technology in the capitalist accumulation process, and which opposes 'idealism' to 'materialism' in an unacceptable manner. This is very much connected to the assertion of the primacy of 'culture' over 'society'. As used by many sociologists to imply some sort of harmonious societal unity, the term 'society' may justly be regarded with suspicion. But if understood as social relations of both dependence and struggle, it supplies an essential mediation between the polarity of 'culture' and 'industry' as these appear in Williams's writings.

Partly for these reasons, one of Williams's most persistent preoccupations, the relations between 'structures of sentiment or feeling' and the nature of day-to-day personal experience, remains elusive. Throughout his writing he argued that, as he put it in *The Long Revolution*, 'What we are looking for, always, is the actual life that the whole organisation is there to express.'

Day-to-day experience involves both continuity and change, change which in the modern era is expressed in linguistic mutations such as are analysed in *Keywords*. Two overlapping traditions of philosophy seem to be particularly relevant to conceptualizing these matters, but neither, so far as I know, was drawn upon by Williams: hermeneutic phenomenology, and the philosophy of the later Wittgenstein. One of the most important developments marked by each of these forms of contemporary philosophy is that they insist that personal experience is known to the self as a 'self' only via the public categories of language. They specifically reject the dualism of private experience and socially formed culture which, it seems to me, Williams's analyses still presuppose, however much he might have insisted they are to be related to one another. It is a mistake to associate these philosophies with the 'linguistic turn' so frequently regarded as a major feature of current social thought. For both stress the interweaving of language and practice, the 'other face' of language in 'Being' or 'what cannot be spoken'. Hermeneutic philosophy has also for a long while raised an issue that is posed rather acutely by *Keywords* and the mode of cultural analysis it expresses: the issue of the historical character of human knowledge.

If the changes in terminology Williams described are more than just changes in terminology – if they are changes in overall frames of experience of meaning – there is no obvious reason why his own analyses of such changes should themselves be exempt from the historical process. Problems of the relativity of human knowledge, which crop up not only in hermeneutics but in the post-Kuhnian philosophy of science, seem integral to Williams's enterprise. *Keywords* does not confront such problems at all.

These comments have particular force as regards Williams's work before the appearance of *Marxism and Literature*. This was a more abstract or 'theoretical' book than anything he attempted previously, and among other things delved into problems of relativism in a fairly direct way.

Marxism at that date was embroiled in a series of debates. As Williams argued in *Marxism and Literature*, in the English-speaking world, it once seemed as though Marxism was 'a settled body of theory or doctrine' and that literature was also 'a settled body of work, or kinds of work, with known general qualities and properties'. The relation between the two could be examined, and Marxism 'applied' to literature. Williams wasn't a 'Marxist' in this sense, and his earlier books were written from the point of view of what he later called 'radical populism'.

Marxism, however, he argued, should be seen as an open and flexible tradition of thought, rather than a dogmatic set of doctrines. At the same time, what 'literature' is has become problematic. In response to these changes, Williams became considerably more sensitive to what he described as the 'danger of relativism', but denied that he had succumbed to it.

He identified his standpoint as one of 'cultural materialism', and although the study expresses a major transition in his thought, the new Williams retained a great deal of continuity with the old. The book again begins with the concept of culture, and the notion of structures of feeling plays a pivotal role. But this time language is seen to be involved in a complex way with these ideas, and Williams tried to integrate a discussion of meaning with an analysis of the base/superstructure problem in Marxism. He began to formulate a viewpoint which sees 'language and signification as indissoluble elements of the material social process itself involved all the time both in production and reproduction'. I think this conception is essentially correct. I am not at all convinced, however, either that Williams managed in the book to elaborate upon it successfully, or that it is compatible with earlier ideas he claimed to sustain.

Williams noted that while on the one hand 'there is no natural seeing and therefore there can't be a direct and unmediated contact with reality', on the other 'it is necessary to recall an absolutely founding presumption of materialism: namely that the natural world exists whether anyone signifies it or not'. This sounds more like some sort of version of Kantianism than anything else. I imagine that Williams did not wish to advocate a Kantian position. Yet the main dilemmas raised by Williams's earlier work remained unresolved in *Marxism and Literature*, and indeed became to a certain degree compounded.

TWELVE

T.H. Marshall, the State and Democracy

Tom Marshall is remembered above all for the brilliance of his work on citizenship. Modest in size, Marshall's classic work *Citizenship and Social Class* (1950) has enjoyed a continuing influence for some half a century. In that book Marshall described a balancing act between the divisive effects of class inequalities and the integrative implications of citizenship rights. Marshall did not use the term 'democracy' all that often, but his analysis of the progressive development of citizenship certainly can be regarded as a theory of democratic evolution.

Marshall's views were strongly shaped by a critical reaction to Marx and Marxism. Marshall wanted to defend the claims of reformist socialism as contrasted to its bolder and violent cousin, revolutionary communism. He wanted to show also that class conflict was neither the main motor of social transformation nor a vehicle for political betterment. With Max Weber, Marshall accepted class inequality as an inherent element of a capitalistic industrial society. Class division, however, in Marshall's view is only one dimension of such a society. The other, integrative, dimension is that of universal involvement in the national community, given concrete form in the welfare state. The term 'welfare state' was first coined during World War II, to contrast the idea of a cohesive and protective national community with the 'warfare state' of Nazi Germany. The new welfare policies were designed to treat all citizens as part of a more inclusive national order and in so doing to recognize state responsibility for caring for those who were in some way prevented from active economic participation. Marshall recognized the influence of the war effort upon the shaping of welfare institutions, but placed them in a much longer evolutionary context. His theory of citizenship rights, nevertheless, was at the same time a theory of the welfare state as the realization of a programme of socialist reform.

Marshall's critical reaction to Marx's interpretation of class conflict is a clear and evident feature of his work. Less obvious, and less explicit, is his critique of Marx's account of democracy. Marx recognized that the universal qualities of democracy run counter to the class-divided nature of capitalist societies. He was able to preserve the primacy of class in his theory by treating democratic rights as narrow and partial. In demographic systems people only get to vote occasionally, every few years: there is little or no participatory democracy. Even more important, democratic rights are limited in two ways. In Marx's time only a small proportion of the British population, essentially male middle-class property owners, had the right to vote. Moreover, political rights made no impact upon the economic sphere. The worker, as sheer 'labour power', sacrificed all control over his or her body when entering the workplace. Many have argued that Marx was undemocratic or even anti-democratic. A charitable reading of his texts, however, would suggest that he believed class revolution to be the means of widening and deepening democratization. A genuine universalizing of democratic rights would be accompanied, in other words, by some form of economic democracy having the participatory traits noted by Marx in his discussion of the Paris Commune.

Whether consciously or not, Marshall provided an alternative interpretation of democratization to that offered by Marx. On the one hand, Marshall was more clearly aware than was Marx of the essential importance of civil or legal rights in a democratic society. Legal rights that guarantee effective freedoms protect individuals both from the overweening power of the state and from the organized use of violence or coercion.

In his discussion of economic rights, however, Marshall in effect picked up Marx's theme of the partial nature of democracy. Marshall was not a proponent of economic democracy, but his advocacy of welfare rights, in the context of his overall analysis of citizenship, can be understood as a theory of democratization.

Welfare rights round out and deepen the 'hollow' character of democracy that Marx diagnosed. When combined with the other two types of citizenship right, rights of welfare provide for a full and 'complete' integration of the citizen into the wider social order. The citizen is no longer simply the 'abstract voter' but instead appears as a flesh-and-blood individual with material needs; as a citizen, she or he has the right to expect that the society will cater for those needs in circumstances of deprivation or disability.

If Marshall spoke little of 'democracy' as such, it is because the burden of his work was concerned with welfare systems and the welfare state. The welfare state, in his argument, becomes part of the general extension of democratization. Yet mechanisms of political democracy tend in his writings to be taken for granted rather than directly explored.

Marshall wrote at a period during which it seemed to almost everyone, supporters and critics alike, that the welfare state would continue its upward trajectory. Hayek was thought of by most as an eccentric and marginal thinker; neo-liberalism, as it later became, might have been a gleam in his eye but was hardly even dreamed of by anyone else. Over the past twenty or so years, of course, welfare systems have been the subject of sustained attack from the neo-liberal right. Some of the policies and programmes that Marshall believed would allow disadvantaged individuals to live a full and rewarding life have been seen by the neo-liberal critics as producing precisely the opposite. Such critics have attacked welfare rights as promoting dependency and apathy. Far from ensuring that the underprivileged have a full place in the wider society, according to them one of the consequences of the rise of the welfare state has been the creation of an excluded underclass.

The collapse of the Marshallian vision, if such has indeed occurred, cannot be laid solely at the door of neo-liberalism. Rather, the neo-liberals provided an – unsound – interpretation of wider changes affecting not only welfare institutions but many other aspects of modern societies also. Marshall concentrated his attention upon Britain. He did not give much attention to transnational events or structures, but it is to these events and structures we must look to explain the difficulties of the welfare state today. Marshall did not, and could not, have anticipated some of these developments. But neither do his writings give much purchase upon either the expansion of democratic concerns in the present day or the troubles that democracy at the same time is experiencing.

Just as Marshall's thinking about citizenship and the welfare state had its origins in the UK, so in some part did neo-liberalism, in the shape of what came to be called Thatcherism. Neo-liberal doctrines, in one guise or another, however, have been influential worldwide. At the same time, there has occurred something of a global expansion of democracy, expressed not only in the fall of Communism but in the decline of authoritarian or military governments in other areas. In the sense of liberal democracy, democratization seems to have become to some degree a global process today. On the other hand, in the heartlands of liberal democracy, the Western capitalist states, liberal democratic institutions appear to be suffering from stresses and strains as substantial as those affecting the welfare state. Many of the population have come to distrust politicians, have little interest in politics and are unable to identify with any existing political party.

Set against the general background of Marshall's work, a number of questions can be asked in this situation: (1) What accounts for the global spread of democratizing processes? (2) What are the main mechanisms of democracy – should democracy be equated with liberal democracy? (3) What connections exist between problems of democratic organization today and problems facing the welfare state?

For reasons already mentioned, Marshall did not really explore the attractions or the limitations of liberal democracy. He was conscious of both, to be sure, and he believed that to establish a strong welfare system without democratic parliamentary institutions would lead to authoritarianism. Marshall does not appear to have seen the cultural foundations of liberal democracy as particularly problematic. Others, however, have done so and some of these include scholars who have drawn extensively upon Marshall's work on citizenship. For such authors the advantages of liberal democracy compared to other types of political order are obvious; the emergence of sound liberal democratic institutions is inevitably a long-term process. For a properly functioning liberal democracy depends upon a wider civic culture – not just the civic rights that Marshall so ably analysed, but a more diffuse political culture conducive to the regular succession of political parties and to non-coercive government.

Such a view of democracy provides a rationale for the spread of democratization in current times, but also suggests that newly democratizing states will have great problems in establishing well-functioning democratic institutions. I shall refer to this position as the fragile flower theory of democratization. It equates demo-cratization with liberal democracy in the context of the nation-state.

According to the fragile flower theory of democracy, if liberal democratic institutions are spreading into many countries it is because liberal democracy is manifestly superior to any other type of political system. Two cheers for democracy, as E.M. Forster said: democracy might be imperfect but it is still superior to any alternatives, and can be seen by everyone to be so with the disintegration of Soviet Communism. Democracy, however, is a plant that needs fertile conditions in order to grow. It needs soil that has been laid down across the generations and like any other fragile growth needs constant nurturance. The fragile flower theory of democracy is also a catching-up theory: for democrat-ization to be successful in areas such as Asia, Africa or Latin America, the conditions that have led to the successful develop-ment of democratic institutions in the Western countries have to be duplicated. Since democracy is a fragile flower these con-ditions are problematic: there cannot be any relatively sudden transition to democratic organization.

Most who have taken such a view have accepted a general association between the development of the democratic civic culture and the progression of capitalistic or market institutions. Markets do not create or sustain democracy in and of themselves. They are the natural complement to democratization, since they cultivate individualism and freedom of choice, even if marketiza-tion cannot in and of itself create the cultural conditions necessary for stable democratic life.

The fragile flower theory is fairly simple and it is intuitively attractive, making sense as it does both of the spread of democracy and of the conditions for its success. There are good reasons, nevertheless, to be somewhat cautious about it. First, there do seem to have been historical circumstances in which liberal democracy has been established almost overnight and where it has persisted in a stable fashion. Thus Germany and Japan were both authoritarian states where, largely through the intervention of the victorious powers after World War II, were set up liberal democratic institutions that took an instant hold. Second, the theory presumes events not fully explained – including especially the fall of Soviet Communism – in order to interpret the spread of democratization. Although there were protest movements in the East European countries, the Soviet Union was not brought down by any sort of 'democratic deficit'. Third, the theory does not cast any light upon the troubles of liberal democracy in those countries that have well-developed democratic institutions. The apparently global triumph of liberal democracy is accompanied by a process of strain or decline. Why should this be so?

The importance of liberal democracy cannot be gainsaid. Even those on the political left who might once have tended to downplay its significance now accept this. To explore its nature, and its current popularity, however, perhaps we need more than the fragile flower perspective. Instead of such a view I would propose what might be called a sturdy plant theory. This is not a catching-up theory of democracy; and it places current processes of democratization in the context of wider changes sweeping through not only the industrialized countries but most of the world as a whole. Such a view does not identify democracy *tout court* with liberal democracy. The very spread of liberal democratic institutions can be understood as part of the same processes that, in their heartlands, tend to compromise or challenge them.

Democracy is perhaps a sturdy plant that can in fact take root in what was previously quite stony soil; it does not necessarily depend upon a long-established civic culture, but rather upon other structural conditions that on occasion can be put in place quite quickly. It is always probably vulnerable, but may have more inherent strengths than other competing types of political system or legitimation.

We should situate democratization in the context of a number of very basic social changes. The first of these is by now very well known and, over the past few years at least, has become as much debated as has democracy. This is the impact of globalization.

The second set of changes is intimately bound up with globalizing processes: these are to do with the impact of de-traditionalization. (See chapter 2.) For some two centuries modernity created something of an effort-bargain with tradition. The philosophers of Enlightenment set themselves against tradition; one of the dominant impulses of modern society, with its heavy reliance upon science and technology, is the overcoming of fixed legacies from the past. Yet modernity in some large part accommodated itself to tradition and vice versa. On the level of large-scale institutions, new ideologies were invented with a heavy shot of tradition including, for instance, various kinds of religious belief and symbolism. Just as important was the persistence of what can be termed infrastructural traditions – traditions of everyday life. In respect of gender, the family, kinship, sexuality and other domains, traditions became altered but also reconstructed during the course of the nineteenth and early twentieth centuries.

De-traditionalization in the current period stems from two main sources: one is the impact of social movements of various types. Thus the feminist movement, for example, actively sought to place in question traditionalized or taken-for-granted aspects of the position of women and gender identity more generally. Tradition encompasses what has been called a 'silent power': it forecloses options at the same time as it supplies guidelines to conduct. When questions that are latent in tradition are brought in to the public domain they have to be discursively justified. Traditional ways of doing things give way to actively promoted and debated courses of action.

Globalizing processes tend to be de-traditionalizing because they bring together a diversity of newly visible worlds and ways of life. Anyone who persists with a traditional way of doing things cannot but be aware that many other alternative life practices exist. A world of cultural cosmopolitanism of this sort is not one where tradition necessarily disappears. Almost to the contrary, tradition is often reconstructed and achieves a new dynamism. Yet it cannot take the forms it once did.

A particularly important aspect of de-traditionalization is the emergence of fundamentalism. In a few short years we have become accustomed to the idea that there are tensions between fundamentalism and democracy. Indeed in the shape of political extremism, ethnic purification and assertive religious dogma, fundamentalisms of various sorts are perhaps the chief enemy of democratic dialogue. Marshall gave no attention at all to this phenomenon. And this is not in any way surprising: for the rise of fundamentalism is actually a quite recent occurrence, reflecting the global changes here being discussed.

Although the term 'fundamentalism' dates from around the turn of the century, it has only come into common currency over about the last twenty years. The widespread introduction of a term in this way where none previously existed, or where its use was marginal, virtually always suggests the arrival of a new social phenomenon. Fundamentalism can be understood as a reaction to radical de-traditionalization – a reaction to the expansion of modernity, but also an attempt to defend tradition as authentic and as having its own indigenous claims to truth. Fundamentalism seeks to defend tradition 'in the traditional way' in a world that is increasingly globally cosmopolitan; in so doing it purifies tradition, often in an aggressive fashion, and at the same time frequently links into the new modes of global electronic communication.

Fundamentalism is complex and I would not want to oversimplify its character. By and large, however, it can be said that fundamentalism can emerge in any domain subject to de-traditionalization. (Chapter 2.) Fundamentalism is essentially a means of authenticating tradition and therefore is not specifically linked to religion. It is an outlook in some sense in genuine dialogue with the presuppositions of industrial capitalist civilization. It poses the question 'Can we live in a world where nothing is sacred?' Fundamentalism is not always dangerous to others, but can easily become so. For it implies a refusal of dialogue, a justification of tradition that resists discursive engagement with others.

The third cluster of changes affecting the contemporary world is connected to increasingly high levels of social reflexivity. 'Reflexivity' refers here to the active engagement with diverse sources of incoming knowledge or information that is an inevitable part of living in a de-traditionalized social environment. Ulrich Beck has justly spoken of the retreat of fate in our lives as intimately bound up with de-traditionalizing influences. When social roles were relatively fixed, for example, it was the fate of most men to expect to leave school or college and go out to work until age 65, which was followed by a period of retirement. Most women could anticipate a life of domesticity, centred upon children and the home, even if a substantial proportion of women were always also in paid work. Anatomy is no longer destiny and gender is no longer fate. In most areas of social life, whether they be affluent or less privileged, most people have to take a variety of life-decisions that cannot be settled by appeal to past tradition. They must make such decisions, some way or another, in the context of diverse information sources and malleable knowledge-claims.

A world of heightened social reflexivity is one infused with diverse forms of expertise, but where at the same time expertise becomes fragmented. It is a world of active involvement yet one that is puzzling and often opaque.

Where these various sets of changes take hold, a variety of institutional consequences follows. In the area of social and economic organization, for instance, the old bureaucratic hierarchies, which once were seen by Weber and others as the height of social efficiency, start to become beleaguered and ineffective. A reflexive citizenry, living in a world where fate is in retreat, is loath to accept the sorts of labour discipline characteristic of earlier periods. What seemed to Weber an inexorable process, submission to bureaucratic dominion, becomes contested and vulnerable. Institutions that appeared so solid as to be unshake-able do not look so at all when suddenly placed in question. Both the fact and the ideology of bureaucratic hierarchy begin to cede place to an emphasis upon the small-scale and upon bottom-up decision-making.

An increasingly active, reflexive citizenry both demands democratization and at the same time becomes disenchanted with politics. Political authoritarianism has scarcely disappeared, and indeed is all too evident in different parts of the world. Yet the counter-pressures are also increasingly strong. Authoritarian regimes become vulnerable for much the same reason that bureaucratic organizations of the Weberian type become social dinosaurs. Calls for 'flexibility' and 'social involvement' are no doubt often ideological; yet where fate no longer rules it is difficult for political authoritarians to rule effectively either. The result is not necessarily enhanced democracy. Such a situation, in some contexts at least, can lead to social disintegration and the virtual impossibility of effective government of any kind.

The consequences for established democratic systems are mixed. The advance of globalization links local and regional systems to events and processes that bypass the national state. (See chapter 12.) Many events that affect people's lives happen either above the level of the nation-state or in the domains of social and technological change in everyday life. It is not only the political or sociological observer who notices these things. They become to some degree the common currency of everyone and form part of their own reflexive awareness of, and reaction to, contingent events.

Disenchantment with politics within the democratic societies in some part reflects the visible discomfort experienced by political leaders. To sustain legitimacy, such leaders must make promises and must assert their capability to control or alter the existing framework of events. Yet the mass of the citizenry can see quite well that these promises have little chance of being effective. I do not think that political disaffection is the only consequence that can flow from such a situation, nor is it the case that the arena of national politics inevitably loses all its effectiveness. On the more positive side, there are possibilities for 'the democratizing of democracy' that both promise greater democratic involvement for many and also address the issue of generating effective political power.

The democratizing of democracy involves various elements. These include an attack upon various forms of political patronage. It is not by chance that corruption cases have come to the fore in many diverse political settings around the world. Such corruption is not necessarily a recent development. Rather, the enhanced 'social visibility' of the political domain means that influences that were once concealed, or even thought generally acceptable, now come into public view and are actively condemned. The democratizing of democracy also implies the downward and upward devolution of power. We do not know as yet what institutional forms such devolution is likely to assume, if it can be realized. Neither existing forms of local government, nor existing supranational organizations, seem fully up to the task. There are real possibilities of developing forms of democratic participation that might enhance local decision-making, as many proponents of a 'revived civil society' have proposed. In the contemporary world, however, local and global happenings are often directly tied to one another. We have to search for democratic forms that are able to grapple with the new connections of the local and the global.

Nobody knows where this situation will lead. Yet the very intensity of recent debates about democracy, involving proposals for forms of democratic organization once thought to be either obsolete or unavailable in a large-scale society, points to a transformed agenda. Participatory democracy was long ago written off by Weber, Schumpeter and others as irrelevant and unrealizable in the settings of modern social life. Yet with the social transmutations now occurring, including especially the downward devolution of power, schemes of participatory democracy have again been widely canvassed. In the short space available to me here, I do not propose to look at the diversity of schemes of democratic renewal now being discussed. I want to mention only one mechanism of democracy, which I hold to be particularly important in the social circumstances I have analysed.

Whether one speaks of liberal democratic institutions or other forms of democracy, democracy involves two partly separate dimensions. One is the representation of interests. Democratic institutions provide a means whereby a variety of interests can find expression and where there is some means of organizing to represent those interests. But democracy also means the chance to have one's say. It means, in other words, the possibility of dialogue. Liberal democratic institutions plainly provide various contexts in which dialogic engagement is possible – in parliaments, in congresses and in other public media. Perhaps the most interesting attempt to reinterpret liberal democratic mechanisms in recent years – that associated with the idea of deliberative democracy – depends upon the idea of resolving issues through dialogue. As usually understood, deliberative democracy falls far short of Habermas's ideal speech situation. In empirical situations of dialogue, it will often be the case that controversial issues cannot be resolved directly; yet discussion can allow us to agree to disagree, and can therefore be a powerful medium for tolerance and conciliation.

Dialogic democracy, or its possibility, should not be seen as limited to formal contexts of democratic participation. Mechanisms of dialogic democratization need to be established – and to some extent are developing – in a number of other major arenas of social life, both local and more global.

The background to the emergence of dialogic democracy in such circumstances is again the sweeping changes diagnosed above. We live now in a much more intensely cosmopolitan world than even three or four decades ago. Cosmopolitanism and difference were until relatively recently often preserved through geographical segregation. Different groups, cultures and regions coexisted in some part through sheer geographical separation. In an age of instantaneous global communication, geographical separation loses much of its meaning and its social significance. Different groups and cultures are brought much more directly into relation with one another, and global cultural diasporas of all kinds form a routine part of the daily experience of individuals who may be separated geographically by many thousands of miles.

New possibilities, indeed demands, for communication and symbolic exchange thus emerge. At the same time, the relation between dialogue and potentialities of social or political violence becomes especially tensionful. Fundamentalisms, with their assertion of the integrity of 'purified' traditions, readily step into the spaces where dialogic relations are ill-formed or lacking.

In all settings of communicative contact, communication can move in two possible directions. On the one hand, as we know both from the literature of global diplomacy and from that of much more intimate personal relationships, communication can be a means of the fruitful exploration of difference. Getting to know the other, whether an individual, group or culture, better can serve to increase one's self-knowledge, heighten communication with the other, and initiate a virtuous circle of mutual understanding. On the other hand, degenerate cycles of communication produce a diametrically opposite effect: dislike feeds on dislike or, worse, hate feeds on hate. Whether assessing conflicts in marriage, or violence between religious or ethnic groups, it is important to recognize that, like love, hatred does not exist in a 'fixed quantum'. Vicious group conflicts, involving the most extreme forms of barbarism, can develop in situations where there was previously a reasonable degree of coexistence between the groups or communities involved. It is not too fanciful to draw a parallel with personal life here. In marriage, tolerance or love, when a relationship deteriorates, can turn into an elemental hatred. A sobering finding of the literature on emotional relationships is that very often the things which attracted one individual to another in the first place – certain traits of personality and behaviour – become those most despised or reviled if the relationship enters a negative communication spiral.

The formation of mechanisms of dialogic democracy in the transnational sphere is a matter of the first importance. As yet we can only dimly foresee what such mechanisms might be. Advocates of 'cosmopolitan democracy', such as David Held, have argued that parliamentary institutions or congresses can be stretched above the level of the nation-state, so as to create regional and international assemblies, such assemblies having a direct tie to the United Nations. We might have to look for somewhat more unorthodox models of dialogic engagement than this, although I shall not pursue the issue here.

In the domain of 'sub-politics' there are at least two arenas in which mechanisms of dialogic democratization become important or vital. One concerns the ever more pervasive role of science and technology in our daily lives. The relation of science to tradition in Western society is an interesting and tangled one. On the face of things, as the prime progenitors of Enlightenment, science and technology set themselves radically against tradition. Yet for a long while science itself was a sort of tradition in modern society. That is to say, science remained fairly insulated from the wider lay community, and scientists got on with testing their findings relatively independently of the broader population. With the acceleration of social change, and the role of technological innovation in creating such acceleration, this insulating barrier breaks down. Science is no longer regarded by the majority as sacrosanct, as having the status of unquestioned authority. In a reflexive social universe, where the essentially sceptical nature of scientific method becomes revealed to view, lay individuals have a much more dialogic involvement with science and technology. Not only do they 'talk back' to science, they routinely engage with its claimed findings.

Individuals diagnosed as HIV positive, or suffering from AIDS, for instance, are sometimes in the forefront of scientific research concerned with their malady. They do not just accept what 'the doctor' tells them, but conduct an active interrogation into the current state of scientific and technological knowledge. They don't wait for the 'normal' processes of long-term testing that a more insulated scientific community used to take for granted. Many issues and problems stem from this situation, including forms of commercial exploitation of the needy or desperate. But in such dialogic engagement there is the promise of greater democracy – the opportunity to forge constructive dialogues between those who produce scientific knowledge and those whose lives are affected by that knowledge.

Another prime context for the advance of dialogic democracy is that of personal life: in the spheres of sexual relations, marriage, the family and friendship. All of these areas of social activity have been subject to de-traditionalizing processes. De-traditionalized personal relations fall within the category of what I term the 'pure relationship'. The pure relationship is an ideal-typical form. Actual contexts of action approximate to it only in greater or lesser degree. The pure relationship is a relationship that is lived for its own sake: it is one that in principle depends upon personal integrity and gaining the active trust of the other. Pure relationships necessarily are dialogic because they do not draw upon traditional ways of doing things or relating to others.

We can speak of the advance of dialogic democracy in the various contexts of personal life to the degree to which certain communicative conditions are fulfilled. These conditions are readily apparent in the therapeutic literature dealing with personal or emotional life. There is a remarkable similarity between what a good relationship is like, as diagnosed in the literature of therapy and self-help, and the properties of formal democracy in the political sphere. A good relationship, in brief, is one in which each individual accepts that the other is independent and equal; problems in the relationship are settled through discussion, rather than coercion or violence; the relationship is an open and mobile one, corresponding to the changing needs of each partner; and negotiation and compromise are central. These traits could very well be taken as constitutive of a democratic polity, at least in the sense of deliberative democracy.

Two cheers for democracy – this theorem applies not only to liberal democracy but to all the other contexts of actual or possible democratization. Democracy is not a panacea: it is a means of enabling individuals to live together in conditions of mutual communication and mutual respect. Imperfect though it might be, a 'democracy of the emotions' in personal life is likely to prove just as consequential as the development of democracy in the more public sphere. As with other contexts of dialogic democratization, the tension between communication and violence is particularly important, yet problematic. It is not yet clear how far dialogic democracy will develop or whether in these spheres as in others forms of fundamentalism, perhaps linked to generic violence, will surface.

I have strayed some way by now from the ideas of T.H. Marshall. Can we bring such a discussion back to focus more squarely on questions of citizenship and the welfare state? There is no doubt that we can. It has often been said that Marshall's account of citizenship rights has been made redundant by the very effects of globalization. To be a citizen, in any meaningful sense, is to be a citizen of a nation-state; and the nation-state is being outflanked by the combined forces of globalism and localism. It is true that citizenship for us cannot carry exactly the weight that Marshall wanted it to bear; yet analysing various possibilities of the democratizing of democracy does allow us to pursue themes that Marshall raised and to elaborate upon them in the context in which we now find ourselves.

A grasp of the problems facing the welfare state, and its likely future, is fundamental to assessing Marshall's long-term intellectual legacy. What Marshall took to be enduring aspects of welfare institutions now look distinctly shaky. Marshall's perspective is dated in a number of respects, but it would be as much a mistake to accept the critiques of the welfare state offered by the neo-liberals as it would be to hold that the origins of its troubles are to be traced to a fiscal crisis. Welfare dependency, at least among some groups and in some situations, is surely a reality; and the fiscal strains of the welfare state are apparent enough. However, I would look at the stresses currently affecting welfare institutions in terms precisely of the social changes that have been the core focus of my discussion in this chapter.

The welfare institutions with which Marshall was preoccupied developed at a time when most social lifestyles were more stable than they are today and when life continued to be lived largely as fate. Welfare systems were thus established on the presumption that the state can guarantee against various categories of risk, each being treated as akin to risks of nature. One might be or become poor, fall ill, become disabled, or be divorced: the state can step in to protect those who are affected by such hazards. In the more active, reflexive, yet disturbingly unsettling world of today, these assumptions do not make sense in the way they once did. Divorce, for instance, is not something that now only affects a minority and it is not something that simply 'befalls' individuals. The problem is not solely, or perhaps even primarily, how to fund welfare institutions: it is how to reorder those institutions so as to make them mesh with the much more active, reflexive lives that most of us now lead. And here new thinking about citizenship has to be integrated with a reappraisal of democracy and its possibilities.

THIRTEEN

Brave New World:
The New Context of Politics

My theme is a world that has taken us by surprise – a world of manufactured uncertainty. (See chapter 2.) Life has always been a risky business. The intrusion of manufactured uncertainty into our lives does not mean that our existence, on an individual or collective level, is more risky than it used to be. Rather, the sources, and the scope, of risk have altered. Manufactured risk is a result *of* human intervention into nature and into the conditions of social life. The uncertainties (and opportunities) it creates are largely new. They cannot be dealt with by age-old remedies; the sorts of reaction we might make to them today are often as much about 'damage control' and 'repair' as about an endless process of increasing mastery.

The advance of manufactured uncertainty is the outcome of the long-term development of modern institutions; but it has also *accelerated* as the result of a series of changes that have transformed society (and nature) over the past four or five decades. Pinpointing these changes is essential if we are to grasp the altered context of political life today. Three sets of changes are particularly important. These are those discussed in the previous chapter, concerning globalization, de-traditionalization and the intensifying of social reflexivity. They help explain, among other things, the decline of socialism. In the shape of Soviet Communism (in the East) and the Keynesian 'welfare compromise' (in the West), socialism worked tolerably well when most risk was external (rather than manufactured) and where the level of globalization and social reflexivity was relatively low. When these circumstances no longer apply, socialism either collapses or becomes turned onto the defensive – it is certainly not any more in the vanguard of 'history'.

Socialism was based upon a cybernetic model of social life, one which strongly reflects the Enlightenment outlook mentioned elsewhere in this book. According to the cybernetic model, a system (in the case of socialism, the economy) can best be organized by being subordinated to a directive intelligence (the state, understood in one form or another). But while such a set-up might work reasonably effectively for more coherent systems – in this case a society of low reflexivity, with fairly fixed lifestyle habits – it does not do so for highly complex ones.

Very complex systems depend upon a large amount of low-level input for their coherence (provided by a multiplicity of local pricing, production and consumption decisions in market situations). The human brain probably also works in such a way. It was once thought that the brain was a cybernetic system, in which the cortex was responsible for integrating the central nervous system as a whole. Current theories, however, emphasize much more the significance of low-level inputs in producing effective neural integration.

The proposition that socialism is in serious difficulties is much less controversial now than it was even a few short years ago. More heterodox, I think, is a second assertion I want to make: that conservatism faces problems of just as profound a kind. How can this be, for has not conservatism triumphed worldwide in the wake of the disintegrating project of socialism? Here, however, we must distinguish conservatism from the right. What has come to be understood as 'the right' today is neo-liberalism, whose links with conservatism are at best tenuous. For if conservatism means anything, it means the desire to conserve – and specifically it means the conserving of tradition, as the 'inherited wisdom of the past'. Neo-liberalism is not conservative in this (quite elemental) sense. On the contrary, it sets into play radical processes of change, stimulated by the incessant expansion of markets. Paradoxically, the right here has turned radical, while the left seeks mainly to conserve – trying to protect, for example, what remains of the welfare state.

In a post-traditionalist society, the conserving of tradition cannot sustain the sense it once had, as the relatively unreflective preservation of the past. For tradition defended in the traditional way becomes fundamentalism, too dogmatic an outlook on which to base a conservatism which looks to the achievement of social harmony (or 'one nation') as one of its main *raisons d'être*.

Neo-liberalism, on the other hand, becomes internally contradictory and this contradiction is increasingly plain to see. On the one hand neo-liberalism is hostile to tradition – and is indeed one of the main forces sweeping away tradition everywhere, as a result of the promotion of market forces and an aggressive individualism. On the other, it depends upon the persistence of tradition for its legitimacy and its attachment to conservatism – in the areas of the nation, religion, gender and the family. Having no proper theoretical rationale, its defence of tradition in these areas normally takes the form of fundamentalism. The debate over 'family values' provides a good example. Liberal individualism is supposed to reign in the marketplace – and the purview of markets becomes greatly extended. The wholesale expansion of a market society, however, is a prime force promoting those very disintegrative forces affecting family life which neo-liberalism, wearing its fundamentalist hat, diagnoses and so vigorously opposes. This is an unstable mix indeed.

If socialism and conservatism have disintegrated, and neo-liberalism is paradoxical might one thus turn to 'liberalism' *per se* (capitalism plus liberal democracy, but shorn of New Right fundamentalisms) in the manner, say, of Francis Fukuyama? I do not think so, for reasons which I shall simply state here, but elaborate upon in what follows later. An ever-expanding capitalism runs up not only against environmental limits in terms of the earth's resources, but against the limits of modernity in the shape of manufactured uncertainty; liberal democracy, based upon an electoral party system, operating at the level of the nation-state, is not well equipped to meet the demands of a reflexive citizenry in a globalizing world; and the combination of capitalism and liberal democracy provides only limited means of generating social solidarity.

All this reveals plainly enough the exhaustion of received political ideologies. Should we therefore perhaps accept, as some of the postmodernists say, that Enlightenment has exhausted itself and that we have more or less to take the world as it is, with all its barbarities and limitations? Surely not. Almost the last thing we need now is a sort of 'new medievalism', a confession of impotence in the face of forces larger than ourselves. We live in a radically damaged world, for which radical remedies are needed. There is a very real and difficult issue to be faced, however: the problematic relation between knowledge and control, exemplified by the spread of manufactured risk. Political radicalism can no longer insert itself, as socialism did, in the space between an abandoned past and a humanly made future. But it certainly cannot rest content with neo-liberal radicalism – an abandonment of the past led by the erratic play of market forces. The possibility of, even the necessity for, a radical politics has not died along with all else that has fallen away – but such a politics can only be loosely identified with the usual orientations of the left. It must cope with a world that has run up against the limits of modernity.

What might be called 'philosophic conservatism' – a philosophy of protection, conservation and solidarity – acquires a new relevance for political radicalism today. The idea of living with imperfection, long a leading emphasis of philosophic conservatism, here might be turned to radical account. A radical political programme – one that takes things by the roots – must recognize that confronting manufactured risk cannot take the form of 'more of the same', an endless exploration of the future at the cost of the protection of the present or past.

It is surely not accidental that these are exactly the themes of that political force which can lay greatest claim to inherit the mantle of left radicalism: the green movement. This very claim has helped to obscure the otherwise rather obvious affinities between ecological thinking, including particularly 'deep ecology', and philosophic conservatism. In each case there is an emphasis upon conservation, restoration and repair. Green political theory, however, falls prey to the 'naturalistic fallacy' and is dogged by its own fundamentalisms. In other words, it depends for its proposals upon calling for a reversion to 'nature'. Yet nature no longer exists! We cannot defend nature in the natural way any more than we can defend tradition in the traditional way – yet each quite often *needs* defending.

A framework for radical politics

Our relation to nature – or what is no longer nature – is one among other institutional dimensions of modern society, connected particularly to the impact of industry, science and technology. Although closely bound up with it, the consequences of industrialism can be distinguished from the partly independent influence of capitalism, defined as a competitive market system of economic enterprise, in which goods and labour power are commodities. If the oppositional force of socialism has been blunted, must a capitalistic system reign unchallenged? I do not think so. Unchecked capitalistic markets still have many of the unhappy results to which socialists have long pointed, including the dominance of economic imperatives over all others, universal commodification and the polarization of wealth and income. The critique of these tendencies surely remains as important as it ever was, but today cannot be developed in an effective way from the cybernetic model of socialism.

Political and administrative power does not derive directly from control of the means of production, whatever Marx might have said on the matter. Standing opposed to political authoritarianism is the influence of democracy – the favourite term of the moment, for who is not a democrat now? The question is, however, what exactly we should understand by democracy. For at the very time when liberal democratic systems seem to be spreading everywhere, we find those systems under strain in their very societies of origin.

The problem of democracy, or so I shall argue, is closely bound up with a further dimension of the modern social order: control of the means of violence. The management of violence is not ordinarily part of conventional forms of political theory, whether left, right or liberal. Yet where, as in current social conditions, many different cultures are thrust into contact with one another, the clash of fundamentalisms becomes a matter of serious concern.

On the basis of the foregoing comments I want to propose a six-point framework for a reconstituted radical politics, one which draws upon philosophic conservatism but preserves some of the core values hitherto associated with socialist thought. I do not pretend to develop any of these in the detail that would be required either to justify them fully or to flesh out their policy implications.

1   There should be a concern to repair *damaged solidarities*, which may sometimes imply the selective preservation, or even perhaps reinvention, of tradition. This theorem applies at all the levels which link individual actions not just to groups or even to states, but to more globalized systems. It is important not to understand by it the idea of a revival of civil society, now so popular among some sections of the left. The concept of a 'civil society', lying between the individual and state, for reasons I should not go into here, is a suspect one when applied to current social conditions. Today we should speak more of reordered conditions of individual and collective life, producing forms of social disintegration to be sure, but also offering new bases for generating solidarities.

A starting point is a proper assessment of the nature of individualism in present-day society. Neo-liberalism places great stress upon the importance of individualism, contrasting this to the discredited 'collectivism' of socialist theory. By 'individualism', however, neo-liberals understand the self-seeking, profit-maximizing behaviour of the marketplace. This is a mistaken way, in my view, of interpreting what should more appropriately be conceived of as the expansion of social reflexivity.

In a world of high reflexivity, an individual must achieve a certain degree of autonomy of action as a condition of being able to survive and forge a life; but autonomy is not the same as egoism and moreover implies reciprocity and interdependence. The issue of reconstructing social solidarities should therefore not be seen as one of protecting social cohesion around the edges of an egoistic marketplace. It should be understood as one of reconciling autonomy and interdependence in the various spheres of social life, including the economic domain.

Consider as an illustration the sphere of the family – one of the main arenas in which de-traditionalization has proceeded apace. Neo-liberals have quite properly expressed concern about disintegrative tendencies affecting the family, but the notion that there can be a straightforward reversion to 'traditional family values' is a non-starter. For one thing, in the light of recent research we know that family life in early modern times often had a quite pronounced dark side – including the physical and sexual abuse of children, and physical violence by husbands against wives. For another, neither women nor children are likely to renounce the rights that they have won, and which in the case of women also go along with widespread involvement in the paid labour force.

Since once again there are no real historical precedents, we do not know how far family life can effectively be reconstructed in such a way as to balance autonomy and solidarity. Yet some of the means whereby such an aim might be achieved have become fairly clear. Enhanced solidarity in a de-traditionalizing society depends upon what might be termed *active trust*, coupled with a renewal of personal and social *responsibility* for others. Active trust is trust which has to be won, rather than coming from the tenure of pre-established social positions or gender roles. Active trust *presumes* autonomy rather than standing counter to it, and it is a powerful source of social solidarity, since compliance is freely given rather than enforced by traditional constraints.

In the context of family life, active trust involves *commitment* to another or others, that commitment implying also the recognition of obligations to them stretching across time. Strengthening family commitments and obligations, so long as these are based upon active trust, does not seem at all incompatible with the diversity of family forms now being pioneered in all the industrialized societies. High rates of separation and divorce are probably here to stay, but one can see many ways in which these could enrich, rather than destroy, social solidarity. Recognition of the prime importance of the rights of children, together with responsibilities towards them, for instance, could provide the very means of consolidating the new kinship ties we see around us – between, say, two sets of parents who are also step-parents and the children they share. Recombinant families may bring in their train a rich nexus of new kin ties, almost like premodern extended kin groups.

2   We should recognize the increasing centrality of what I shall call *life politics* to both formal and less orthodox domains of the political order. The political outlook of the left has always been closely bound up with the idea of emancipation. Emancipation means freedom, or rather freedoms of various kinds: freedom from the arbitrary hold of tradition, from arbitrary power and

from the constraints of material deprivation. Emancipatory politics is a politics of life-chances and hence is central to the creation of autonomy of action. As such it obviously remains vital to a radical political programme. It is joined today, however, by a series of concerns coming from the changes analysed earlier – the transformation of tradition and nature, in the context of a globalizing, cosmopolitan order. Life politics is a politics not of life-chances but of lifestyle. It concerns disputes and struggles about how (as individuals and as collective humanity) we should live in a world where what used to be fixed by either nature or tradition is now subject to human decisions.

Life politics includes ecological problems and dilemmas, but understands these as linked to wider questions of identity and lifestyle choice – including some of the key issues raised by feminism. It would be a basic error to see life politics as only a preoccupation of the more affluent. In some respects, in fact, the opposite is true. Some of the poorest groups come up against problems of de-traditionalization most sharply. Thus women are leaving marriages in large numbers and seeking to recast their lives – a high proportion of marriages in most Western countries are now actively broken up by women, a sea change of great significance. Many, however, become part of the 'new poor', especially if they are lone parent heads of households. Cast down economically, they are also called upon to pilot new forms of domestic life and kin relations.

The emergence of life politics helps explain why some types of issue – such as abortion – come to appear so prominently on the political agenda, but life politics also impinges on more 'standard' areas such as work, employment and unemployment. Like so many other areas of social life, work was until quite recently experienced by many as fate. Most men could expect to go out to work at a relatively early stage of their lives and continue to do so until retirement age. For many women, the complementary prospect was confinement to the domestic milieu. Protest against such 'fate' was first of all mostly emancipatory in impulse. This was true of the union movement, dominated by men, which developed most strongly among manual workers, who more than anyone else experienced work as a given set of conditions, offering little autonomy of action. It was also true of earlier forms of feminism.

In current times, even among more deprived groups, neither paid work nor domesticity is usually approached as fate (unemployment, perversely, more often is). There is a wide reflexive awareness that what counts as 'work' is much more broadly defined than it used to be, and that work is a problematic and contested notion. Given changes in the class structure, few people now automatically follow the occupations of their parents or those typical of homogeneous working communities. Even – or perhaps one should say especially – against the background of a shrinking labour market, it becomes clear that there are decisions to be made, and priorities located, not just about trying to get one job rather than another, but about what place work should have as compared to other life values.

3   In conjunction with the generalizing of social reflexivity, active trust implies a conception of *generative politics* which comes to the fore today. Generative politics exists in the space that links the state to reflexive mobilization in the society at large. For reasons already discussed, the state can only to a limited degree function as a cybernetic intelligence. Yet the limitations of neo-liberalism, with its idea of the minimal state, have become very apparent. Generative politics is a politics which seeks to allow individuals and groups to make things happen, rather than have things happen to them, in the context of overall social concerns and goals.

Generative politics implies:

(a) seeking to achieve desired outcomes (a phrase that, however, covers a nest of difficult problems) through providing conditions for social mobilization or engagement;
(b) creating circumstances in which active trust can be built and sustained, whether in the institutions of government as such or in other related agencies;
(c) according autonomy to those affected by specific programmes or policies, and in fact aiming to develop such autonomy in many contexts;
(d) encouraging the development of ethical principles of action, rejecting the indifference of (some versions of) socialism to ethics, but also the unhappy neo-liberal marriage of market principles and authoritarianism;

(e) decentralizing political power: decentralization is the condition of political effectiveness because of the requirement
for bottom-up information flow and recognition of autonomy. The push and pull between decentralized power and
the political centre, however, is not a zero-sum game.
Decentralization can enhance the authority of the centre,
either because of political trade-offs or because of the
creation of greater legitimacy.

Generative politics is a defence of the politics of the *political
domain*, but does not situate itself in the old opposition between
state and market. It works through providing material conditions,
and organizational frameworks, for the life-political decisions
taken by individuals and groups in the wider social order. Such a
politics depends upon building active trust both in the institutions
of government and in connected agencies. Appearances perhaps
to the contrary, generative politics is in the present day the main
means of effectively approaching problems of poverty and social
exclusion.

Generative politics is not a panacea. The shifting character of
the state, and the fact that more or less the whole population lives
in the same 'discursive space' as state and government agencies,
produce major new political dilemmas and contradictions. For
example, where the national polity has become only one among
other points of reference for an individual's life, many people
might not often 'listen' to what is going on in the political domain,
even though they may keep mentally 'in touch' on a more
consistent basis than before. 'Tuning out' may express a distaste
for the antics of politicians, but may also go along with a specific
alertness to questions the person deems consequential. Trust here
might mingle with cynicism in an uneasy combination.

4   The shortcomings of liberal democracy, in a globalizing,
reflexive social order, suggest the need to further more radical
forms of democratization. Here I would reaffirm the importance
of dialogic democracy. Among the many forms and aspects of
democracy debated in the literature today, two main dimensions
of a democratic order can be distinguished. On the one hand,
democracy is a vehicle for the representation of interests. On the
other, it is a way of creating a public arena in which controversial

issues – in principle – can be resolved, or at least handled, through dialogue rather than through pre-established forms of power. While the first aspect has probably received most attention, the second is at least equally significant.

The extension of dialogic democracy would form one part (although not the only one) of a process of what in the previous chapter I called the democratizing of democracy. Where the level of social reflexivity remains quite low, political legitimacy continues to depend in some substantial part upon traditional symbolism and pre-existing ways of doing things. All sorts of patronage and corruption can not only survive but, within the political leadership, become accepted procedure. In a more reflexive order, however – where people are also free to ignore more or less the formal political arena if they so wish – such practices are liable to be called into question.

Greater transparency of government would help the democratizing of democracy, but this is also a phenomenon which extends into areas other than that of the formal political sphere. Outside the arena of the state, it may be suggested, dialogic democracy can be promoted in three main contexts. In the area of personal life – parent–child relations, sexual relations, friendship relations – dialogic democracy advances to the degree to which such relationships are ordered through dialogue rather than through embedded power. What I have referred to as a democracy of the emotions depends upon the integrating of autonomy and solidarity mentioned earlier. It presumes the development of personal relationships in which active trust is mobilized and sustained through discussion and the interchange of views, rather than by arbitrary power of one sort or another.

Thus parents' authority would no longer be a 'given', a fact of life for them and their children alike; it would become more actively negotiated on both sides. To the extent to which it comes into being, a democracy of the emotions would have major implications for the furtherance of formal, public democracy. Individuals who have a good understanding of their own emotional make-up, and who are able to communicate effectively with others on a personal basis, are likely to be well prepared for the wider tasks and responsibilities of citizenship.

Dialogic democracy can also be mobilized through the activities of self-help groups and social movements. Such movements and groups express, but also contribute to, the heightened reflexivity of local and global social activity today. In contemporary societies, far more people belong to self-help groups than are members of political parties. The democratic qualities of social movements and self-help groups come in large part from the fact that they open up spaces for public dialogue in respect of the issues with which they are concerned. They can force into the discursive domain aspects of social conduct that previously went undiscussed, or were 'settled' by traditional practices. They may help contest 'official' definitions of things; feminist, ecological and peace movements have all achieved this outcome, as have a multiplicity of self-help groups.

Some such movements and groups are intrinsically global in scope, and thus might contribute to the wider spread of forms of dialogic democracy. Given that the idea of a world government is implausible, mechanisms of dialogic democracy operating not just through states and international agencies, but also through a diversity of other groupings, become of central importance. For a long while democratizing influences on a global level were seen in the conventional terms of international relations theory. The international arena was considered as 'above' the level of nation-states. In this conception, democratization would mean the construction of the institutions of liberal democracy writ large. The 'empty' or 'anarchic' areas connecting states, in other words, would have to be filled in. Such an idea has not of course become irrelevant, but looks to be of more restricted importance where globalization and reflexivity are so deeply intertwined. For many globalizing connections do not flow through the nation-state, but in large part bypass it.

5 We should be prepared to *rethink the welfare state* in a fundamental way. In many countries what remains of socialist ideology has become concentrated upon protecting the welfare state against the attacks of the neo-liberals. At least one book has been written[1] invoking philosophic conservatism to defend welfare institutions – as institutions that have a proven track record and have withstood the 'test of time.' And indeed there may very well be basic features of the welfare state which should be preserved against the potential ravages of cut-backs or of privatization. In terms of trust and solidarity, for example, welfare provisions or services quite often embody commitments

that would simply be eroded if a more market-led, 'business' orientation were introduced.

Yet the welfare state was formed as a 'class compromise' or 'settlement' in social conditions that have now altered very markedly; and its systems of security were designed to cope more with external than with manufactured risk. Some of the major problematic aspects of the welfare state have by now been identified clearly enough, partly as the result of neo-liberal critiques. The welfare state has been less than wholly effective either in countering poverty or in effecting large-scale income or wealth redistribution. It was tied to an implicit model of traditional gender roles, presuming male participation in the paid labour force, with a 'second tier' of programmes directed towards families without a male breadwinner. Welfare state bureaucracies, like bureaucracies everywhere, have tended to become inflexible and impersonal; and welfare dependency is probably in some part a real phenomenon, not just an invention of neo-liberalism. Finally, the welfare state was consolidated in the postwar period at a point where chronically high levels of unemployment seemed unlikely to return.

The reconstruction of welfare institutions is a complex matter, which I could not pretend to discuss adequately in the space available here. A radical rethink of the welfare state, however, would probably involve disentangling its key components. A new settlement is urgently required today; but this can no longer take the form of a top-down dispensation of benefits. Rather, welfare measures aimed at countering the polarizing effects of what, after all, remains a class society must be empowering rather than merely 'dispensed'. They must be concerned with just that reconstruction of social solidarity mentioned earlier, on the level of the family and that of the wider civic culture. And such a settlement has to be one that gives due attention to gender, not only to class.

Coping with manufactured uncertainty creates a whole new spectrum of problems – and, as always, opportunities – for the reform of welfare. Here one should think of reconstruction along the lines of models of *positive welfare*. The welfare state grew up as a mode of protecting against misfortunes that 'happen' to people – certainly as far as social security is concerned, it essentially picks up the pieces after mishaps have occurred.

Positive welfare, by contrast, places much greater emphasis upon the mobilizing of life-political measures, aimed once more at connecting autonomy with personal and collective responsibilities.

An example would be the area of health care, now so deeply caught up in the fiscal dilemmas of the state. Health-care systems are still mostly based upon treating illnesses once they have been contracted. A common reaction of critics of such systems is to advocate giving a greater role to preventative medicine, and no doubt this is right and proper. More far-reaching, however, is the suggestion that we must abandon what has been called the 'biomedical' model of health and illness, in favour of one which places a greater stress upon holism and, more particularly, which connects health to environmental conservation and protection. Such an approach would involve a new appreciation of the interrelation of positive health with the transformation of local and global lifestyles. Reducing ecotoxicity, which demands collective action as well as the assumption of new personal responsibilities, would be a health-care measure more profound in its implications than anything attempted in current systems of health provision.

6   A programme of radical politics, for reasons already given, must be prepared to confront *the role of violence* in human affairs. The fact that I have left this question until last does not mean at all that it is the least important. It is, however, one of the most difficult of issues to deal with in terms of received political theory. Neither socialist thought nor liberalism has established perspectives or concepts relevant to producing a normative political theory of violence; while rightist thought has tended to think of violence as a necessary and endemic feature of human life.

The topic is a big one. The influence of violence, after all, stretches all the way from male violence against women through casual street violence to large-scale war. Are there any threads that connect these various situations and that therefore might be relevant to a theory of pacification? I think there are, and they bring us back to the themes of fundamentalism and dialogic democracy.

In any social circumstances, there are only a limited number of ways in which a clash of values can be dealt with. One is through geographical segregation; individuals of conflicting dispositions, or cultures hostile to one another, can of course coexist if they have little or no direct contact. Another, more active, way is through exit. An individual who, or group which, does not get along with another can simply disengage or move away, as might happen in a divorce.

A third way of coping with individual or cultural difference is through dialogue. (See chapter 2.) Here a clash of values can in principle operate under a positive sign – it can be a means of increased communication and self-understanding. Understanding the other better leads to greater understanding of oneself, or one's own culture, leading to further understanding and mutuality. Finally, a clash of values can be resolved through the use of force or violence.

In the globalizing society in which we now live, the first two of these four options become drastically reduced. No culture, state or large group can with much success isolate itself from the global cosmopolitan order; and while exit may be possible, in some situations, for individuals, it is not available to larger social entities.

The relation between dialogue and violence, strung out along the edge of possible fundamentalisms, thus becomes particularly acute and tense for us today. This reduction of options is dangerous, but it also offers sources of hope. For we know that dialogue can sometimes replace violence, and we know that this can happen both in situations of personal life and in much larger social settings. The 'gender fundamentalism' that violent men sustain towards their partners, and perhaps towards women in general, can at least in individual cases be transformed through greater self-understanding and communication. Dialogue between cultural groups and states is both a force acting directly against fundamentalist doctrines and a means of substituting talk for the use of military power.

The dark side is obvious. Violence plainly often stems from clashes of interest, and joustings for power; hence there are many quite strictly material conditions which would have to be altered to contest and reduce it. Moreover, the centrifugal forces of dispersal within and between societies in the present day might prove too great to manage without explosions of violence, on the small and larger scale. Yet the connections I have explored between autonomy, solidarity and dialogue are real; and they correspond to observable changes in local settings of interaction as well as in the global order.

Coda: the question of agency

What of the question of agency? If it be agreed that there is still an agenda for radical politics, who is to implement it? Does 'radical politics' still mean the same as 'left politics'?

The answer to the second of these questions is surely 'no'. Since the right, however, has largely thrown in its lot with neo-liberalism, the future success of leftist parties is likely to depend upon how far they can colonize the terrain I have sought to identify. Left parties will have to work in tandem with many other groups and movements if they are to stake out this territory and hold it. And they will have to mix repair and restoration with a cautionary acceptance of the imperfectibility of things.

FOURTEEN

The Labour Party and British Politics

Ideas

A few years ago, doom and gloom prevailed in Labour Party circles. In 1992 it appeared that the party would at least deny the Tories an overall majority. Margaret Thatcher was no more and John Major seemed, to say the least, an unlikely person to bring about a fourth Conservative triumph. What led to subsequent Labour despair wasn't just that against all predictions from the massed ranks of pollsters he did so, but that Labour's share of the vote remained stuck at only just over a third.

Immediately, the scavengers started picking over the dead body of Labour's hopes. Was Britain becoming a one-party state, a sort of Anglo-Saxon Japan, Italy or Mexico? And the old question from the 1960s was dusted down and posed once more: can Labour ever win again? Or, more specifically, could Labour win outside a Labour–Liberal Democrat alliance?

Two Labour leaders later, the fog miraculously lifted. Conservative Party sages started to warn that, if things weren't turned around, it was the Tories who could be out of power for a generation.

Hopes raised high can be dashed, as the 1992 general election showed. The childbirth approach – one more push – could lead to just the same disillusionment again. So what should Labour do now? The question has many parochial implications, but can't be approached apart from the broad dilemmas that every socialist party now faces. Between 1990 and 1994 I was invited to no fewer than five separate conferences in various countries with the same trite, but apparently irresistible, title: 'What's left?' Well, what *is* left for Labour when socialism seems all but dead and buried? The way to begin to respond to this question, I shall suggest, isn't through an exhaustive trawling of socialist traditions in the hope of finding ideas that still seem relevant. It is through asking what's happened to conservatism. For the troubles of the Tories come from much deeper sources than squabbles over Maastricht.

The origins of the fractured state of conservatism lie in the increasing distance which has opened up between conservatism and the right – terms which once meant more or less the same thing. (See chapter 14.) Many different versions of conservatism, of varying degrees of sophistication, exist. Yet conservatism, in any guise, means nothing if it doesn't mean 'to conserve'. Specifically, conservatism is about the preservation of tradition, of organic connections between past, present and future. Conservatism was once synonymous with the right, because the protection of tradition was the same as defending hierarchy and minority rule. This was a defence mounted not just against socialism, but much more forcefully against capitalism, that great destroyer of stability and aristocratic hierarchy. For with the overall rush of capitalist enterprise, as Marx so famously put it, 'all that is solid melts into air'.

The right today still sees itself as conservative. But the conservatives have come wholeheartedly to endorse that which they once despised – competitive capitalism and the rule of the market. As a result, their position and outlook on the world have become thoroughly self-contradictory. For nothing is more corrosive of established traditions, habits and forms of social cohesion, just as Marx pointed out, than the wholesale cultivation of market relations. The present-day conservative still wants to conserve – to protect the 'traditional family', traditional symbols of state legitimacy, religion and the identity of the nation. Yet these are being eroded, smashed open even, by the very market forces modern conservatism fosters.

On the one hand, then, there is economic libertarianism, which includes within it an active embrace of global competition; on the other, a retreat into established structures and habits, demanding traditional authority, morality and compliance. The fact that the 'back to basics' campaign was so lamentable wasn't so much to do with the sexual antics of some Tory parliamentarians as with its inherently self-defeating nature. Free markets and a strong, increasingly centralized state – the combination is so contradictory when examined coolly that only the forcefulness of Thatcher's personality could have made it seem plausible for long. No wonder, perhaps, that her critics were seemingly just as much in awe of her as were her admirers. Yet it was Thatcherism that destroyed Thatcher, and helped to destroy conservatism.

Ideologically, conservatism in the present day has no way to go. Thatcherism always had a certain quality of high-minded ruthlessness about it. But the more marked its paradoxes have become, the more this quality has dissolved into a sort of foot-shuffling, yet dogged, worship of market forces. Thatcherism without Thatcher is an embarrassment. More privatization, a further cutting back of public expenditure, plus strategically timed reductions in direct taxation: what a formula for politicians who at the same time bemoan the advance of social disintegration and moral decay! Yet the route back to one-nation Toryism is blocked, even if the political will were there to follow it. For one-nation conservatism depended upon forms of tradition, deference and habit which free-market conservatism has helped thoroughly to undermine.

Now this might be the point at which Labour should start to refurbish itself. Why not step in and occupy the conservative centre ground which the right has made it impossible for the Tories to hold? Let's – it might be said – oppose the capitulation to the market, let's recreate communities, and let's stress duties and obligations rather than following the usual leftist preoccupation with rights. Labour, it would follow, should look to recreate family life, civic virtues and mutual obligations.

Present-day communitarians – people who advocate the recreation of social communities – like Amitai Etzioni in the United States, have a very broad idea of community in mind. Etzioni speaks of the communities he wants to develop as like a set of Chinese boxes. The smaller communities, such as families and neighbourhoods, nestle within the larger ones, like towns and cities, which in turn exist within larger regions, up to and even perhaps beyond the national community. A resurgence of community on all these levels is seen by Etzioni as part of a general moral project – that of balancing rights with responsibilities. Echoing the indictment of American society made in the nineteenth century by Tocqueville, Etzioni argues that a proliferation of rights undermines mutual dependence. Etzioni's is a more liberal version of David Selbourne's 'principle of duty'.

Does talk of the recovery of community in this way make any sense? I think it does, but not in the way in which the communitarians argue. The diagnosis, for one thing, is only partly correct. It isn't the expansion of rights which has undermined social cohesion and a sense of responsibility for others, but the corrosive effects of market forces. And, except in a loose sense of the term, the attempt to revive the idea of community isn't the way to go. To say that 'individuals thrive only in strong communities' may serve a purpose, perhaps, as a slogan against neo-liberalism. But it is quite implausible to think of a modern society as being, or becoming, a set of boxes of communities, if 'community' means a strongly bounded group with a clear set of shared values. Communities in this sense can be more divisive than integrative and are usually authoritarian too. After all, where are the strongest communities in Britain to be found? In Northern Ireland. Closely knit communities almost inevitably breed insiders and outsiders. We must work with different models of social cohesion from the notion of community today. It won't do to suppose that we are suffering from a surfeit of individualism, or of rights; or that communitarianism, coupled to a reassertion of civic duties, forms an adequate response.

We need, first of all, an assessment of what the social and economic changes now sweeping through the industrialized countries are. There *is* a new individualism abroad, of which all political parties must take stock, but it isn't either just the result of Thatcherism or an expression of a selfish free-for-all. Basic mistakes of Thatcherism were to equate the new individualism with the self-seeking of the marketplace, and to opt for a theory (that of Hayek) according to which, through the market, multiple egoisms come to serve the public good.

The new individualism is a mixture of positives and negatives. In the increasingly global order which is the context of our daily activities, we all have to construct our lives more actively than ever was the case before. Even without the corroding effects of markets, traditions and pre-established habits lose their hold.

The result is a mixture of emancipation and anxiety, fuelled by new sorts of uncertainty. As I put it in Chapter 12, our lives are less and less lived as fate. It is no longer the fate of a man necessarily to become a breadwinner, and to work each week from young adulthood to retirement. It is no longer the fate of women to settle for a life of domesticity. Marriage is not any more a 'state of nature', but a negotiated relationship – one of implicit if not real equality, from which either party can relatively easily withdraw. We all have to grapple, for better or for worse, with the implications of these changes, and this grappling is exactly what the new individualism is. Labour should seek to harness the new individualism rather than counterposing it to archaic definitions of community and duty. At the same time, it must separate such individualism, conceptually and in practice, from the operation of market forces.

Consider as an example the position and prospects of those whom many continue to insist upon labelling 'pensioners' – people aged over 65. The new individualism is making large inroads into the lives of older people, and is changing the nature of what old age actually is. A 'pensioner' – the term suggests someone weak and infirm, who has to be provided for by the state. Yet the proportion of people aged 65 to 75 who need regular institutional care today is no higher than that for those aged 25 to 35. Older people also own a substantial proportion of the wealth of the nation. Whatever concrete decisions are taken about pensions, why not start from the premise that older people are a major resource for the wider society, rather than a 'problem' which has to be coped with?

Reconnecting the generations, after all, should be a basic part of political programmes which have as their concern the fostering of social cohesion; and this implies welcoming diversity rather than repressing it. At the moment older people are in a 'welfare ghetto' which is in effect a form of welfare dependency. Recognizing the impact of the new individualism might mean abolishing involuntary retirement, plus other innovations. The importance of overcoming potentially divisive struggles between older and younger people shouldn't be underestimated. In the US, for example, there has been serious talk of a 'war of the generations', while in Holland two 'older people's parties', with programmes that infuriated many younger voters, secured some seats in the national assembly.

The family, of course, is where many currents of social change today – affecting gender, sexuality, marriage and work – converge. 'Go back to the traditional family!' says the right, at the same time as its economic policies increase the strains upon family life. Yet there's no route back to the traditional family, which is in any case a myth that simply dissolves if subjected to historical scrutiny. As Stephanie Coontz has shown of the US in her book *The Way We Never Were*, the traditional family, in which both parents were regularly around, and in which mothers were free to devote themselves to their children, rarely existed.

The communitarian idea of creating strong families isn't a stupid one. Etzioni emphasizes that a revival of the family today would have to recognize the equality of the sexes, shared domestic chores and shared parenting. The slogan 'children first' makes a great deal of sense in this context, especially when children are so strongly over-represented among the 'new poor'. Yet strong families won't look much like the traditional family of conservative mythology and are bound to embrace diversity; and it isn't true that strong families inevitably produce a more cohesive wider society.

Traditional families were primarily centred not upon marriage, but upon a wider array of kinship ties and obligations; it was these in fact which made families strong. It isn't beyond the bounds of possibility to suppose they might do so again – after all, when rates of divorce, but also remarriage, are high, people are often involved in a complex of new kinship ties. If we model the 'strong family' after traditional families, single mothers aren't the threat to family stability some rightist critics take them to be. The absence of a husband doesn't mean that such mothers or their children are isolated. On the contrary, many are at the centre of rich networks of kin relations, which they actively help build.

Strong families, however, don't necessarily make for strong communities, and for the same reason as the very notion of community is suspect. In Italy, for example, the family is strong, but civic integration is weak. 'Family privatism' can be just as much a danger to wider civic cohesion as any other form of enclosed group or community. A tolerance of family diversity should be part of a cosmopolitanism upon which – rather than upon community – the wider social order now depends. By cosmopolitanism I mean a preparedness precisely *not* to be too swayed by, or dependent upon, the ways of life of any group or community of which one happens to be a member. For the key to social order today – locally, nationally and on a global scale too – is being able to get along with, and perhaps positively to value, ways of life which are different from one's own.

What's left? These observations get us some way towards an answer, in the situation in which Labour now finds itself at least, but not nearly far enough. It's no use pretending that socialist practice can somehow be overhauled and brought up to date, perhaps by the magic wand of community.

When, some twenty-five years ago, Eric Hobsbawm gave his famous lecture on 'The forward march of Labour halted', he concentrated on the slackening rate of union membership, and took for granted the association between the coming of socialism and the ascendancy of the working class. How much has changed since then! The 'forward march of labour', with its military overtones, seems to belong to a different time altogether. The confident forward march has become an undisciplined retreat. Virtually none of the ideas in which Hobsbawm and so many others placed their faith has survived. And over the past quarter of a century, the size of the manual working class has diminished by not far short of half. The socialism of the Labour Party, unlike that of the revolutionary left, wasn't based upon the centrality of class struggle. But it did share, as the very name of the party makes apparent, a preoccupation with class division; and it was explicitly a 'class party', notwithstanding the role of intellectuals and other non-working-class groups within it.

The call for a return to ethical or even Christian socialism can't hide the fact that the basic doctrines which shaped the party are now obsolete. Just look at the list: the planned or 'rational' direction of the economy; the 'socialization' of the means of production; the coming to power of the working class itself; the progressive expansion of the welfare state; the gradual disappearance of private capital – the list could go on. The conservatives aren't about to change their title even though the policies they have adopted have swept away most of what they once wanted to conserve. Labour doesn't need to do so either, and no doubt 'socialism' will still figure in its official lexicon; but the word simply can't mean what it did.

Class divisions haven't been overcome by the changes which have helped to make socialism, as a system of economic management, no longer relevant. The diminishing size of the industrial working class, to be sure, in combination with the increasing fluidity of international capital, has altered the shape of the class structure – as have the years of Thatcherism. Equally important, however, is that the salience of class – its relevance to social action and to institutions – has changed.

This brings us back to the new individualism. Class once expressed itself precisely as community. Working-class groups often formed communities, whether in local villages or towns, or in clubs and educational associations. The remnants still exist, of course, but class division now much more often takes on individualized or 'biographical' form. The 'new poor', for example, such as children, single mothers or the chronically unemployed, don't form a community with one another. They share in common only their exclusion from worthwhile participation in the labour market.

The result is that class isn't usually experienced any longer as class, but as other forms of advantage and disadvantage, many of which are to do with consumption rather than production. For this reason, and not only because of the shrinkage of the working class, it makes no sense today for Labour to define itself as a class party.

What should the party stand for, then, when so much has changed? Can socialism have some sort of meaning as an ethical outlook, perhaps one somehow linked to the communal? Socialism has meant so many different things in the past, apart from its concerns with economic management, that the field is fairly open. That there is a necessary place for ethics in the political arena today would be difficult to deny, particularly in a society where almost everything is becoming opened up to the market.

Christian socialism, even when understood in the ecumenical version of R.H. Tawney, surely won't do in a pluralistic social order, where different religions and ethnic groups – indeed, communities – must coexist. If the word 'socialism' is still to be used to define a general political perspective, I would suggest that it be identified with an attitude of care. Care implies an ethics of responsibility, for oneself, for others and for the fabric of the material world. Care is the opposite of egoism, but shouldn't be equated with altruism. For care of the self – a responsible attitude towards self and body – is at the origin of the ability to care about, and care for, others.

An ethics of care preserves core elements of socialist values if one sees socialism as always having been concerned with human interdependence. Care for others implies accepting responsibility for their well-being, in order not to dominate them but to protect and nurture them.

The word 'care' lends itself to empty sloganizing, and needs to be given substance to have any purchase at all on hard reality. An ethical attitude alone, as Marx pointed out many years ago, doesn't generate political strategies and can sometimes actively inhibit them. What about the contesting of inequality? What about the critique of arbitrary systems of power? After all, most socialists, in contrast to the early communists, have taken great pains to see themselves as hard-nosed and realistic.

Equality and democracy should surely continue to be central imperatives in Labour's political outlook. These still serve to identify a left when in many other respects Labour's political thinking must give short shrift to dogmas of both left and right. Political realism now means casting off those very dogmas, and political radicalism means being unafraid to think in a root-and-branch way about them.

A turn towards 'community' on the part of the Labour Party would be disastrous if the term were used as a more acceptable version of 'the state' – and therefore simply justified some sort of return to Old Leftism. The new individualism is here to stay, as are the global economy and cultural order with which it is closely intertwined. Socialism is dead as a set of economic doctrines, but the aspiration for a more solidary and participatory society is still very much alive. Indeed, I would say that, contrary to the popular wisdom of the moment, such an aspiration is heightened by the arrival of the new individualism.

Individualism here has nothing particularly to do with markets or with consumerism. It is about the disappearance of what I earlier referred to as life lived as fate. The more active and energetic life which individuals follow today is not the enemy of either social solidarity or acceptance of social responsibilities. On the contrary, it tends to presuppose these, and a political programme relevant to present-day circumstances would be concerned to develop them further.

We can't bring communities back to life in anything like the traditional sense, much less revive duties. Yet we can and should seek to foster new forms of social solidarity, cohesion and civic culture. Such new forms may often look unfamiliar, because they are no longer subject to the constraints of tradition or place. We shouldn't assume, for instance, that the only viable type of solidary family is the (so-called) traditional family.

The appeal of the idea of community comes from the sense which many people have of the need for repair or renewal. That sense is more than a misplaced yearning for an idealized past of security and stability. It originates in a consciousness of the damage which economic development, when dominated by the untrammelled forces of the market, can bring about. Talk of strong families, resurgent localities, a reconstructed civic culture – these express a need to redevelop organic connections between the past and the future and to reintegrate the generations. Such notions were once distinctively conservative ones, but where conservatism has turned against itself they suddenly become radical.

It shouldn't be surprising that these are the very themes brought to the fore by green political theory. Should we therefore anticipate the greening of the Labour Party? Not much of a vote-winner there – or so it would seem from the fate of the green parties themselves, particularly in Britain. But I wouldn't be so sure. The most important and interesting forms of ecological thought today don't concern themselves with a return to nature, or set themselves against all economic growth. They continue the critical encounter with capitalism which was always the guiding thread of socialism, but in other ways; and such a critical encounter is what even an ex-socialist party should still be interested in too.

Policy orientations

The contradictory nature of modern conservatism offers Labour great political opportunities. Yet the difficulties of creating an alternative political agenda are formidable. How can we have what Tony Blair calls a 'dynamic market society' without undermining the very communal values he wants to foster? Aren't national governments now anyway more or less condemned to impotence in the face of global market forces? Even if they aren't, how can Labour sustain the ideals of equality and social inclusiveness for which it stands, given that nationalization is no longer an option and the welfare state is in trouble?

Talk of community won't help much, for reasons I gave earlier. There are repair jobs to be done, and hopes for social and civic renewal aren't just wishful thinking. Any such attempts will flop or become oppressive if they don't run with the grain of the new individualism. At the same time, they must somehow cope with those more global influences to which in fact the new individualism is a response.

What should Labour's big idea be? I think it should indeed be the idea of renewal, or civic restructuring, even if the other parties want also to muscle in on the act. But to stand any chance, such a project will need a preparedness to think radically in five main areas: the modernization of the state; the process of wealth creation, as opposed to distribution; the reform of welfare institutions; coping with unemployment and a cluster of problems surrounding it; and pursuing an egalitarianism which is probably the very condition of civic refurbishment. Of course, all of these are large issues, and I shan't pretend to discuss them in more than a partial way.

Modernizing the state is likely to be a key area of Labour's appeal. It's said that the matters brought to public attention by Charter 88 and other groups pushing for constitutional reform are of concern only to a small part of the population – they have little electoral weight. But I don't think this is true, for reasons that actually connect with the problem of whether national governments can any longer effectively govern at all.

Creating a binding constitution, developing more secure human rights legislation, introducing a comprehensive Freedom of Information Act, and reform of the House of Lords, among other changes, should all be on the agenda. Modernizing the state, however, has to be coupled to democratization through devolution, whether or not this goes along with proportional representation. Democratizing through the devolution of powers

– the opposite direction from that in which Tory governments have moved – is not only ethically desirable, it's necessary to sustaining the very legitimacy of government at all levels.

The influence of national government has become drained through the effects of two sets of changes noted earlier: globalization and the new individualism. All states now have to deal with a citizenry of 'clever people' – people who are active in changing lifestyle habits, but who also, as a result of the influence of electronic media particularly, inhabit the same 'discursive space' as the government does.

Processes of governance won't, and can't, be the same as when there existed a more passive population with more fixed patterns of life, and more geared to traditional symbols of deference. If many feel more cynical about politics than they used to do, it isn't only, or even mainly, because of the sniping attitudes of the media, but because of the floundering character of governance itself.

All isn't thereby lost. To have an effective influence in the society it is supposed to govern, however, national government is going to have to get used to a sort of spiralling process of double consultation. Government today must often 'reach down' into quite local, even personal, contexts of action in order to 'reach up' to the more global organizations and processes with which, increasingly, it must deal. For instance, new regulations about children's rights might have to be negotiated both with international organizations and with local groups to whom they apply or who have to implement them. Processes of double consultation imply pressing for 'upward' democratization whenever possible – in, for example, the European Union – while 'downward' democratization necessitates the devolution of power, to regions and localities.

State modernization and devolution, radical though they might be in the context of Britain, aren't the only changes needed to revive political legitimacy. As a result of globalization plus the new individualism, the mechanisms of political trust have changed – as have in fact trust mechanisms in industry, in other types of organization, and even in our emotional lives. The emergence of a clever citizenry goes along with the centrality of active trust to government legitimacy. (See chapter 13.) A climate of active trust demands visibility and, not to put too fine a point upon it, integrity. Where those in leading positions in the country aren't bound, and seen to be bound, by the principles they try to make binding on others, it isn't surprising that political legitimacy becomes fragile.

A party which aims to foster double democratization can't afford not to take a radical stance in other areas too. Labour now has to become a party of wealth creation, not one concerned above all with distribution. But it is crucial to shift the definition of what wealth is away from sheerly economic wealth; and to bring squarely into the public domain other measures of wealth creation than GNP. There is no other means by which recognition of the necessary role of markets can be squared with programmes of environmental and civic renewal. Social wealth is about quality of life, and there are many ways in which subservience to the economic actually destroys social wealth. Here we should look to separate *productivity* from *productivism*, where productivism is understood as any situation where the social costs of economic growth outweigh the benefits.

Redressing inequalities should be seen as an inherent part of combating productivism. For the social costs of inequality are high – and, of course, these can engender high economic costs too. Consider, as one example, the effects of inequality upon health. It is well established that variations in levels of health between countries, as measured for example by mortality rates, aren't related so much to expenditure on the health-care system as to their levels of inequality. What matters is not economic inequality as such, however, but its psychosocial effects – it is the experience of deprivation, and its impact upon equality of life, which count.

The welfare state has long been the main vehicle through which the Labour Party has sought to counter inequalities. There is a good deal of evidence, however, to show that the welfare system has never been particularly effective in this respect. Redistribution through the welfare state has been mainly across the life-cycle, rather than from one class or income group to another.

Labour must be prepared to think radically about the future of the welfare state. In the short term, defending existing welfare systems, particularly the National Health Service, is important and commands a high measure of public support. It has a wider logic too, when set in the context of Tory reforms. Introducing market principles into settings which work in large part through an ethics of care dissolves forms of trust which aren't prompted by monetary considerations. Once corrupted they are hard to recapture.

Yet it won't do for Labour to base its longer-term policies either on shoring up the welfare state as it is, or proposing – somehow – to spend more on everything than the Tories are prepared to do. There's no point in making shibboleths of either the welfare state in general or the NHS in particular. Both must be looked at against the backdrop of the socio-economic transformations I have mentioned earlier, particularly if the idea of social and civic renewal is to be anything more than rhetoric.

Analysis, as always, is the key to prognosis. The crisis of the welfare state is ordinarily seen as a fiscal one – and this is the terrain upon which debates about welfare systems are currently conducted by the various parties. As viewed from the left at any rate, the strains of the welfare system are seen as part of the 'can't pay, won't pay' mentality described (surely inaccurately) by Galbraith as the culture of contentment. But I don't think this is correct; something of a sea change in interpretation is demanded here.

The difficulties of the welfare state, particularly as regards social security and health care, should be understood not so much as a fiscal crisis, but as a crisis of risk management. The welfare state has always been above all a security system, designed to combat the hazards which individuals or groups face. It developed, both pre- and post-1945, mainly as a means of dealing with external risks – misfortunes which affect people through no fault of their own. Thus individuals find themselves deserted by their spouses, living in poverty, out of a job, sick, disabled, getting old and so forth.

Manufactured risk, however, is risk of a mobile character, which can't easily be calculated in an actuarial way. What we 'make happen' becomes much more tangled up with what 'happens to us'. A whole welter of uncertainties and anxieties are thereby created, which affect both the social and natural worlds. Nature becomes so thoroughly infected with manufactured risk that it isn't nature any more. The big transition here is the point at which we no longer worry so much – as human beings have had to do for centuries – about what nature might do to us, but about what we've done to nature.

Does this seem light years away from the mundane troubles of the NHS? Well, it isn't. One of the major difficulties with existing health-care systems is that enormous amounts of money are spent upon treating illness as a form of external risk. Like most social security provisions, they are designed to pick up the pieces when things go wrong, as if the reasons why things go wrong were out of anyone's hands.

Now of course in many situations this is still a valid assumption. The causes of a range of illnesses, for instance, are either contested or unknown, while in other cases there may be no effective treatments. Yet in health care, as in social security, manufactured risk and the new individualism create conditions for the cultivation of new forms of responsibility, social integration and environmental repair. The issues here bite much more deeply than emphasizing preventative medicine rather than medical treatment. They are to do with encouraging lifestyle habits which see health as a positive goal, and with environmental care, rather than concentrating only on either the avoidance of illness or its treatment.

In the area of health and illness it's obvious enough that there are difficult decisions to be taken, ethical as well as financial. Some forms of necessary medical equipment are very expensive to provide; advances in treatment may add to costs, rather than reduce them, as the realm of what is treatable expands. Care for the frail elderly often has to be continuous and can't be cheap. Even the best-funded health system will have to face many problems of rationing, which might become more acute, not less, in the future. But the dilemmas that must be resolved don't only, or even primarily, lie in the narrow area of state provision versus privatization.

They lie in the connections between communal health care and personal responsibility that the new individualism has opened up. Illness is something which happens to us if we're unlucky, isn't it? Actually, no, it isn't. In common with most other aspects of our lives, health and illness are less and less a matter of just fate – except perhaps for the very elderly.

Let's suppose first of all that we take positive health as an overriding value, not avoidance of illness. One's capability to pursue positive health is influenced by a number of factors which concern either personal or collective responsibilities – responsibilities we have either towards ourselves and our own bodies, or to others. Most illnesses are not biologically given. They depend upon who one is, how one lives, and the state of the surrounding social and physical environment.

Forms of health care oriented to manufactured risk should look to create a new fusion of personal and collective responsibilities for positive health – most of these wouldn't work through the health-care system as usually defined. Attacking poverty, controlling environmental pollution, promoting personal lifestyle responsibility and democratizing access to health-care knowledge – these are the directions in which in the future we should move. All these factors are related to one another, and all have a direct bearing upon social and civic renewal.

How is any of this going to shorten the waiting list for hip replacements? It isn't, of course, at least in the short term (although hips and other joints deteriorate less if a person takes modest, but regular, physical exercise throughout life). None the less, combining lifestyle responsibility and active environmental policy can add up to cold cash-saving. All illnesses associated with smoking, for example, which causes 10,000 deaths a year in the UK, are in principle avoidable. Campaigns against smoking in the US, especially combined with other measures countering risks of heart disease, show what can be achieved.

Some estimates claim that as many as 80 per cent of illnesses once generally thought to be more or less inevitable accompaniments of old age are lifestyle-related – they derive from, or are connected with, how the individual lives, dietary patterns and environmental toxicities. Although no one knows the truth of the matter, some scientists argue that a high proportion of cancers have their origins in avoidable environmental toxicity. And we do know that pollution creates, or worsens, many cases of lung disease.

So far as the democratizing of health care goes, the richer countries can learn something from policies originally developed in relation to the poorer ones. *Where There is No Doctor*, by David Werner, is one of the best-known manuals of health care aimed at the very poor in developing countries. Werner emphasizes the following principles: health care is not only everyone's right, but everyone's responsibility; informed self-care should be the main goal of any health programme; medical knowledge should not be the guarded secret of a select few, but should be freely shared by everyone; people with little formal education can be trusted as much as those with a lot – and they are just as clever; basic health care should not be delivered but encouraged. All these principles are generalizable.

Consider again the 'problem' of the ageing population, supposed to be such a source of difficulty for the welfare state. A radical approach would go well beyond the question of what kinds of pension system are appropriate and how they should be funded. I don't mean to say that there aren't such dilemmas, but again the terms of reference of the debate should be shifted. There is a useful transition here to considering questions of unemployment and poverty.

It isn't usually noticed that many people over 65 would be unemployed if it weren't for the way in which compulsory retirement cooks the books. To be unemployed is to want to have a paid job, but be unable to find one – or more accurately, one that makes use of an individual's skills and capacities. In surveys of those aged 65 or more, 40 per cent of men and women without paid work say that they would like a job if they could get one. Were the conventional idea of retirement done away with, the result would seemingly be a net reduction in the number of jobs available per person in the population. In other words, the outcome would be to add to the overall level of unemployment. But would it? Almost certainly not, if the abolition of orthodox unemployment were accompanied by policies allowing much earlier retirement if desired, time off in mid-career to be 'repaid' later, and numerous other similar possibilities which exist.

Whenever possible, treat a problem as an opportunity – it's a good maxim of psychotherapy, but it also applies to political policy-making. Now that as many women as men – in fact slightly more – are in paid jobs, 'full employment' can't possibly mean the same thing as it did in the heyday of Keynesianism. There may be short-term schemes which can help to reduce official rates of unemployment; a diversity of remedies are around, although the most important influences are still likely to come from the global economy. However, far more people are in paid work today in Western societies than used to be at the peak of 'full employment' in the Keynesian welfare state. The question now isn't 'full employment or not?', but 'employment under what conditions and for whom?'

Fighting unemployment, even in the medium term, is inseparable from a series of other concerns which must be at the top of the political agenda – concerns which affect particularly sexual equality, the family and environmental protection. We should understand paid employment as being not only about the production of wealth, but about its distribution – and about its consequences, in the form of social wealth. Policies aimed at an equitable distribution of paid work mark the direction in which to go.

One possible scenario: no advances are made towards greater sexual equality, or work-sharing in the home, or dual parenting. Result: 'flexibility' means the creation of many 'McJobs', mainly held by women; levels of overall unemployment remain high, with men making up a high percentage of the long-term unemployed; men at the same time dominate the best-paid jobs, which often demand a slavish devotion to paid work.

Another possible scenario: there is a move towards sexual equality, which carries with it greater mutual involvement in domestic tasks, including the care of children. Result: flexibility means a diversity of situations in which paid jobs are combined with other tasks and pleasures; unemployment doesn't necessarily have a negative meaning, and in any case is understood in social rather than purely economic terms; there is a more equitable distribution of occupations between the sexes.

The first scenario is what we have, the second what we should aspire to. But a transition from one to the other will depend just as much upon what happens outside the area of employment as inside it. Here the theme of the new individualism, and its relation to civic renewal, returns with full force. Women's claims to autonomy, and to equality, are an elemental part of that individualism. The entry of women into the paid labour force in large numbers has placed in question a whole cluster of other structures in contemporary society. Civic renewal will depend in a profound way upon making progress towards a new settlement between the sexes, and not only because of the connections which (as Beatrix Campbell has shown) exist between unemployment, frustrated masculinity and crime.

Among other measures, reform of the welfare system is important. Welfare schemes in Britain still depend upon the assumption that men are the providers, women the (often unpaid) carers. Welfare reforms should aim not only at springing the poverty traps that can result, but at ending the situation in which the possibility of full-time or even half-time fathering is in effect strongly discouraged.

Successful engagement in global competition carries with it a number of bottom-line demands, particularly concerning the structure of business enterprise and technology. Yet global competition isn't, or shouldn't be understood as, only a scrabble for economic development. What is at issue is social or lifestyle competition. Official rates of unemployment between different countries are often contrasted as though the comparisons had a clear meaning. But they don't unless one compares also, among other things, the absolute numbers in a labour force, who wants paid work and who doesn't, and what other kinds of work are carried on by whom.

If tackling unemployment is seriously to be compatible with civic renewal, strategies to promote the redistribution of work and paid jobs should take precedence over the quantity of jobs created. The large majority of the jobs generated in the UK in the 1980s were in services; 90 per cent were in casual or part-time work with no career prospects. As André Gorz has shown, personal service jobs have little or no effect of 'productive substitution'. In early periods of economic growth, industrial production and technology allowed many tasks which were previously done in an intensive way to be carried out much more efficiently. The mechanization and industrialization of agriculture, for example, allow far more food to be produced, far more efficiently, than earlier systems could.

Most of the new personal service occupations, however, do nothing which one couldn't do oneself. They simply mean that one individual buys free time by transferring tasks to others. This is essentially what happens with servants, and Gorz suggests that the result in modern conditions is the creation of a large 'servant class', mainly composed of women. Job creation hence doesn't produce savings of working time across the whole society, but instead transfers working time to the benefit of those who have more to spend.

The issues involved here are undeniably difficult and the dangers of increasing social schism are great. Each year in the UK since the early 1980s, 3 per cent of jobs have disappeared, mostly as a result of technological innovation. Information technology is progressively becoming cheaper and more 'intelligent'. Thus people are forced out of jobs completely, or wages have to be lowered to match the reduced costs of the technology.

Yet it isn't utopian to suppose that work time could be distributed more equitably – between men and women and between the affluent and the poor. We should take seriously the case that the casualization of work and the dualization of society between the affluent and the 'new poor' are perverse responses to the freeing-up of time which technological downsizing produces. A structural approach to countering unemployment wouldn't concentrate only upon the unemployed or those in casualized work themselves. It would focus upon the more affluent, with the aim of freeing up work time without a transfer to paid services. The needs to which casualized personal services respond are two-fold: avoidance of drudgery and saving of time. Unappetizing tasks there will always be, but drudgery becomes so in part because of time pressure. Lack of time comes from the dominance of paid work over other aspects of people's lives – in other words, from productivism. Reducing working time, particularly if it were accompanied by more shared parenting, hence would have a positive outcome.

It is exactly this endeavour which can contribute to a revival of family structures and to the goal of civic renewal. There's no going back to the so-called traditional family, but solidarity in diversity is not a utopian aspiration. We can aim at reconstructing family life, and in a way which will give force to the injunction 'children first'; and we can aim at recovering wider forms of social cohesion. These things won't come about, however, through tightening the divorce laws, much less from flights of fancy about civic duties. They'll only happen in the context of a restructuring of jobs, work and family obligations.

Strategies and options

For twenty years it was the right who were the radicals, usurping Labour's traditions of political innovation and change. If Labour can break out of the protective shell which it has built for itself, the prospects for political reconstruction in Britain are alluring indeed – and disturbing for the other two parties. I've argued so far that there is a coherent ideological stance which Labour can adopt; and that a series of integrated policy orientations flow from it. But how should Labour deal with the more concrete problems it must face in order to move towards its more long-term objectives?

First, Labour at this point should consolidate the definitive break with Keynesian welfare-statism – as well as with Old Leftism – which the new leadership has made. The economy is sluggish and may remain so. (It may not, as the integrated global economy is new, and no one knows how it works.) Given low growth rates, however, there isn't enough government revenue to introduce new spending plans. The temptation is strong to say: we'll reflate, get the economy moving and as things improve there will be more to spend. The result, however, would be to threaten all that Labour in government might seek to achieve.

Second, union reforms should continue – but with positive aims in view, not the negative ones that have dominated since 1979. Tony Blair has indicated that he won't go back on Tory regulation of wage-bargaining mechanisms, and indeed he shouldn't. Yet overcoming short-termism within the union movement is as important as it is elsewhere in the society. Sustaining close links with a revived union movement doesn't necessitate that Labour present itself as a class party. New forms of industrial partnership are probably the very condition of reversing the decline in union membership, a phenomenon of many years' duration. A strong union movement should still be Labour's aim; as the experience of other European countries shows, this can help reduce, rather than create, chronic industrial conflict.

Third, Labour shouldn't be afraid to challenge the power of the City, and should couple this to active support for the long-term regeneration of manufacturing industry. A positive attitude towards manufacturing, together with an investment programme for transport and communications, are absolute musts.

Fourth, fiscal reform must be on the agenda. Here the party has to be prepared to be innovative. Tax-cutting in an overall sense can't even be contemplated when state resources are already thinly spread and when there are so many 'good causes' around. It obviously doesn't follow, however, that the distribution of taxes and tax benefits should remain intact. The main objective of fiscal changes shouldn't be to increase government revenue, even if this were thought clearly desirable. It should be to integrate the fiscal system with constitutional change and democratization on the one hand, and with a positive transformation of the welfare state on the other. How to reverse the tendency towards the emergence of a new 'excluded poor' – impoverished groups set apart from society's mainstream – is the biggest challenge, but one which must be squarely faced.

Let me expand on each of the above issues in turn.

A motto should be inscribed above the door of every Labour policy-maker: 'I will not flirt with Keynesianism!' What is needed is a fundamental change of economic outlook. Labour should now, in a principled not a pragmatic way, seize the economic high ground by building its policies around sustaining low inflation while seeking to generate long-term infrastructural investment. The party faces an uphill battle, both internally and in the international financial world, if it is to shed its tax-and-spend reputation. Winning that battle, however, is the key to financial stability in the event of a Labour election victory.

Keynesianism, of course, isn't the same as public expenditure as such. Pretty obviously it should be Labour's task to dissolve the residues of the Thatcherist formula, 'private enterprise good, public enterprise bad'. Yet I think it doubtful that a 'modest return to Keynesianism' could work even at the European level. Europe-wide regulation of economic activity, including the Social Chapter, is likely to prove vital to the future of the European national economies. But there isn't much reason to suppose that Keynesianism at the level of the EU is any more plausible than Keynesianism in one country.

However benign its longer-term involvement with the union movement may be, Labour in power will have to nerve itself for tough confrontations ahead – for such confrontations will probably be unavoidable. No matter how direct Labour's economic dependence on the unions, however, 'one member one vote' has shifted the whole climate both within the party and in the country at large. Any way of further loosening that dependence would be desirable, even if the prospects are not bright. Only a tiny proportion of the population belongs to a political party in any Western country; it's doubtful that a mass membership drive is going to transform the party's finances permanently.

The theme of industrial partnership has recurrently surfaced in policy documents Labour has produced across the years. As *Meet the Challenge, Make the Change* expressed it, 'Economic success depends on good working relationships and partnership in industry.' Well, yes, but are such relationships possible to achieve if the dragon of mass unemployment happens to be slain? For the relative weakness of union bargaining power today reflects not only diminishing membership, but the discipline which large-scale unemployment places on wage-claims.

The immediate question confronting a Labour government would be that of maintaining pay restraint. Realistically speaking, whatever gloss might be put on the matter, the Tory policy of keeping down public sector pay increases as a brake upon others would have to be maintained. The unions don't any longer represent the 'united working class', if they ever did, and if Labour is to fight entrenched sectional interests the unions can't be exempted. Given the internal composition of the Labour Party, and the extensive hankering for Old Leftism, the problems here are to say the least extremely difficult and without the deployment of a great deal of political nous could prove insurmountable.

Whatever happens, however, inflationary pressures can't be tackled only on the ground of industrial relations. For difficulties in controlling inflation in this country have come from a particular 'culture of investment' which became entrenched over a period of time. A number of institutions and styles of economic action were locked into it – the housing market, patterns of consumption in relation to saving, together with various forms of financial speculation. Can these patterns be altered, or have they been already? There is good reason to be hopeful. Britain has a much higher proportion of owner-occupiers than most other industrial countries, and for years housing was far and away the most reliable means of saving. Both the housing boom and the slump that followed have had serious consequences, with which it will be difficult to cope. Yet it does seem as though the expectation that housing investment will inevitably outperform other sorts of investment has been thoroughly blunted. Given that any future escalation in property prices is contained, there will be a positive output for other forms of consumption and saving. Getting the housing market going again while avoiding price surges, however, is going to be hard to achieve.

Price and wage stability, plus the control of corruption, should be dominant concerns informing Labour's attitude to the City. Should the party launch a renewed prawn-cocktail offensive, or should its stance be more critical and adversarial? Labour was supported by the *Financial Times* in the 1992 election campaign, and does have friends in the City. The paradoxes and limitations of neo-liberalism haven't escaped those who make their living from market dealings.

Finance capital isn't quite the bogey it once appeared to many on the left, but Labour should have the courage of its convictions and should be prepared to confront organized City interests. 'The unions shouldn't run the country' – no, but neither should the City. The themes of civic renewal, responsibility and social cohesion apply with just as much force to the centres of power as to other groups, and where new legal regulation is needed, it must be introduced. In the financial sector as well as elsewhere the obvious things should be attempted: tax loopholes should be closed, and if there are effective measures to cap top executive salaries and benefits that gallop ahead of inflation, then they should be used. Even *The Economist* recently suggested that many British bosses are heavily overpaid. It is power in the boardroom rather than market competition which settles their salaries and handouts. Studies show only a slight relation between pay and movements in share prices. Golden goodbyes have been paid to executives leaving firms whose performance has been poor or even abysmal. Performance-related pay may be difficult to institute, but cultivating responsible practices and long-termism should clearly be the aim. Business leaders in the City and in industry must accept their responsibility to lead by example.

The relation between the City and manufacturing industry, of course, has long been problematic. City interests have tended to dominate over those of industry, a situation which some have seen as at the origin of Britain's relative economic decline. Today, however, the City–industry relation has to be interpreted in a different light and a different range of problems confronted.

Financial and industrial capital have both become much more intensively globalized than they were even a couple of decades ago. The big UK companies operate in global terms, buying and producing in the cheapest markets and selling wherever they can. The City is a prime site in the new global economy of money created over the past twenty years as a result of global telecommunications. The global economy of electronic money is so fresh, and is evolving so rapidly, that it is difficult to grasp its dynamics, let alone formulate practical policies within a single national state which might effectively control its impact.

The City, it's said, is a big earner for the British economy, and in terms of jobs and profits generated this is true. The total value of the goods and services produced in the new economy of money is enormous – enough to buy the entire year's output of the UK economy is traded in three days in London. Yet much investment which might otherwise find its way into industry becomes swept up in the rush of money trading.

Could a Labour government do anything about this situation? Should it, if it could? I would answer 'yes' to both questions. No government would have much influence working on its own, but a firm contribution to Europe-wide measures might be very important. Money chasing money isn't, as Marx thought, unproductive; but money trading, in the end, follows the manufacture of real products, because this is what it presumes. If manufacture increasingly moves to the Far East, so will the centre of the global money economy.

Speaking in national terms, the omens for a close cooperation between an incoming Labour government and manufacturing industry are good. Labour has consistently defended the claims of manufacture in the face of the rush for services which Tory governments have either welcomed or at least tolerated. The problem, plainly, is for Labour to break with a past in which ineffective industries and businesses have gobbled up public money and still flopped.

There isn't really a clear model to point to in other parts of the world. The state intervenes actively in support of certain industries, and attempts forward planning, in Japan and the successful Asian economies. But for various reasons it doesn't seem likely that similar strategies could be followed in this country. In Germany, some industries have been protected which here haven't been able to withstand sudden blasts from global markets. Although local communities dependent on a particular industry or company should surely be shielded from sudden mass redundancies wherever possible, one could not say that state protection of industry in Germany has a good economic rationale.

In the UK, productivity growth, and not state protection of weaker industries, is what is needed, but it isn't at all clear how the country can remedy what is an historic weakness. Manufacturing productivity in the UK still lags about 30 per cent behind Japan and 45 per cent behind the US; and Britain is well down in the OECD rankings of international competitiveness.

More skills, more technical education, more training – these are the magic potions which many hope will revive British industry. Investment in skills and training is supposed simultaneously to create productivity gains in manufacture and elsewhere, and cope with unemployment. A country's investment capital in the future, it is said, is going to be tied up increasingly with the skills and experiences of its population, since capital is now so mobile, raw materials can quickly be brought in from elsewhere and technology can be purchased or rapidly copied. So investment in people, geared to 'employability' rather than employment, will be vital. Labour, it is argued, should seek to initiate a 'supply-side revolution'.

The ambition to make 'flexibility' mean something other than cheap, disposable labour-power – one of the aims of the Social Chapter – is surely right and proper. Whether education and skills have the magical properties some think, however, is more dubious, particularly if technical and vocational training become the central reference-point for the educational system as a whole. In an increasingly knowledge-based society, education is bound to be a fundamental component of a country's prosperity. Yet it doesn't follow that technical training and skills will lead to

diminishing levels of unemployment. The issue of unemployment, as I have pointed out previously, goes well beyond the
status of the paid workforce. 'Employability' may enhance the
adaptability and, where needed, mobility of the workforce, but
won't in itself create jobs.

Measures of social wealth must here be brought clearly into
view. That Britain lags behind some others in terms of skills and
technical training there is no doubt. But as it moves towards
becoming a lifetime process, education should surely retain a
humanistic core. Education should be aimed at producing that
cosmopolitanism which I have discussed earlier. It should help
enhance a wide spectrum of life-values, rather than only serving
to 'narrow down' or technicize.

Education requires investment, as does improving the infrastructure of transport and communications – as do also health,
social security, pensions and the many other provisions which fall
within the rubric of the welfare state. There's the rub, as
everyone, including every voter, knows. In some areas investment might be forthcoming from the private sector, or from a
combination of business and state capital. But government
expenditure is already overstretched and the country as a whole is
in hock. What to do?

That there are no easy answers to such a question is the easy
answer with which all politicians begin their speeches. Well, there
aren't any easy answers, as left-of-centre parties have discovered
all across the world. The Old Leftists within the Labour Party
have theirs, and to some they seem straightforward enough.
Income tax should be raised for those who are comfortably off –
although beginning at a much higher level than was proposed in
John Smith's pre-election budget in 1992. There should be new
wealth or inheritance taxes, while VAT should be introduced for
services which are skewed towards the more affluent, notably
private education and private health care. These measures would
be redistributive downwards, and would go along with tax cuts for
the low paid. At the same time, universal welfare benefits would
be maintained and extra funds channelled into the NHS.

While some of these proposals are worth taking seriously, they
only scratch the surface of the possibilities involved. They are the
thinking of the 1950s facing the problems of the 1990s. More

radical fiscal proposals are possible and almost certainly necessary, as public debate has increasingly come to recognize. Tax-cutting – in the sense of reducing income tax – is the lodestone of Tory electoral strategy. Labour can and should outflank the conservatives on the issue. The idea of reducing basic rate income tax to below 20 per cent in the pound doesn't seem a starter in practical terms. Yet even if only meant as a Tory-teaser, the proposal is a stimulus to debate.

Where social life has become more and more structured around the new individualism, forms of taxation in which there is a discretionary element will find more public acceptance than those which are involuntary. And where government legitimacy depends more and more on visibility and active trust, earmarked taxes should at least be considered. Labour shouldn't adopt an attitude of blank hostility to schemes such as those which the Liberal Democrats have canvassed and which have been discussed or instituted in some other European countries. Earmarked taxes for education and for the NHS may face concerted Treasury opposition, but could meet with public approval as well as significantly increase revenue. A specific health tax, or using taxation income from alcohol and tobacco for some NHS funding, or a combination of the two, are plausible possibilities. So long as they don't have regressive consequences, energy, pollution and road-use taxes, whether hypothecated or not, should all be seriously debated. Of course, in the end reducing various kinds of tax breaks may turn out to be the most practical way to go.

Whatever new sources of revenue might be put in place, there would be no point in slotting them back into a tax-and-spend framework. Radical reform of the welfare system is both possible and necessary. Reform of the welfare state, as I've suggested before, should be prompted not only or even mainly by fiscal considerations, but by the need for structural reorganization in relation to the changing make-up of the social order today. Targeting benefits may be anathema in some Labour circles, but it is the only effective direction in which to move, and it can be redistributive in favour of low-income groups.

'Targeting' – the word is an awful one, suggesting passive groups of individuals at whom benefits have to be aimed. What it means, or should mean, is getting help to those who need it most – and in sufficient quantity. Benefits should be increased rather than reduced for the needy; but many who receive benefits, including large numbers of older people and the children of affluent families, do not fall into such a category at all.

Pensions, which amount to nearly 40 per cent of social security expenditure, must come under scrutiny. Private pensions can be hazardous, as we all know following the activities of Robert Maxwell. Almost 60 per cent of the over-65s already have private pensions of some sort, however, and that proportion should be encouraged to grow. Safeguards can protect pension investors against the unscrupulous, and it is a myth that state pensions are inevitably more secure. Governments haven't the same control over private pension funds as they have over public ones; but just for that reason they aren't so easily able to cut them when unforeseen fiscal embarrassments loom.

A substantial chunk of the corporate wealth of the country is tied up in pension funds. Shouldn't those who 'own' them also control them? Several strategies are possible and should at least be publicly debated. Frank Field, for instance, has suggested that 'pension serfdom' could be overcome via a new system of tripartite ownership of pension funds – employer, worker and pension-holder interests would each be represented.

Policies directed towards older people, as I have suggested earlier, have to be empowering, not based merely on catering for individuals as dependants. The same applies to welfare reforms concerned with attacking the widening socio-economic divisions in Britain. The polarization of affluent and poor has been more marked here than in most other industrial societies over recent years. 'No South Bronx in this country!' is the slogan suggested by Sir John Banham in his blueprint for social and economic reconstruction. He is surely right, but the trends in Britain and some of the Continental countries are worrying. Some taxi-drivers refuse to venture into Manchester's Moss Side – and their counterparts in Frankfurt or Rotterdam feel much the same way about entering Gallusviertel or Nieuwe Westen.

While in most European countries the gap between rich and poor has widened, in absolute terms living standards of the poor in Europe have improved over the last twenty years. The most deprived inner-city areas are not as segregated as those in the US, and the standard of local services is better. Racism, however, is every bit as prevalent and the same cycle of violence, social exclusion, chronic unemployment, drugs and everyday despair is to be found. There isn't yet a deprived underclass of American dimensions in Britain, and a minimum requirement of a new government should be to keep things that way. Just as in the areas of health and pensions, however, we can be sure that effective answers won't come simply from trying to bolster existing welfare state mechanisms. Rightist authors say that welfare provisions aren't the solution to urban blight, but part of the problem. No one on the left has listened, but perhaps they should start to do so. Breaking cycles of deprivation isn't going to happen solely through external intervention, no matter how well-meaning. It's going to demand local organization, local initiative, and civic reconstruction which starts from below. Leftist writers, after all, make much the same emphases when criticizing external aid programmes in developing countries. 'The aid which kills' is the title of a study by one author on the issue. In less dramatic ways, policies which worsen what they were meant to cure can happen in industrial societies too. Who can doubt, for example, that the building of council tower-blocks destroyed more than it remedied?

The 'no easy answers' easy answer to economic polarization and to the emergence of an underclass is to blame Thatcherism and leave it at that. There's no doubt that some of the changes made by recent Conservative governments to social security have contributed, particularly in the case of the young. A series of restrictions on young people's rights to benefit were introduced from the 1980s onwards. Some such changes have certainly been destructive of family bonds. For instance, young people became ineligible for 'board and lodging payments' after a certain period if they stayed in their local area.

Thatcherism, however, has served to worsen trends which can be observed in many other countries besides Britain and which are influenced by global economic factors. A reversal of some of the welfare changes made by the Tories will help somewhat. For instance, advance payments for rent for the homeless could be reintroduced, and certain other benefits reinstated. Problems of

urban decay, racism, ethnic segregation and homelessness, however, bite very deep. They won't respond to half-hearted measures and quite clearly have to be approached in the context of
broader questions of social division and unemployment. We're
back here to the issue of the structural sources of civic renewal,
the redistribution of work and re-establishing continuity in family
life. The trickle-down effect which the neo-liberals sought didn't
happen. But couldn't there be a different kind of trickle-down
from policies which promote egalitarianism in a cluster of
connected institutional domains? At any rate, welfare reforms
concerned to reduce poverty and prevent class polarization won't
make much impact unless they are part of a wider drive against
inequality.

In recent years, the Labour Party hasn't exactly been a hotbed
of new thinking, or of any kind of radicalism. The ideological
reforms which the party so painfully made from the mid-1980s
were supposed to make the party 'electable', but if they have
done so it was at the cost of most of the dynamism the party
possessed. We must hope the next two or three years won't see a
further set of soggy compromises and loss of political edge. The
danger is that, having witnessed the failure of neo-liberalism,
the Labour leadership will think that it's enough just to swing the
pendulum back again towards just a little bit more state intervention or fiscal redistribution – masquerading as the 'community'.
This isn't where the main questions to be faced lie at all. The
limited level of discussion of green issues in the party is a case in
point. Ecological thinking is identified in a straightforward way
with environmentalism, as though the two were the same. Yet the
green themes of care, continuity and social cohesion are exactly
those which the idea of community raises. Contesting productivism while promoting productivity is the only route to follow if a
low-inflation, low-growth society is also to refurbish itself and
give substance to values of participation and equality.

A revision in political outlook such as I've suggested can't be
inward-looking, given the twin influences of globalization and the
new individualism. All the issues I have discussed here reflect
very much broader global divisions and global dilemmas, which
every national government has to confront – dilemmas of an
ecological kind, and of world economic polarization. Labour
should adopt a much more global outlook than it has hitherto. It

won't be enough just to avoid the little Englander (Britisher?) parochialism which afflicts the Tories, and it won't be enough to concentrate only on Europe. A clearly developed international policy stance is essential in a world whose dynamics have become puzzling, but which impinges upon us in an immediate and continuous way.

Notes

2 Living in a Post-Traditional Society

1 U. Beck and E. Beck-Gernsheim, *The Normal Chaos of Love*, Cambridge: Polity Press, 1995.
2 A. Giddens, *The Consequences of Modernity*, Cambridge: Polity Press, 1990.
3 P. Dicken, *Global Shift*, London: Chapman, 1992.
4 U. Beck, *Risk Society*, London: Sage, 1992.
5 A. Giddens, *The Transformation of Intimacy*, Cambridge: Polity Press, 1992.
6 N. Baker, *The Mezzanine*, Cambridge: Granta, 1990, p. 45.
7 R.B. Lee, *The Dobe !Kung*, New York: Holt, 1984, p. 49.
8 Ibid., p. 49.
9 P. Boyer, *Tradition as Truth and Communication*, Cambridge: Cambridge University Press, 1990.
10 E. Shils, *Tradition*, London: Faber, 1981.
11 M. Halbwachs, *The Social Frameworks of Memory*, Chicago: University of Chicago Press, 1992, p. 39.
12 Cf. A. Giddens, *The Constitution of Society*, Cambridge: Polity Press, 1984, pp. 45–51.
13 Boyer, *Tradition as Truth and Communication*, ch. 5.
14 Ibid., p. 112.
15 Shils says that there are 'factual traditions', without normative content. For me these fall into the category of customs. Shils, *Tradition*, pp. 23–5.
16 A. and T. Harris, *Staying OK*, London: Pan, 1985, p. 19.
17 S. Freud, *The Interpretation of Dreams*, London: Hogarth Press, 1951.
18 Giddens, *The Transformation of Intimacy*.
19 M. Weber, *The Protestant Ethic and the Spirit of Capitalism*, London: Allen & Unwin, 1976, p. 72.
20 Ibid., p. 182.
21 Ibid., pp. 84–6.

22 See, for instance, D. Bell, *The Cultural Contradictions of Capitalism*, London: Heinemann, 1979.
23 A.W. Schaeff, *Codependence: Misunderstood, Mistreated*, New York: Harper, 1986, p. 21.
24 Ibid., pp. 25–6.
25 M. Scarf, *Intimate Partners*, New York: Aullantine, 1987, p. 42.
26 Ibid. Quotations that follow are from this source.
27 A. Giddens, *Modernity and Self-Identity*, Cambridge: Polity Press, 1991.
28 S. Helmsletter, *Choices*, New York: Product Books, pp. 100–3. This is a selection from a list of 100 day-to-day choices in the original.
29 Ibid., p. 104.
30 W. Wordsworth, *The Prelude*, Book One, lines 1–8.
31 B. McKibben, *The End of Nature*, New York: Random House, 1989.
32 C. Ponting, *A Green History of the World*, London: Penguin, 1991, ch. 5.
33 J. Broome, *Counting the Cost of Global Warming*, London: White Horse, 1992.
34 R. Sheldrake, *The Rebirth of Nature*, London: Rider, 1990, p. 153.
35 Ibid., p. 154.
36 Lee, *The Dobe !Kung*, pp. 47–8.
37 G. Simmel, 'The stranger', in Simmel, *On Individuality and Social Forms*, Chicago: University of Chicago Press, 1971, p. 143. On this question see also the important discussion in Z. Bauman, *Modernity and Ambivalence*, Cambridge: Polity Press, 1991, pp. 56–61.
38 Bauman, *Modernity and Ambivalence*, p. 60.
39 M. Weber, *Economy and Society*, Berkeley: University of California Press, 1978, vol. 1, pp. 226–7.
40 Ibid., p. 215.
41 John Agnew, *Place and Politics*, London: Allen & Unwin, 1987.
42 Cf. A. Giddens, *The Nation-State and Violence*, Cambridge: Polity Press, 1985.
43 Ibid.
44 E. Hobsbawm, 'Introduction: inventing traditions', in E. Hobsbawm and T. Ranger, *The Invention of Tradition*, Cambridge: Cambridge University Press, 1983.
45 C. Davies, 'The Protestant Ethic and the comic spirit of capitalism', *British Journal of Sociology*, vol. 43, 1992.
46 Giddens, *The Transformation of Intimacy*.
47 For a discussion, see Giddens, *The Consequences of Modernity*.
48 See R. Hyam, *Empire and Sexuality*, Manchester: Manchester University Press, 1990.
49 N. Barley, *Not a Hazardous Sport*, London: Penguin, 1989.
50 Ibid., p. 138.
51 Ibid., p. 142.
52 R. Hewison, *The Heritage Industry*, London: Methuen, 1987.
53 M. Gluckman, *Custom and Conflict in Africa*, Oxford: Blackwell, 1970.
54 D.I. Kerzer, *Ritual, Politics and Power*, New Haven: Yale, 1988, p. 37.
55 R. Benedict, *Patterns of Culture*, London: Routledge, 1954.
56 Giddens, *The Transformation of Intimacy*.

4 Functionalism: *Après la Lutte*

1 Robert K. Merton, 'Manifest and latent functions'; Ernest Nagel, 'A formalization of functionalism with special reference to its application in the social sciences'; both in N.J. Demerath and Richard Peterson, *System, Change, and Conflict*, New York, 1967.
2 Arthur Stinchcombe, *Constructing Social Theories*, New York, 1968.
3 Emile Durkheim, *Suicide* (Glencoe, IL, 1951), London, 1952, p. 44.
4 D.F. Aberle et al., 'The functional prerequisites of a society', in Demerath and Peterson, *System, Change, and Conflict*, pp. 324 and 326.
5 Ibid., pp. 323 and 327.
6 Ibid., p. 319.
7 The quotation is from Radcliffe-Brown, 'On the concept of function in social science', now in *Structure and Function in Primitive Society*, London (Glencoe, IL), 1952.
8 Cf. Ludwig von Bertalanffy, 'General System Theory', in Demerath and Peterson, *System, Change, and Conflict*; also Walter Buckley, *Sociology and Modern Systems Theory*, Englewood Cliffs, NJ, 1967.
9 Claude Lévi-Strauss, 'Réponses à quelques questions', *Esprit*, vol. 11, 1963.
10 Kingsley Davis, 'The myth of functional analysis as a special method in sociology and anthropology', in Demerath and Peterson, *System, Change, and Conflict*.

7 Four Myths in the History of Social Thought

1 Talcott Parsons, *The Structure of Social Action*, New York, 1937 (second edition, 1949).
2 Robert A. Nisbet, *The Sociological Tradition*, London, 1967, pp. 12–13.
3 Robert A. Nisbet, *Emile Durkheim*, Englewood Cliffs, NJ, 1965, pp. 23–5.
4 'Les études de science sociale', *Revue philosophique*, vol. 22, 1886; 'La science positive de la morale en Allemagne', ibid., 1887 (in three parts); 'Le programme économique de M. Schäffle', *Revue d'économie politique*, vol. 2, 1888.
5 'L'individualisme et les intellectuels', *Revue bleue*, vol. 10, 1898, p. 9.
6 *Education and Sociology*, Glencoe, IL, 1956, p. 89. (I have modified the translations.)
7 'Sociologie et sciences sociales', *Revue philosophique*, 1886, p. 469.
8 Letter to Davy, quoted in George Davy, 'Emile Durkheim', *Revue française de sociologie*, vol. 1, 1960, p. 10.
9 Ralf Dahrendorf, *Class and Class Conflict in Industrial Society*, Stanford, 1959, p. 159. It should be noted, however, that the 'problem of order' is defined here in a less specific, and a more ambiguous, way than it is understood by Parsons.
10 *Socialism*, New York, 1962, p. 240.

11 *Emile Durkheim*, p. 28.
12 Colette Capitan, 'Avant-propos' to Bonald, *Théorie du pouvoir politique et religieux*, Paris, 1966, p. 10.
13 A.V. Dicey, *Law and Public Opinion in England*, London, 1962, p. 7. For a survey of some of the nineteenth-century English 'conservatives', see Benjamin Evans Lippincott, *Victorian Critics of Democracy*, Minneapolis, 1938.
14 *Professional Ethics and Civic Morals*, London: Routledge, 1957, p. 99.
15 'L'individualisme et les intellectuels', p. 8.

9 The Suicide Problem in French Sociology

1 A.M. Guerry, *Essai sur la statistique morale de la France*, Paris, 1833; E. Lisle, *Du suicide*, Paris, 1856; A. Legoyt, *Le Suicide ancien et moderne*, Paris, 1881; A. Quételet, *Sur l'homme et le développement de ses facultés* (2 vols), Paris, 1835; *Du système social et des lois qui le régissent*, Paris, 1848; A. Wagner, *Die Gesetzmässigkeit in den scheinbar willkürlichen menschlichen Handlungen*, Hamburg, 1864; T.G. Masaryk, *Der Selbstmord*, Vienna, 1881; E. Morselli, *Il suicidio*, Milan, 1879; E. Ferri, *L'omicidio-suicidio*, Turin, 1883. Studies of suicide published in English borrowed extensively from the French and German writers: F. Winslow, *The Anatomy of Suicide*, New York, 1882; W.W. Westcott, *Suicide*, London, 1885.
2 'Not only are suicides, each year, of almost the same quantity; but, separating rates for groups in terms of the instruments used, we find the same constancy.' Quételet, *Du système social et des lois qui le régissent*, p. 88.
3 The phrase is taken from S. Miller, *The Guilt, Folly and Sources of Suicide*, New York, 1805, p. 14.
4 E. Esquirol, *Des maladies mentales*, Paris, 1838, vol. 1, p. 639.
5 Durkheim, *Suicide* (Glencoe, IL, 1951), London, 1952, p. 46.
6 M. de Fleury, *L'Angoisse humaine*, Paris, 1924. Prior to de Fleury's book, Bayet's important historical survey of suicide appeared, written from a broadly sociological standpoint, and explicitly indebted to Durkheim. A. Bayet, *Le Suicide et la morale*, Paris, 1922.
7 De Fleury, *L'Angoisse humaine*, p. 79.
8 M. Halbwachs, *Les Causes du suicide*, Paris, 1930.
9 Ibid., p. 238.
10 Ibid., p. 426.
11 P. Courbon, review of Halbwachs's *Les Causes du suicide*, *Annales médico-psychologiques*, new series 1, March 1931, p. 322.
12 F. Achille-Delmas, *Psychologie pathologique du suicide*, Paris, 1932.
13 Ibid., p. 234.
14 Ch. Blondel, *Le Suicide*, Strasbourg, 1933. Immediately prior to the publication of Blondel's book, Bonnafous made a spirited defence of the *thèse sociologique* in a review article of Delmas's work. M. Bonnafous, 'Le suicide: thèse psychiatrique et thèse sociologique', *Revue philosophique*, vol. 115, May–June 1933, pp. 456–75.

15 C. Drombrowski, *Les Conditions psychologiques du suicide*' (MD thesis), Geneva, 1929, p. 32.
16 G. Gurvitch, *Essais de sociologie*, Paris, 1939, pp. 141–2. The same essay is reprinted, with minor alterations, in G. Gurvitch, *La Vocation actuelle de la sociologie*, Paris, 1950. Gurvitch's work is not without its critics. Cuvillier has been perhaps the most outspoken. See particularly A. Cuvillier, *Introduction à la sociologie*, Paris, fifth edition, 1954, ch. 4, pp. 84–124; and *Où va la sociologie française?*, Paris, 1953.
17 R. Bastide, 'Le suicide du nègre brésilien', *Cahiers internationaux de sociologie*, vol. 12, 1952, pp. 72–90. See also his 'Sociologie et psychologie', in G. Gurvitch, *Traité de sociologie*, Paris, 1962, pp. 71ff.
18 C. Lévi-Strauss, 'French sociology', in G. Gurvitch and W.E. Moore, *Twentieth Century Sociology*, New York, 1945, p. 509.
19 Durkheim, *Suicide*, p. 46.
20 Quoted by Durkheim, ibid., p. 311.

11 Literature and Society: Raymond Williams

1 Raymond Williams, *Politics and Letters: Interviews with New Left Review*, London: New Left Books, 1979.

13 Brave New World: The New Context of Politics

1 T. Tannsjo, *Conservatism for Our Time*, London: Routledge, 1990.

Index